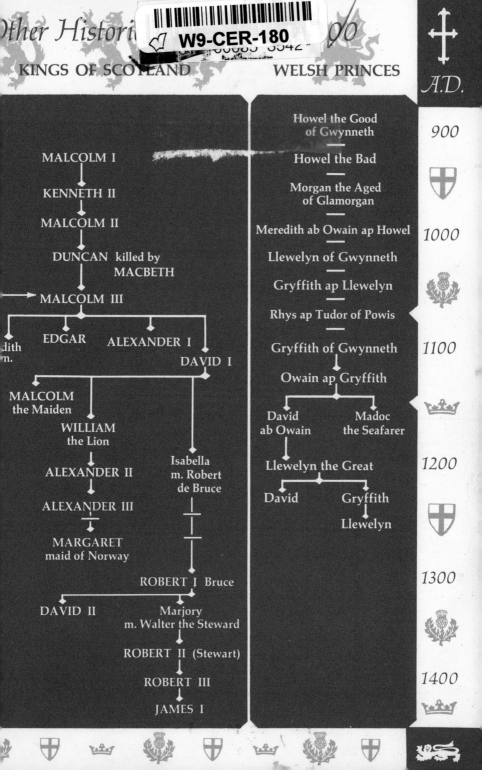

Other Histori... ...00

KINGS OF SCOTLAND

WELSH PRINCES

A.D.

900

MALCOLM I

KENNETH II

MALCOLM II

DUNCAN killed by MACBETH

MALCOLM III

dith m.

EDGAR   ALEXANDER I

DAVID I

MALCOLM the Maiden

WILLIAM the Lion

ALEXANDER II

Isabella m. Robert de Bruce

ALEXANDER III

MARGARET maid of Norway

ROBERT I Bruce

DAVID II   Marjory m. Walter the Steward

ROBERT II (Stewart)

ROBERT III

JAMES I

Howel the Good of Gwynneth

Howel the Bad

Morgan the Aged of Glamorgan

Meredith ab Owain ap Howel

1000

Llewelyn of Gwynneth

Gryffith ap Llewelyn

Rhys ap Tudor of Powis

Gryffith of Gwynneth

1100

Owain ap Gryffith

David ab Owain   Madoc the Seafarer

Llewelyn the Great

1200

David   Gryffith

Llewelyn

1300

1400

ENGLISH SURNAMES

C. M. Matthews

ENGLISH SURNAMES

CHARLES SCRIBNER'S SONS
New York

A—9.67 [MC]

PRINTED IN THE UNITED STATES OF AMERICA
LIBRARY OF CONGRESS CATALOG CARD NUMBER 67-24062

Contents

929.4

CONTENTS

III Names of Relationship

IV Local Names

Appendices · Classified Lists of Surnames

Preface

Many years ago at the university, in New Zealand, I had the good fortune to read English under Professor Arnold Wall, an outstanding academic figure in the Antipodes and a fine scholar by any standards. His greatest friend was Ernest Weekley, the leading authority at that time on English surnames. These two had shared that interest when at Cambridge together reading for the same degree and in later years, from their professorial chairs on opposite sides of the globe, had corresponded regularly on the subject. Thus it happened that I received from Professor Wall not only something of his passionate feeling for the English language but also, at the same time and at long range, a share in Weekley's enthusiasm for the origins of surnames.

Weekley's books, excellent in their day, are now outdated, for since then more medieval sources have become available for students and much research has been done on them. But the interest inspired in me at that early stage in my career never faded, and when in later years, living in England, I came to spend much time on local history research I was greatly stimulated by discovering that multitudes of early medieval surnames exist still, in taxation rolls, manorial documents and so forth, a seemingly endless supply inviting one to further study. As years passed I became an avid reader of these medieval sources, delighting in comparing the names of that period with those around me in the modern world and frequently surprised to find them so similar. It is as a result of this long period of study and rumination that I now venture to put in writing my observations, conclusions, and queries on the subject.

The task of giving a general view of such a large field would hardly have been possible without the work done by certain research scholars, noted in the bibliography, whose carefully compiled lists, indexes, and dictionaries have provided an enormous amount of reliable material in a convenient form. As all surviving texts from the Anglo-Saxon period have been carefully edited, it has been possible for scholars to note all recorded pre-Conquest personal names. Of course many existed that are not recorded, but the work done by Searle, Redin, and von Feilitzen forms a solid foundation of Old English names as a basis for further study. In the Middle English period the situation is very different. Many thousands of names exist in original sources, large numbers of which are still unpublished and even unread. During the last hundred years Bardsley, Weekley, Ewen, Fransson, Ekwall, Reaney and others have made valuable collections of early surnames with learned annotations, but the scope for further research remains enormous. Outside a small group of scholars this fascinating subject is little understood, and my aim is now to interest a wider public.

In the face of such a large subject I have tried to confine myself to English language names, and though it was found impossible to omit the Welsh and Scots entirely I have glanced at them as lightly as possible, hardly mentioned Ireland, omitted altogether the distinctive names of the Isle of Man and the Channel Islands, and hardly touched on the large subjects of surname distribution and local variation.

Aiming at the study of themes and patterns rather than individual etymologies, I have concentrated chiefly on the commonest names because it is clear that those that exist in the largest numbers are the ones that arose in many different places simultaneously and represent the truth about medieval life most closely. In seeking to find out as accurately as possible how and when and why so many people were called Brown and Green, King and Kemp, Wright, Hall, Hobbs, Higgins and so on, we come nearer to the minds of our forefathers than by hunting after rarities. For this reason I have consistently noted the numbers of names, taking the London Telephone Directory as a standard of measurement, and have found that they often draw attention to matters of significance. The rarer names are often entertaining and fill out the details of the medieval scene, but the common ones give us its salient features.

The question of spelling has been a difficulty. Writers on the Anglo-Saxons generally use the simpler later forms of their names, especially in cases where they are well known. But when the names themselves are under discussion it is necessary to give both early and late versions and also modern survivals in the form of surnames. In a dictionary they can be tabulated logically, but in a book of this kind, which turns from one period to another, the forms must vary according to the context in which they are used, and some inconsistency is unavoidable. Likewise, to avoid repetition, I have often used a noun in its surname spelling – Taylor for instance – when also implying the craftsman. When only one form has been given, the best known spelling has been used, but in a subject of such great variety no rigid rule could apply in every case.

I should never have completed this book without the forebearance, encouragement and practical help of my husband and my daughter Carola, to whom my affectionate thanks are due.

C.M.M.

January 1966   *Gussage All Saints*
Dorset

Preface to the American Edition

In preparing this edition I have – besides making a few small corrections – added new material to the Appendices, including lists of the leading surnames in four American cities (page 346), and also a complete chapter about American surnames in general. Another new feature takes the form of endpapers, showing the royal families who reigned in the island of Britain during the period when surnames were being formed, and whose immense personal influence is still reflected in our modern directories. This I hope may serve as a handy reference for dates and periods throughout the book.

My thanks are due to the editors of *Horizon*, in which part of the material for Surnames in America first appeared, and of *History Today* who published in London the original article that led to the writing of this book, and also to Mr Thomas J. Davis III, Editor of the History Department of Charles Scribner's Sons, for his help and patience.

C.M.M. *1967*

Part One

HISTORICAL BACKGROUND

Introduction

The great mass of English surnames rose as a spontaneous growth. Never regulated by law, seldom consciously chosen or deliberately given, they simply evolved out of everyday speech because they were needed, and like any other natural phenomenon were subject to modification and the law of survival of the fittest.

In just the same way, though at an earlier date, our place names had evolved naturally from the spoken word, echoing the colloquial phraseology of their day. Each of these two groups of name-words has much to teach us. As our place names link us with those invading tribes of Angles and Saxons at the time they were first settling in this land, so our surnames echo the common speech of their descendants some six or seven centuries later at a time when a new phase of national life was beginning after the Norman conquest.

Place names have received much attention from scholars and are well understood. The subject of surnames is much more unwieldy, slippery and harder to get hold of. Much valuable work has been done on it – particularly, and surprisingly, by Swedish scholars – but it cannot be said that it has been thoroughly mastered in the way that the late Professor Ekwall mastered our place names. The latter have the great advantage of being immutably fixed in position, so that there is a good chance of finding them in early records and recognizing them by their locality. Without early forms of a word its etymology is mere guesswork. But the bearers of surnames have always been mobile, becoming ever more so with the passage of time, which makes it much harder to pin down early examples of their names and know that they are the ones we are looking for. On the other hand the forming of surnames is not nearly so remote from us as that of place names, and as England is wonderfully rich in records from the eleventh century onwards it is in fact possible to follow the development of the majority of our names, though one cannot attach a particular modern family to a particular medieval one with any certainty without a genealogy, which is a hard thing to prove.

And let us be clear at once that in speaking of the antiquity of our surnames we are not laying any stress on those that 'came over with the Conqueror'. Some names of Norman origin are very interesting, but they are a small number compared with the vast mass of English surnames, many of which are older than the Norman and most of which are of humble origin. Many scholars have worked on the Domesday Book statistics, trying to calculate the number and classes of the population at that time, which is the very time when surnames were beginning to be used. The evidence is too incomplete for accurate figures, but all are agreed that at least three-quarters of the total population of that time were of villein or lower status, that is to say peasantry. By the same token at least three-quarters of our surnames come from the lower classes. They echo the lively voices in the market places of the growing towns and the rough talk of the servants and men-at-arms in the castles, rather than the courtly conversation of lords and ladies, though that is to be found too, but above all they relay to us the familiarities of village life in the country, where the majority of our ancestors tilled the soil.

Those who set great store on their gentility need not be discouraged by this conclusion. England has always been a land of opportunity. Hundreds of peasant families had increased their holdings and become country gentry by Tudor times, or made their fortunes in trade and married into the nobility. Likewise younger sons of noble families could sink very rapidly to the bottom of the scale. Every noble family would find some peasants among its ancestors if all its lines could be followed back. Even the Queen herself is only six generations removed from a London plumber, behind whom must lie hundreds of ordinary people. Conversely the humblest people have probably some noble strains in their ancestry, perhaps kings and queens if only they knew it. We are all made of a great mixture and the surname we each have inherited belongs to just one of the ingredients. So in this study of surnames, whatever interest may lead us on, let us at least abandon that of snobbery, the most untrustworthy of all guides when searching for the truth.

C. L. Ewen has estimated that there are at least a hundred thousand current surnames of British origin. I can well believe him, if one includes all the different spellings of each name. When some day a comprehensive dictionary of them is published it will be an enormous book. In the meantime the best is Dr P. H. Reaney's Dictionary to which I am much indebted. My purpose in this book is not so much to give individual meanings as to look at our names as they stand in their masses and in smaller groups, and see what we can learn from them. There is significance in their incidence as well as their nature, and the common ones can tell us more than the rarities, for they tell what great numbers of people were saying and doing at that special time in our history when the casual designations of neighbours stuck fast. They give us a chance to listen in to the small-talk of the Middle Ages, the jokes, the pet names, the descriptions of six or seven hundred years ago, miraculously crystallized into permanent form.

We see and hear these names all around us in such enormous quantities that the author struggling with too much material must select for comment only those names which seem most significant. We can also find them in medieval rolls, preserved among our national muniments, where they were set down by monks and clerks in the twelfth or thirteenth centuries. In these records the names are generally in Latin or Norman French or a mixture of the two, Radulphus de Campo, Robertus filius Walteri, Henricus Piscator, Petrus le Blound. We see here what the clerk of that time thought the correct form for an official document, but in the modern names we hear what was actually said, *Field*, *Watson*, *Fisher*, *Blunt*.

Here again, among medieval sources, the mass of material is embarrassing. A large team of scholars is needed to deal with it and as yet no such team has been organized, though a few individuals have achieved much. All that the present writer can hope for is to give a general view of this fascinating subject, so familiar and yet so little noticed, a subject which can unfold for us the whole panorama of medieval life, if only we can interpret it aright.

Chapter 1

PRE-CONQUEST NAMES

English surnames became fixed and hereditary in the period between the battles of Hastings and Agincourt, a fact which we will try to establish more explicitly later. But many of them had their roots in a much earlier time; indeed the more one studies them the more they recede into the past, so that, to understand them properly, we must look back before the Conquest.

Generally speaking the Anglo-Saxons had only one name each. Of course they sometimes added or substituted nicknames, for human inventiveness was no less than now, but such things were transitory and died with the individual. However in the last century before the Conquest new ideas were in the air, conditions were changing and second names of the sort which might develop into surnames were beginning to appear with some frequency. In order to understand these beginnings we must give some thought to Old English names and the changes that came over them.

Anyone who begins a study of Anglo-Saxon personal names – and hundreds of them appear in charters and wills as well as in better known literary works – must be struck at once by two very noticeable points about them. The first is how completely they belong to their own language and to that of the closely related Scandinavian race. Apart from a slight Celtic element, which was well absorbed at an early date and is not easily distinguishable, there is an almost total absence of names from any other culture than their own right up to the time of the Conquest.

It was not that names from the Classics and the Bible were unknown to the Anglo-Saxons. At the time of the Conquest they had been Christian for about four centuries, and during part of that time England had been renowned throughout Europe for its saints and scholars. Exquisite copies of the Gospels had enriched its monasteries; missionaries from Devon had converted many of the heathen Germans; English princesses had married continental royalties – and vice versa; and Charlemagne had chosen an Englishman, Aelhwine (or Alcuin) of York, as tutor to his sons and reorganizer of his monastic school at Tours, which he planned as a centre for the revival of learning. And yet this learned and religious race never gave its children names from the Graeco-Roman or Biblical world.

The only way in which such names were used in pre-Conquest England was by priests or bishops who sometimes took Biblical names, or made-up Latin ones like Deodatus or Boniface, at their ordinations or consecrations. But this custom was never very common and became rarer in the later Anglo-Saxon period. At the time of the Conquest the Bishops and Abbots of England had names such as Wulfwig, Aldred, Wulfstan, Aelfric or Aethelwine. The native tradition of naming was too deeply embedded to be changed even by Christianity.

But that being so, why and how did this whole system of Saxon names vanish so completely? Before 1066 everyone in England had a name like Cuthbeorht or Leofwine or Ethelnoth, or possibly one of those shorter ones like Penda or Offa which sound even more remote from us; and then we seem suddenly to move into a different world where men are called William and Richard and John. For thousands of people history becomes readable only at that point.

The truth is that the change was not nearly so rapid as we might suppose. Those far off centuries are somewhat telescoped for us, and the Saxon people, passing for a time into obscurity, had few of their names recorded with any prominence during that period. Their native names lasted long enough for hundreds of them – literally – to be preserved in our surnames, as will be shown later. But the change was remarkable none the less. In two centuries after the Conquest the great majority of the native names had vanished, and, considering how tenaciously they had been clung to at an earlier stage, it is strange indeed. This is the more so as the language of which they were a part was to survive triumphantly. Submerged for a time under a layer of Norman French it rose again, somewhat modified by the experience, but enriched and full of vitality. Not so the English personal names. The average Englishman today knows those of a few kings and saints, thanks largely to the efforts of scholars and the antiquarian zeal of the Victorians, but the majority of pre-Conquest names are gone.

How was it that the Normans, who failed to impose their language on the English, did impose their names? Or to put it differently, why did the English, who so obstinately continued to speak their own language, accept the names of their hated conquerors? There is no easy answer to this question. However one looks at it, it remains a strange phenomenon. The only way in which we can come nearer to an understanding of it is to look again at the Old English names. We will find that a change was coming over them in the tenth century. They were in a transitional stage when the Conquest struck them, which may account in part for their inability to stand firm.

The second and even more striking point that we notice about the Old English names is their enormous number. Cerdic, Creoda, Ceawlin, Ceolwulf, and so on; they seem to be never repeated. We see here a totally different philosophy of names from that to which we are accustomed. For the last nine hundred years or so we have been inclined to call our sons after their fathers or their grandfathers or some other relative, or, failing that, after some saint, king or hero, but the Anglo-Saxons did not do that. A name was a man's private property, respected by his family, and not lightly to be given to others, and the more a man was honoured the more his name was kept for him alone. This led to the constant creation of new names. Not that the same name was never repeated. Men's minds ran in similar channels and names expressing popular ideas reappeared in different places and times, but each family regarded the names of its own immediate progenitors as sacred.

In the early Anglo-Saxon period we find a great many short, simple names like Aelle, Beda, Penda, Ine, surviving from ancient times, and beside them names composed of two words placed together as Cyneric, Oswald, Sigebeorht. Gradually these two-theme names became more and more popular until by the ninth century they are firmly established as the standard form of name, at any rate for the upper classes. Among the words used in the making up of these names some few were already obsolete, living on only in this way, but the majority of them were ordinary nouns and adjectives in current use – many are still so – expressive of noble qualities or symbolic objects. These name-themes chosen by our remote ancestors give us a good idea of their taste and aspirations. As we would expect, their favourite qualities were of a warlike nature. The list of name themes on page 337 shows how many were connected with fighting. The wolf was decidedly their favourite living creature. But good counsel (raed) was frequently included as a most desirable attribute, and kindly human qualities were also valued. It is not by chance that, in the last century before the Conquest, when the Anglo-Saxons had suffered much from Danish invasions, such mild themes as Leof (beloved), God (good), Frith (peace) and Wine (friend) became the most popular of all. Throughout the whole period ran a strong poetic vein and one of the favourite name-words was 'beorht' or 'bright' which means, as it still does, shining or beautiful.

Some of these theme words such as Aethel (noble or royal) were always placed first. Some few were always last, but most of them could be in either position – Beorhtric or Ricbeorht – and this resulted in an enormous variety of names with the possibility of coining more at will. Sometimes the themes were combined in such an apparently haphazard way that modern writers on the subject have been led to state that by the eighth or ninth century their meanings, when used for name making, had ceased to have any significance. But I am unable to agree with this view. Almost all the words so used were still in current use, so that their meanings could not be ignored. To take a parallel modern example; if we name a daughter Rose we may do so because it is a family name, but we cannot be unaware of the flower. In the same way a Saxon calling his son Wulfstan could not fail to think of the fierce courage of a wolf and the hardness of a stone.

The two themes did not have to fit together logically or grammatically. They were simply two separate words put together to make a name. Very often they did combine well, as in Leofric (beloved ruler) or Godwine (good companion), though if the father stood out for a fierce quality and the mother wanted something milder – or vice versa – the result could be very incongruous, as with a name like Wigfrith (war-peace). Perhaps in such a case they hoped to fit their child for all contingencies; I cannot believe that they had no feeling for these simple, strong words that they put together.

The point to bear in mind is that the Anglo-Saxons, in common with others of the same language group at that time, did not call their children after people, but after ideas. Courage, power, love, the cunning of the elves, the brightness of the sword, these were the sort of attributes they had in mind with which to endow a child.

Side by side with this strong tendency to create an individual name for each child, to differentiate him from all his family and those around him, there was also a vague desire pulling in the opposite direction, to link the family together in some way by name, in fact to do the very thing which surnames were to accomplish so successfully hundreds of years later. The first expression of this idea was to have all the names of one's family beginning with the same letter, as has been the custom of the Egyptian royal family in recent times. We see this in the early annals of the house of Wessex, where in the first six generations following the legendary Cerdic twenty-two out of the twenty-three recorded names begin with 'C', and all are different. Then, after a few mixed names, the family changed to 'E' and 'A' as its most favoured initials.

Another attempt to bring some unity into the names of a family, while at the same time keeping them all different, was to give one theme of the mother's or father's name to some or all of the children, and this was practised widely for several centuries, but never consistently, most of the leading Saxon families having their favourite name-themes. Thus Aethelfrith, King of Northumbria, called his eldest son Eanfrith, and five more sons each had a name beginning with 'Os'. But this system was not confined to the dynasties of the great. A lady who died in Dorset in about 995 kindly left bequests in her will to many of her slaves, including Wulfrun (a woman) and her son Wulfric, and to Eadstan and his son Ceolstan. She also mentions Cynestan and Herestan who were probably of the same family, as well as other slaves with the simple old-fashioned short names which abounded in this class, like Bica, Aeffa, Beda and Snel.

It is this practice of combining similarity of name with

differentiation (something like the modern system of naming race-horses) that has proved the bugbear of the Saxon period for generations of schoolchildren. Bogged down among Eadgars, Eadwigs, Egberts and Egfriths, they have abandoned the struggle, contenting themselves with feeble jokes about Eggnog and Eggflip.

The royal house of Wessex, since we can follow it closely for many generations, is very useful for illustrating the feelings of the Anglo-Saxons about names. It made the point abundantly clear that though they honoured their ancestors they did so by leaving their names severely alone. All their genealogies lead back to the half-mythical Cerdic, but there is no record that they ever used this name again. The king who brought the family to power in more historic times was Egbert (Ecgbeorht, sword bright). It was an apt name for a warrior king and crops up in various other parts of the country, but not again in the royal house of Wessex. His son Aethelwulf favoured the school of continuity and called his first four sons Aethelstan, Aethelbald, Aethelbert, Aethelred and his daughter Aethelswyth; and then abandoning his plan unexpectedly named his youngest son Aelfraed. What prompted this we do not know. It would be absurd to suggest that he had a presentiment that this child would have more than ordinary wisdom (Aelfraed means fairy counsel). However that may be, Alfred, like the youngest son in a fairy tale, outlived his brothers and became the hero and 'darling' of his race, and his name was avoided by his own family for a full century afterwards.

Alfred named his own son Eadweard, the first part of which came from his wife's family and has been variously translated as riches and prosperity. 'Weard' means guardian. It is reasonable to suppose that he was thinking of the riches of civilization which he had fought so hard to save, and that he wanted his son to preserve them. I cannot believe that so thoughtful a man did not choose this name deliberately, very conscious of its meaning.

Henceforward the theme word, Ead, was the favourite first element for Alfred's descendants as long as the male line lasted, and the whole name Edward was eventually to become the best known and most honoured of the Anglo-Saxon names. It was this, rather than his own name, that Alfred bequeathed to us. After this his descendants rang all the changes on Ead-

and Aethel-, and all but the most determined students lose heart.

But towards the end of the tenth century the old taboos about names were breaking down. King Edgar called his two sons Edward and Ethelred, both names that had been used in his family before, though several generations earlier. His son Ethelred (the Unready) continued the same policy, naming all his sons after ancestors, one of them even after Alfred. We can imagine the more old-fashioned of his subjects shaking their heads and saying that no good could come of such naming. Apparently it did not. The unfortunate prince Alfred, the only one of Alfred the Great's royal descendants to bear his name until George III gave it to his youngest son, was cruelly murdered; gallant Edmund Ironside died young; and generally affairs went from bad to worse. The King proved most Unready; but the new style of name-giving had come to stay. From that time all the princes of the house of Wessex were called after honoured ancestors, down to Edgar Atheling who fled to Scotland.

Not only in the royal family, but in all the contemporary records, we see the same thing happening, and some names definitely emerging as popular. This is a change very pertinent to our subject, for as long as everyone had a name that differed from those of all his family and neighbours there was no need for surnames, but as soon as the same names began to be repeated within a community, then second names appeared automatically to distinguish one from another.

We see these early surnames in the Anglo-Saxon Chronicle and other writings of the period, chiefly in charters and wills. Some are the kind of nicknames men have always given each other, whether in admiration, scorn or fun – Tofi the Proud, Aelfmar Darling. Others are plain statements of fact, with no other purpose than identification – Eadric Little, Ednoth the Staller, Aelfward Kentish. In one of Cnut's charters two of the witnesses are Tovi the White and Tovi the Red. In modernizing such names it is usual to include the definite article, but in the original language, though sometimes written in that way, they are more often just 'Tovi hwita' and 'Wulfsig blac'. It seems that already these nicknames were being spoken as simply as modern surnames.

They were indeed surnames, but not yet family names. They were personal and temporary and would not pass on to the next generation. Swedish scholars who have done much work on this subject have coined the term 'by-name' for them, to distinguish them from hereditary surnames, but I do not find this expression convenient in use, as one can seldom know exactly when a temporary name becomes permanent. The one state merges so naturally into the other. Consequently I call them 'surnames' from the time they first appear, with the qualification that the earlier ones are sure to change.

The name Tovi (or Tofi) mentioned above is a Danish one, and reminds us of the thousands of Danes who settled in England from the ninth century onwards and whose names added to the great number already in use. They were very much of the same types as the Old English ones, many of them having cognate forms in English. Thus the Danish Harald and the English Herewald merged together as the more familiar Harold. In the last century before the Conquest Danes and English were mixing freely, and names of both origins were to be found all over the country. Godwin, most powerful of the Anglo-Saxon earls, married a Danish woman and gave his four eldest sons Danish names, Sweyn, Harald, Tosti, Girth. Like the English, the Scandinavians were adopting the new style of name-giving, repeating rather than avoiding the names of their forbears, and were much given to the use of nicknames. Thus Harald Harefoot (who must have been a fast runner) was distinguished in speech from his grandfather Harald Bluetooth, and from the Norwegian king, Harald Hardrada.

Altogether there was a bewildering number of names current in England at this time. As well as all the two-part names of the Cuthbert/Winbold type which seem capable of endless new permutations, and the Danish versions of much the same themes, there were still hundreds of the old type, short names belonging to both languages used chiefly among the lower classes. Some of them, like Cutha and Wine and Aeffa, were obviously mere abbreviations of the longer names, others apparently had an independent life of their own, Binni, Hucca, Toki, Dodda; they seem endless. M. Redin of Lund, who has made a valuable study of these in his *Uncompounded Anglo-Saxon Names*, has collected

736 of them, but in his interesting preface he stresses that these are far less numerous than the formal two-theme names. This will give some idea of the numbers that we are contending with. It was high time that there was a change.

As has already been made clear the change had set in. A system of fewer names, supported by surnames as required, was on the way by the year 1000. Even if there had been no Norman Conquest it would have established itself in its own time. But the Conquest did come and the slow movement was swept forward by a tidal wave.

Chapter 2

THE MELTING POT

Much of what has been said about Anglo-Saxon names would apply to those of all the Teutonic races who spread across Western Europe in the Dark Ages. But on the Continent the idea of repeating the names of great men began to develop earlier than in England, though it did so slowly. By 800 the Franks had had three Childerics and three Pippins and by 900 they were embarking on their long succession of Charles and Louis, to whom immediately they gave nicknames, the Bold, the Simple, the Fat and so forth. But the English in their isolation from Europe had come more slowly to this idea.

The Normans, who were of the same racial group as the English, were still barbarians when they burst into Europe in the tenth century. But such was their extraordinary energy, both physical and mental, that in less than a century they had consolidated their territory, become ardent Christians, mastered the arts and skills of their more civilized neighbours, surpassing them in most respects, and had discarded their own language in favour of French. Among other innovations they adopted a French pronunciation for their Nordic names, picked up some more names popular with the Franks, and took whole-heartedly to the new idea of calling a child after his father or patron. This new system of names tuned in perfectly with the close-knit feudal spirit on which their strength was based; the loyalty of each man to his lord, each lord to an overlord, and all to the king, could now find a new expression in names which were no longer barriers but bonds.

When William invaded England he had with him dozens of men who already proudly bore his name or that of his father,

26

Robert, or his grandfather, Richard, and he had already given these three names to his own sons. (Richard was killed young while hunting.) His barons also had typical Norman names such as Geoffrey, Roger, Walter and Hugh, and we may be sure that the young knights who followed them were eager to express their loyalty by naming their sons for their lord or their king.

It is not surprising that these new names, loosed on England at the highest level, soon became fashionable with all who accepted Norman rule. What is remarkable is that their ultimate victory was so complete. But this success was not won quickly. For well over a century after the Conquest the native names are still to be found in large numbers, as we should expect. The Norman yoke, tolerated by some, was bitterly resisted by many. There were rebellions, reprisals and widespread suffering; but side by side with this there was acceptance on a large scale too, and some degree of co-operation. At this date Norman and English names can be clearly distinguished, except for a very few that are common to both, and the proportions in which they occur give valuable evidence as to the position of the English at this painful period in their history.

In his study of *Early London Personal Names* the late Professor Ekwall gives much evidence on this subject. In administrative records in London soon after the Conquest he finds the names of the two races side by side everywhere. A list of the Canons of St Pauls in 1104 shows seven English names to eleven Norman, and in 1130 the majority of Aldermen were still English. By this time many Englishmen had Norman names but the reverse hardly ever happened, and therefore an Old English name is a strong indication of race. Londoners had grown somewhat used to Normans in high positions during the reign of Edward the Confessor, and one might assume that they would be more ready to co-operate with them than the rest of the country. But there is evidence telling much the same story everywhere. In Domesday Book among the holders of land under the new régime we see hundreds of English names, at least one-third of all the names given, though not much more than an eighth of the land, since all the richest prizes went to Normans. One can never be accurate about numbers of people in Domesday Book because the same name is often repeated in several places, and without fixed surnames it is impossible to know if it refers to the same man or another. However there is clear evidence of hundreds of Englishmen holding land under King William, many of them described as 'the king's thegn', which means that they had taken the oath of allegiance to him. There certainly was co-operation and perhaps less nursing of hatred than romantic writers would have us believe. Nothing succeeds like success, and among young Englishmen there must have been many who admired the Norman vigour and adopted Norman fashions very readily.

We must also bear in mind that William's army contained many young bachelors eager to marry and found families to hold their new lands for ever. Kipling, with his poet's eye for truth, has shown us such a one in the young knight who sang, 'Now England has taken me'. Soon there was a new generation of young Williams and Richards and Roberts and Hughs growing up to inherit these lands, many of them with English mothers, and not all of them hated.

So the names fanned out over the country and filtered down rank by rank to the humblest, and when a peasant fifty years after the Conquest named his child William, he was not thinking of the harsh king whose army had burnt down his grandfather's hut, but of the lord of his own manor who, though somewhat to be feared, was perhaps in some respects also to be admired as the greatest man in the small world of the village. If there had been a moderate number of highly popular native names, they might have stood their ground beside the new ones. But this was not so. The English name system was still too diffuse and variable to produce strong individual champions of this sort. The movement in this direction was too late; and the many Old English names fell a prey to the fewer names of the new leaders.

Every man must have a lord. That was the basic principle of Norman England, and poor men, fearful for their lives and their families, subscribed to it anxiously, praying God that their lord might be a merciful man. If one could recommend one's son to him by naming the child after him, that was clearly a good thing to do, and so the new names multiplied fast.

Many stuck to the old names for generations, but it is a tribute to the success of the Norman kings and the social system they imposed that less than two hundred years after the Conquest William was the commonest name in England.

No sooner had the Norman names come flooding into England than another new idea followed in their wake. If a name could be used to commend a child to a living patron, how much better to commend him to a saint in Heaven, even to one of the blessed Apostles if one dared to look so high. This idea also came with the Normans but it was new to them too, comparatively new indeed in Western Europe, where the same spirit of respect that had for centuries restrained men from using the names of their ancestors had held them back from taking the names of saints and Biblical personages. But once the ice was broken such names began to grow in popularity.

In Domesday Book among the hundreds of Norman names, the Gilberts and Williams and Hughs that occur on every page, we see the occasional Biblical name. Adam, Joseph, David, Solomon, Daniel, John, Peter, Matthew, Thomas and Stephen all appear, but with very few examples. Altogether they total less than 1% of all the names given. A century later (taking 1,000 names at random from the Index of the Pipe Roll of 1186), Biblical names have climbed to just over 8%, and in the following century they go forward rapidly.

In a somewhat similar test we can see the Norman and Biblical names together ousting the Old English ones. The Pipe Roll, a record of accounts of the Exchequer, has a convenient index of names in which all those that are set down with a patronymic (Richard the son of Ralf) are grouped together under the heading 'filius'. Thus in this group we have two generations conveniently arranged together, for whatever year we choose. If in this list we take 1166, one hundred years after the battle of Hastings, we find that among the fathers' names 42% are still of the Old English type, but of the sons of these same men only 15% have English names. In 1200, about a generation later, the number of old style names among the sons has fallen to barely 3%, all the rest being Norman or Biblical with the proportion of the latter slowly increasing. In fact we see the old names going out fast. Such entries as 'William son of Wulfric' and 'Peter son of Hereward' tell the story. Fifty years later we search the records almost in vain for any pre-Conquest names at all.

If the change-over to Norman names by the English people typifies their acceptance of the rule of their conquerors, so their adoption of Biblical names at much the same time shows that

29

religious fervour which gradually raised their spirits above the harsh conditions in which they lived, and enabled them to endure. Alongside the great castles and cathedrals which are the chief visible monuments to medieval life in England, we have the Norman and Biblical Christian names which seem to share the same long-lasting qualities.

At this important moment in our history, when one of the manifestations of the national upheaval was a total change in the name system, leading on to the development of surnames, we are fortunate enough to have one of the most remarkable early records in Europe. Domesday Book is a sort of General Directory for 1086, which enables us to make a review of the name situation as it was twenty years after the Conquest. For every manor, and that means at least every village, we are given the names of the new owner who in most cases is a Norman, though by no means always, and his English predecessor, sometimes with several additional names of lesser men. As has been mentioned before, accurate figures are impossible owing to frequent repetitions, but roughly speaking we are told the names of several thousand landowners at the time of the survey and as many from the time of Edward the Confessor, enough material to give a very good idea of the way in which both Normans and English were designated at that time.

One thing instantly noticeable is that the Old English names have been already modified into simpler and more manageable forms than those in which we have met them earlier. The noble Aethel- has become Ail-, El- or Al-, many diphthongs have been reduced to simple vowels, and many consonants dropped so that instead of the long-winded Aethelbeorht, Aethelmaer, Leofwine and Sigeweard, men are already calling each other Ailbert, Elmer, Lewin and Siward. The same name appears in half a dozen spellings, for the Norman clerks merely wrote down what they heard in their own way, but in doing so they make it clear to us that the pronunciation of such names had been much modified, and for the better, since the classic Anglo-Saxon period, and that traditional spellings still used by monks in their Chronicles had not kept pace with the spoken word.

Another point which we cannot fail to notice on looking through Domesday Book is that almost all the Normans have surnames, or second designations of some kind, and very few of the English. On the one hand we see Geoffrey de Mandeville, Henry de Ferrers, Robert Malet, Ralph de Mortemer; on the other Ailmar, Godric, Brictward, Edsi. But this gives a false impression. We must remember that this famous list was written by Normans for Normans. On the one hand are the conquerors, the new holders of the land, who must be treated with respect, and also carefully identified so that there can be no mistake about the land they hold and the tax they pay for it, and on the other the dispossessed who no longer matter, many of them already dead. We must be thankful that King William thought it worthwhile recording their names at all. It was only done to identify the land in question. Ten hides formerly held by Wulfric could be distinguished from those adjoining that were held by Turchil. Had these men needed further identification it would have been forthcoming.

In an earlier draft of the great Survey which survives for Ely and Cambridgeshire, the majority of the English owners (about three-quarters of them, which is as high a proportion as for the Norman tenants) are given surnames. But these were cut out from the final version, presumably to save space. Among the English who made their peace with the new king and appear in this final survey as still in possession of their old lands, as many have second names as the Normans; Alward the Goldsmith, Alvred de Marlborough, Wulwi the Huntsman, Alwold Chamberlain, Alwin Dodesone. In fact there is no real evidence to suggest that the Normans were in any way ahead of the English in the matter of surnames at this time.

The Norman surnames of Domesday Book consist for the most part of the names of the places from which they have come. Though they are busy raising their castle keeps on their new English estates, they still call themselves de Bec, de Courci and de Montfort. Many others are distinguished by the names of their fathers, Ralf son of Hugh, Richard son of Gilbert and so on. Most of these presumably are young men who had no estates of their own in Normandy. Then there are those who have won their place among the landowners by useful service, Hugo the Steersman (Stirmannus), who may have proved his worth on that memorable Channel crossing; Tezelin the Cook (Cocus);

Odo the Crossbowman (Arbalisterius), Durand the Barber (Tonsor), and many more.

The smallest group of surnames but perhaps the most interesting consists of personal nicknames. William Malet took his from the iron mace or hammer wielded in battle, though there are other possible sources for this much discussed name. Humphrey Vis de Lew (Wolf Face) probably prided himself on his fierce countenance. Osbern Giffard had a fat face (O.F. giffard, fat-cheeked), but none of his family seem to have minded this as the name has multiplied and lasted to the present time. Many are straightforward personal descriptions, Blond (the fair), Musard (the dreamy), Basset (the short). My favourite name in all Domesday Book is Roger Deus Salvet Dominas, or Roger God-save-the-ladies. The clerk put it into decent Latin, but he himself would have uttered his favourite toast in Norman French, unless like Roger Bigod, one of William's closest counsellors, he had already learnt to swear in English.

In fact in Domesday Book we see the four types into which surnames can always be classified, those of locality, relationship, occupation and description, the last including nicknames, and we see them both in French and English. The greatest difficulty in writing about names at this stage is to maintain any consistency in language. Most of the names are latinized, which generally consists of no more than the addition of -us to the Norman French or English name. On the whole I have omitted this encumbrance and translated other Latin words unless there is a particular reason for leaving them. But how can one be consistent when the original is such a mixture?

Let us now skip 880 years and take up a modern telephone directory; that of London is the best for the purpose, being the largest and most representative. Almost every surname in Domesday Book will be found in it, some few in precisely the same form, but most of them modified in spelling. The aristocratic Norman names from places, the *Percies* and *Mortimers*, are there of course, and so are the *Cooks* and *Chamberlains*, while names of the 'son-of-Richard' type are in great profusion and variety.

Some of the nicknames have changed a good deal, but hardly one is missing. *Giffard* is unaltered, but can also be found as

Jefford. The Old French 'blund' or 'blond' has become *Blunt*, just as 'grand' became *Grant*. Even the villainous sounding Vis de Lew is still present as *Vidler*. This may sound like a guess, but it is well documented all the way. God-save-the-ladies was really too much of a mouthful to stay the course, and yet something very like it is with us in part. In French it would begin 'Dieu garde-', and there are several *Dugardes* in our directory. These might be thought to be of modern French origin were it not for a number of medieval examples of the same name, such as Agnes Dieugarde from the Stafford Poll Tax of 1381, showing the inter-mediate stage.

But though the Domesday surnames are nearly all with us still, it does not follow that their present bearers are descended from these very landowners of 1086. In times past genealogists were very ready to make pedigrees back to the Conquest or earlier, but now they are so cautious and careful that they will hardly allow more than a handful of lines to be proved so far back. Many can be traced to the thirteenth or even twelfth century, but the last step that would unite them with the Domesday Book gentry is over uncertain ground.

It was just in this early Norman period about the reign of William Rufus, for which records are most lacking, that names were inclined to fluctuate and change before settling down for ever. It was, by this time, well established that a man with any pretensions to importance needed a second name, but the idea of its continuing as a family name for all his male descendants had not been grasped. Undoubtedly many who proudly bore the names of Norman villages did keep them and pass them on to their descendants as cherished certificates of origin. But others, who built themselves castles in England far more splendid than their wooden keeps in Normandy, took the names of their new estates. Meanwhile new arrivals from Normandy brought the same Norman names with them again.

Likewise the young men who in Domesday Book have no other distinction than being the sons of their fathers, must all of them have taken the names of their new English manors, unless they acquired nicknames that stuck very fast. And exactly the same may be said of those who had as it were risen from the ranks. They would be cooks and steersmen no longer, but lords of manors by the names of which they and their progeny would

33

be known. But in both cases the earlier names continued too. There were still plenty more people called sons of Richard and Robert, plenty more cooks and chamberlains.

One would think that of the four types of name the nicknames would be the most personal and least likely to pass on, but the evidence tells us otherwise. They seem, in fact, to have been among the earliest to become hereditary. Certainly some of the surnames of this type, of the invading Normans, like *Mallet* and *Giffard*, for which long genealogies have been proved, were already hereditary before they landed in England. Of many others we cannot be sure of the unbroken descent. The names were there in England in the eleventh century, and are here still, but popular nicknames once established could be used again for other people with the same characteristics. To go back a little to our own hero-king, Edmund Ironside, his male line soon died out but we have *Ironsides* with us still. Likewise there are *Wakes*, though probably not descended from Hereward. The Conqueror's famous minstrel, Taillefer (or Cut-iron) was the first man killed at Hastings and no one of that name held land in 1086, and yet there were Taillefers in England in the thirteenth century as there are *Telfers*, *Telfords*, and *Tullivers* today. A famous nickname like a title of honour could be bestowed by popular acclaim on anyone who truly earned it.

To sum up we may say that the surnames used in England in the eleventh century have lasted amazingly well. They are with us in enormous numbers as good as new, but many of them drifted about a little before settling on one family for as long as its male line would endure.

Domesday Book gives us a foretaste of our surnames. The chief ingredients are in the melting pot. In the next two centuries many more will be added and all will simmer together until the 'jelly' sets. This metaphor cannot be pressed too far, for when one makes jam it sets at one moment, and with our surnames the setting period varied over three hundred years. As we have seen, a number of names at the time of the Conquest were already hereditary. But even in well-documented cases where we know the name has survived in the same family from the Conquest, we do not know that *all* the sons took it in those early generations.

It was perfectly natural for the eldest son of Richard of Clifford, for instance, when he inherited the castle his father had built on the Welsh border, to inherit its name too. This kind of name was a statement of fact. He was 'of Clifford'. But his younger brothers, carving themselves fortunes elsewhere and perhaps gaining good estates where they won an importance of their own, would be known by the names of these new homes.

Likewise, in a different sphere, the son of a smith was likely to inherit his father's forge and the trade to which he had been brought up, and the name Smith with it, but the same man's other sons, employed as cooks or shepherds, would be known as such.

It is not until truth is dispensed with, and the sons and grandsons of the Cliffords living far from their ancestral home, and the descendants of the smith engaged in totally different trades, are all called *Clifford* and *Smith*, that the jelly is really set. And this happened at different times in different social spheres and different parts of the country.

As may be expected it happened sooner among the upper classes than the lower, and sooner in the South than the North; for the South was more prosperous and civilized than the North which suffered terrible devastation at the hands of William I, from which it recovered but slowly. But though one might think that it also happened sooner in towns than in the country, the very opposite seems to be the case.

When one comes to think of it this is readily understandable. Country people are more conservative than townsfolk and have longer memories. Anyone who has lived in a small village knows how easily a young fellow could be called Smith, even though he was working with the cows, simply because his great grandfather had been the smith and was still remembered by the older generation. It would be very different in a busy town where new people were always arriving and an obsolete trade-name could be definitely misleading. We have here an anomaly. For once the conservatism of the country made more fertile ground for a new principle – that of fixed surnames – to flourish in, than the more practical go-ahead mentality of the town.

But for each individual the setting process came in one lifetime. A man's neighbours spoke of him as Robin Black in spite of his fair hair simply because his father had been called Black. They would never have done such an unnatural thing if it had

35

not become so much a matter of course that it happened without thought. When did this custom spread so strongly across the country that it affected even the humblest classes? How nearly can we date the change from transitory to permanent surnames? To find the answer to this question we must turn to the medieval records.

Chapter 3

MEDIEVAL RECORDS

England is wonderfully rich in medieval records. Owing partly to the organizing ability of a few extremely capable kings, partly to the industrious habits of the great monasteries, and partly to the comparatively peaceful nature of our internal history, in which sacking, burning and total destruction were less frequent than on the Continent, vast accumulations of ancient parchment have survived. Much of this has been worked over by scholars and published by learned societies; much exists only in the original, the ink faded, the parchment often stained or torn, but still miraculously available to the modern student; more still remains in various archives, some hardly accessible, waiting for the industry of new generations.

This being said, it must be admitted that for the first century after the Conquest the evidence is scanty for the people as a whole. Domesday Book, splendid record though it is, has one great drawback for our purpose in that it refers only to the land-owning classes. Those mentioned are not all of noble birth by any means; as we have seen they include cooks, barbers and bow-men, and a great many young fighting men who had few possessions but their horses and armour when they set out across the Channel. But none the less they are the successful men of their day, the ruling class. Of the peasantry who made up the great mass of the population it is much harder to find evidence. But such evidence does exist here and there and must be constantly sought out to counterbalance the names of the gentry which tend to appear so much more frequently in official documents.

There is, for example, among the records of the Abbey of Bury St Edmunds, a detailed list of tenants of Abbey lands dating

from soon after the Conquest. Such rent rolls or custumals as
they were called, giving the names of manorial tenants with the
rents and services they owned for every foot of land, exist in
large numbers from two or three centuries later, but are very
rare from such an early date. Mr D. C. Douglas, who has made a
study of the Abbey records, calls this 'the earliest extensive list
of peasant names up to now discovered in any English document', and dates it provisionally as belonging to the reign of
William Rufus.

That the men and women named in this list are of humble
class is shown by the small amounts due from them, mostly
about fourpence a year with customary labour. Two villages together, Barton and Packenham, make up just a hundred names,
of which nine or ten are Scandinavian in origin; one only
(Robert) is Norman and all the rest are Old English, so we know
we are dealing with the native peasantry, hardly influenced by
the Conquest. Surely, one might think, these people are too remote from us for their surnames to affect our present ones. But
not at all. They are the same names. Like those of the gentry in
Domesday Book they can nearly all be found in our directories.

Of the hundred individuals mentioned, sixty-nine have surnames or second designations of some kind. Only six of these are
occupational and five of them, given in Latin, are clearly just
statements of fact, but one, *Hayward*, which occurs three times
(Wihtric Heiward, Godwi Haiwart and Brihtmar Haiward),
seems to have established itself already as a proper name rather
than a common noun which could be translated. (The hayward
looked after hedges and enclosures.) Thirty-two of the surnames
are patronymics like Godric filius Turstani (Godric son of
Thurstan), and sixteen are nicknames, all very English and
mostly still in use. *Brown*, *Frost* and *Long* are very familiar. Two
men with more individual names, though rather long for lasting,
were Aedric Hopehevene and Godlaf Crepunder Huitel. The
former must have had some pious expression about hoping for
heaven constantly on his lips. In the latter case 'huitel' or
'whittle' is a Middle English word for a cloak or blanket; but
whether Godlaf was inclined to creep under one habitually or
had only done so on some particular occasion we can never know.
Such names could only survive if abbreviated, perhaps to *Hope*
or *Whittle*. But in speaking of names of this date 'surviving' I do

not wish to imply that they were hereditary, only to make the point that however far back we probe into the past, we find surnames already in use, and frequently the same ones that we still have. The poor seem to have had them just as much as the rich. After all they cost nothing, and could add a bit of merriment to a hard working life.

An interesting rental from the next century is that of a manor created by William I as a useful appurtenance to the great Abbey which he founded to commemorate his victory near Hastings. We are told in the twelfth-century Chronicle of Battle Abbey that a number of men were brought to the place from the surrounding country, and to each was allotted a house and portion of land. This list, made about a hundred years later, names the descendants of those hand-picked peasants. Their rents average about sixpence or sevenpence a year with labour.

Under the eye of this royal patronage we should expect to find the strongest possible Norman influence, but out of the 108 Christian names at least sixty-five are Old English or Scandinavian (a few names are of uncertain origin). Even in circumstances such as these it took a little longer for the peasantry to adopt the new names whole-heartedly. Eighty-five have surnames of some sort, of which thirty-three are occupations (mostly in Latin) and twenty are nicknames, nearly all in the vernacular. In contrast to the Bury list there are few patronymics. There are hardly any place names in either.

To give an idea of the character of such a list, here are the first fifteen names, omitting the tedious Latin termination to each Christian name, and giving some explanation to the surnames where needed, and some of their modern versions.

Brihtwin bedellus	(beadle or bailiff)	*Biddle* or *Bailey*
Reinbald de Bece	(of the beech tree)	*Beech*
Aelfric Dot	(from the O.E. Christian name Dodda. This clerk has a regular tendency to write 't' for 'd' in O.E. words)	*Dodd*
William molendarius		*Miller*
Edward Gotchild		*Goodchild*
Ralph Ducg	(the spelling disguises a simple farmyard nickname)	*Duck*

Gilbert textor		*Weaver*
		or *Webster*
Dering Pionius	(Paeony, a nickname for a man with a red face?)	
Legard	(a man without a surname)	
Elfin Trew		*True*
Godieve	(a woman's name)	*Goodeve*
Godwin filius Colsueni	(the son of Colswein)	*Cole*
		or *Colson*
Godwin Cocus		*Cook*
Edward purgator	(scourer)	*Scorer*

We must also remember that any of these people's Christian names could make surnames for the next generation.

In old-fashioned history books kings used to be neatly labelled bad or good, strong or weak, and to the student working through medieval records it is soon apparent that the strong kings were those who had good business methods. They wanted money and they got it in an orderly way, and saw that good accounts were kept. Thus the strong kings have left good records.

It was with a financial purpose that William I had the Domesday survey made; William Rufus left few useful records; Henry I, an extremely efficient man, started the system of Exchequer Accounts, known as the Pipe Roll because its enormous rolls looked like pipes. It lapsed during the anarchy of Stephen, but the energetic Henry II soon started it again and organized the Exchequer on such a firm basis that the Pipe Roll runs in unbroken line from the first year of his accession right down to the nineteenth century. It gives a detailed account of the king's receipts from rents and fines, and much of his private expenditure; and its early sections, printed and well indexed by the Pipe Roll Society, are invaluable as a source of names of the upper and middle classes.

Several other important series of rolls also date from the twelfth century, but since nearly all are concerned with property and jurisdiction about it, their use is limited for our purpose in that they refer chiefly to the landed class, even more than does the Pipe Roll. Much better for a cross-section of the whole population are the Assize Rolls, some of which survive, from soon after 1200. These give detailed accounts of the cases which came before the judges on their rounds and deal with all classes of society, but largely with the less fortunate. We read here of murder, robbery, rape, runaway serfs, and simple accident, litigation about property, and appeals of bondmen who are trying to prove that they ought to be free. Often we touch rock bottom in the social scale and in many of the cases two generations of a family are mentioned, so that it is then possible to see whether surnames are being passed on or not.

What we see in these early thirteenth-century records is that virtually all, even the poorest, have surnames, or at least have them when they are needed for an important matter like a legal case, and it is clear that already an appreciable number are hereditary, but that many others are not. It is easy to find plenty of examples from 1200 onwards where a son continues his father's surname, but there are even more where the situation is too fluid, too uncertain for one to be able to make statistics on the subject.

A typical entry is as follows from the Lancashire Assizes of 1246: 'Thomas, son of Siward the Otterhunter, fell from a horse in Yarrow water and was drowned. William, son of Siward, found him. Verdict misadventure. Value of the horse 3s for which Matthew the Sheriff is to answer.'

It is impossible to tell here whether the unfortunate Thomas, had he lived, would have kept the surname of Siward (which has survived as *Seward*), or used one derived from his father's occupation, probably abbreviated to *Hunt* or *Hunter*, and the same applies to his brother. The Sheriff appears elsewhere in the same roll as Matthew de Redeham. This latter seems a more personal name and more likely to be perpetuated than the official 'sheriff', but then there are plenty of *Sherriffs* with us today to attest to the fact that this kind of official name often did become hereditary.

It is just worth noting that Siward, who himself had a typical Old English name, had christened both his sons after the new Norman fashion. This is the regular pattern at this date.

In the same roll we see that 'Robert le Eir' claimed land in right of his father. But the court ruled that his father, 'Richard le Eyr', had been only a tenant and not the owner of the land in question. In this case the name had been definitely passed on, but it seems that neither of these so-called 'heirs' had been successful in proving their right of inheritance. Perhaps it was the fact that they had tried to claim it as such and that the son had gone to law about it that fixed the names among mocking neighbours. The modern form of this surname is generally *Eyre* or *Ayre/s*, though as a common noun it settled down as 'heir'.

But to return to our 'strong kings', the greatest benefactor to the modern student of names is Edward I, the Lawgiver. From the beginning of his reign (1272), records of every kind become more plentiful. His statutes regulating land tenure had the result that from then onwards manorial records were properly kept and preserved, so that to this day hundreds of Manorial Court Rolls exist dating back to the late thirteenth century. These parchment rolls in crabbed dog-Latin give the minutes of manorial courts which dealt with the smallest agricultural problems, and lists of tenants so low in the social scale that they often owned nothing but rights of common pasture. This material exists in vast quantities, most of it still unpublished, much even unread. To have such early rolls in one's hands, original evidence of the life and work of ordinary people hundreds of years ago, is in itself a fascination, but one that involves a good deal of time and trouble. Manorial Court Rolls are full of repetition and are apt, just when one is becoming interested, to become illegible or incomplete. In fact their charm is tempered with tedium, but they are full of the names of common people and their descendants. Again we can find plenty of examples of names that are hereditary from the time the rolls begin, and others that vary from one generation to the next.

When Edward I came to the throne as an eager young prince recalled from the Holy Land, ambitious to achieve great things in England after his father's mismanagement, his first impulse was to find out exactly what his resources were and what money he could rely on. For this purpose he instituted an inquiry into all rents and taxes owing to the Exchequer throughout the land, the results of which are set out in the Hundred Rolls of 1275. These were printed and made available to students early in the last century, with an index containing approximately seventy thousand entries, and this convenient report on the whole country was much used as a quarry for names by Canon Bardsley, the first serious writer on the subject. Most of the early examples in his *Dictionary of Surnames* come from the Hundred Rolls.

But better still for our purpose, though most unwelcome to the king's humbler subjects at the time, Edward, determined to conquer Wales and Scotland, and needing much money for the purpose, followed up this inquiry with a notable series of taxes which affected almost the entire population. Once again the absolutely bottom stratum of society eludes us, for there was a level fixed below which those who possessed virtually nothing were exempt, but the net is spread much wider than ever before. The tax was on moveable goods, everything a man possessed except his wearing apparel. In 1296–7 the exemption point was fixed at 9s and as in that year a pig was valued at 1s, an ox or cow at 4s 10d and a quarter of wheat at 2s 5d, the basic figure would soon be reached and exceeded even by poor men. The original returns gathered in county by county and known as the Lay Subsidy Rolls (Government circles then as now were adept at wrapping a hard fact in a long word) are kept at the Public Record Office. They are the best evidence of all for the formation and fixing of our surnames, for they come at the very time when the names were sticking fast, and are presented in convenient form by parishes without any repetition. Each name occurs only once and that in the place where the man lived, and nearly every town and village is represented. Therefore one can see in each community a complete set of householders from the lord of the manor to the peasant. A whole series of these nation-wide 'subsidies' followed each other in rapid succession from 1283 onwards, paying for the conquest of Wales and the attempt to conquer Scotland.

Edward I not only left us a wealth of records, but had actually a large if indirect influence on the fixing of surnames. His legislation reorganized and clarified the system of land ownership, establishing the system of primogeniture as the basis of English inheritance, and copyhold tenure for manorial land. These arrangements affected all classes. The humble peasant with only one virgate of land was as anxious to claim it by right of being his father's eldest son as the rich man inheriting a large estate. The land could be claimed and awarded only at the Manorial Court, being held 'by copy of the Court Roll', which meant that the life tenant's name was inscribed there on permanent record.

43

This system provided a direct incentive to men to keep the same surname that had been put down on the roll for their father or grandfather. And even younger sons – having in mind the uncertainty of life – might think it just as well to use the name too, even if it was Whalebelly or Chickenhead.

This is an added reason why the Edwardian subsidies are so important to our subject. They occur at the very time when our surnames, that had long been inclined to settle, became suddenly much more stable.

One more great historic tax must be mentioned here, the Poll Tax which precipitated the Peasants' Revolt in 1381. It had been planned in the last years of Edward III to raise money to carry on the war against France, but the old king died and his grandson, the boy Richard II, had to bear the brunt of what followed. This time the authorities had dared to go to the extreme limit and tax everyone. Only known beggars were exempt, and that for the obvious reason that there is nothing to be got out of beggars. But all the rest of the population over the age of fourteen were to pay a minimum of a groat (fourpence) a head (or poll). Now at last we see the whole picture, the servants, the poor relations, the unmarried women, the hangers-on, people whose names have never been written down before and will not be again until the first Parish Registers start in 1538.

Actually we do not see quite so many of these names as we should. A study of the lists of Suffolk and Essex, for instance, reveals an extraordinary absence of single women or widows in some villages, the obvious explanation being that it went so much against the grain for poor people to pay taxes for their old aunts and grandmothers, whom they supported out of kindness or necessity, that they naturally suppressed their names as much as possible. This point is made very clearly by the late Charles Oman in his *Great Revolt of 1381*. The central authorities receiving much less money than they had expected from the tax (no one at that date knew what the population really was, and they had been very hopeful) repeated it in rather heavier form three years later. But by this time the peasants had learnt wisdom and plucked up more courage in evading what seemed an iniquitous imposition, and in the second set of returns the falling off in the numbers of dependants, particularly the womenfolk, was so marked in some places that the dullest-witted official in Westminster who applied his mind to it would become suspicious. The officials were more than suspicious. They sent out commissioners to inquire into the evasions. The peasantry resisted their inquiries; stones were thrown, mob orators arose; and the Peasants' Revolt burst suddenly into flame.

For us, looking at these lists of names nearly six hundred years after they were written down, with our special task in mind, the historic events with which they are connected are less important than the names themselves. But it is impossible to handle these faded rolls without remembering the passions that were running so high when the ink was fresh. As has been indicated there were two sets of returns, the first rather fuller than the second, but there is little to choose between them as far as we are concerned, for both are far more detailed than anything we have seen before. They survive in very imperfect form; far fewer are extant than for the earlier subsidies of Edward I and II; for many counties hardly anything remains except totals from each parish; and yet the detailed legible rolls that do remain are sufficiently widespread to give a representative cross-section from most parts of the country. If all were extant the number of names would be nearly two million, and therefore the toiling investigator is thankful that the hand of chance has picked out a more manageable number. It is probably as fairly representative as any carefully planned Gallup Poll.

What we see in these lists is that, in spite of the new lower class material, surnames have a more modern and settled look than we have seen before, though there is considerable variation from one part of the country to another. All over the South, East Anglia and the Midlands the 'setting' process seems complete, the signs of which will be discussed in the next chapter. But in the North, particularly in Yorkshire, the returns show a highly individual character indicating that though the surnames of the better class people are probably permanent those of their servants are decidedly fluid. The local assessors, veering as usual between Latin and English, incline to the latter and produce many names in the vernacular of such an unsophisticated freshness that we may feel sure they were coined on the spot to meet the requirements of the moment, many of them like John Robertstepson, and Alice Priestsysterservant being far too unwieldy to stand the test of any time. In many cases the relation of the name to a current state of affairs is clearly apparent. The name, Matthew de Lofthouse, for instance, is followed by William Matthewman and Magota Matthewwoman, and other servants have names formed from those of their masters in just the same way. Many surnames of this type have become permanent. We have *Jackman*, *Harriman*, and so on. But in these Yorkshire lists we see them, or rather hear them, freshly spoken as statements of fact, whereas in most other parts of the country at this date even the servants' surnames are inherited from an earlier generation.

In spite of the very deficient state of its extant remains this Poll Tax of Richard II is of special interest to us, because it comes at a critical time in the history of the country, and of surnames. The fourteenth century was one of enormous change and activity, comparable to the nineteenth for its surge of new ideas. The Black Death, disastrous though it was, helped the surviving peasantry to break old bonds and attain freedom and mobility; the triumphant war against France expressed a new feeling of national consciousness and power; and the Poll Tax, coming towards the end of this momentous century, shows that one of the many manifestations of its lively and creative spirit was the system of surnames, fixed in a form that has served us ever since.

In this brief survey of the chief original sources for the growth of our surnames, we seem up to this point to have been groping in semi-darkness. The records that have helped us most to see our surroundings and are used most in this book are firstly Domesday Book, which has the great merit of throwing light backward as well as forward, and secondly the series of Subsidy Rolls (the early Edwardian ones being best for our purpose), culminating in the Poll Tax. This last, though deficient in many ways, gives us more detail than we have seen before, and ushers us into a period when at last we are in full daylight and among friends. All the way from the time of the Conquest we have met hardly anyone we really know, except kings and archbishops, although we have been conscious of a great concourse of more ordinary people moving beside us in the darkness; but now, in the last twenty years of the fourteenth century, there are familiar faces on all sides, and familiar voices talking English. Wat Tyler is demanding rights for peasants; John Wycliffe is crying out for an English Bible; Geoffrey Chaucer is writing English poetry in the intervals of attending to court business; William Langland is walking on the Malvern Hills dreaming of his allegorical ploughman; Dick Whittington is walking the streets of London dreaming of more practical matters, and whether he had a cat or not he is as real a person as any of them.

All these people, and others that we meet at this time, rich or poor, have firm surnames used in the modern way. There is no evidence that Wat Tyler made tiles himself, indeed it is unlikely that he did so, unless he had inherited the trade as well as the name from his father or grandfather. The word 'chaucer' meant a maker of 'chaussees' or hose, but Geoffrey certainly never made any such thing, nor did his father who was a wine merchant, nor as far as the evidence goes did his grandfather. Such names except in the North had descended from several generations back and nobody expected them to be statements of fact any more.

In the fifteenth century, records are plentiful, but diffuse and variable in quality. Such Subsidy Rolls as survive have a higher exemption level and therefore include a narrower range of names than the Edwardian ones. The next really big landmark among our sources is the starting of Parish Registers in 1538 when at last names begin to be available from every part of the country in hundreds of thousands from all classes. The 'jelly' has been firmly set for some time, and the names differ from our own only in the earlier forms of spelling which are often very useful in showing their origins. Another advantage of these early registers is that, although there had been a good deal of movement of population in the two centuries before they began, it was as nothing to the general mixing up of people that has taken place since, and many family names were still in or near their place of origin. Finally, these first parish registers have the merit of showing us a mass of names that are predominantly English. The main flood of Welsh, Scottish and Irish influx has not yet poured into it, nor have immigrants from the Continent amounted to anything like their modern proportions. In these sixteenth-century registers more than 90% of the surnames are those coined in England in the Middle Ages, and can be studied as such without alien complications. All the same, useful as they are, they lack the excitement of the earlier records in which we see our surnames in their very moment of formation.

Chapter 4

SIGNS OF PERMANENCE

All through the foregoing review of original sources there have been two separate themes for us to follow: firstly the proportion of the population who have surnames at all, and secondly the question of whether these names are permanent.

The first question is fairly easy to answer by straightforward statistics. At the time of the Conquest and up to 1100 about 45% of all recorded men, humble as well as great, Saxon as well as Norman, have second names. By 1200 this figure has gone up to at least 90%, but during these two centuries it must be admitted that the records have been predominantly upper class, and though as many of the proletariat as possible have been included the proportion is nothing like correct. By 1300 the range is much wider and the figure is something like 99%. It is rare to find a man without a surname. Whether each man knew what the clerk had written down, and kept to it for further use is quite another matter. In many cases it may have been rather like the identity numbers we had during the war which many of us could never remember. But that need not engage us now. We are simply counting names as they appear, and it is perfectly clear that by 1300 it was normal to have two names and positively essential on those rare occasions when one's identity was to be established in writing. Our evidence of this time comes from the Subsidy Rolls, and when they were compiled it was in the interest of each man as he paid his few pence to have his name written down in full so that no one could ask him to pay again.

In 1381 we have the evidence of the Poll Tax and in this the figure for recorded surnames has fallen slightly. This is because the net is cast even wider to include the bottom layer of society and in some places the tax-collectors have failed to enter the surnames of the servants, even when they have them. In the last chapter we saw that on this occasion in Yorkshire servants were generally given surnames, some of them very new-looking and temporary. In other parts of the country the reverse is often the case: where surnames are given they are of well-established types, but all too often the assessors getting through an unpopular task as quickly as possible evidently thought it quite sufficient to lump a man's household briefly together. In some villages all dependants of either sex are conscientiously named; in others in the same county the usual form is to write, 'Robert Whytlock. Margarita, uxor ejus. Alicia, filia ejus. Walter et Katherina, servientes ejus'. The last two may have had another name each, but it must have seemed to the man who made the list that having said they were Robert Whitlock's servants he had made their identity sufficiently clear. In the same village (Stowe Langtoft in Suffolk) the parson's three servants were all called John, and in this case surnames were written down for each of them, John Holboy, John Mason and John Clement, probably all inherited names (there were Holboys in this village a hundred years earlier), but they might not have been mentioned if the Christian names had been sufficiently distinctive. In fact at this date surnames were always forthcoming when required, though their importance for all classes had not yet been fully realized.

The second question is a much harder one to answer. How can we distinguish the permanent name from the temporary? How can we say at any particular date that surnames in general are fixed?

We shall never arrive at an answer by following individual families. However much time we might spend on such a task the results would remain only drops in a very large bucket. For such a wide question we must look for more general indications.

An obvious line is to try to find records for the same village at different dates and see how many names have remained the same. In the Sussex Subsidy Rolls of 1296, in five small villages taken at random, there were 126 different surnames. In 1332, in the same villages, a full generation later there were only 107 different surnames and forty-three of them were the same as at the earlier date, although most of the Christian names had changed. This would seem to indicate that in these villages the permanent name was the accepted thing; for natural causes – failure of children to survive, and the movement of families, even into the next village – would in any case prevent the continuance of many names.

But this kind of experiment is not satisfactory unless carried out on a large scale, which is easier said than done. Tests for villages in Suffolk and Hertfordshire showed very similar results in some cases, but in others nearly all the names had changed. The unknown conditions are too incalculable. Death and disaster made all too frequent appearances. Between the Edwardian lists and the Poll Tax of Richard II the Black Death intervened, and though one can find villages where a quarter of the surnames continue after that great calamity, there are others where all the old ones have gone. The surviving names are full of human interest but do not answer our question.

However there are many clear indications that surnames are sticking fast, signs that can be observed even in one list, and are plentiful in the reign of Edward I. One is that for the most part people have only one additional name. A little earlier one can find frequent examples of two or more phrases added to a man's Christian name to make sure of his identity. From Great Amwell in Hertfordshire in 1289 we have 'Richard, son of Alice, at the Lane', and 'William the fisher of Thele', but by 1317 the next generation are called only, 'at the Lane' and 'Fisher', and in the Subsidy Rolls of this time the vast majority of people have one surname only.

Another useful sign in the Edwardian subsidies is the appearance of several taxpayers with the same name in one moderately sized parish. As long as surnames were being tailormade for individuals it followed automatically that the inhabitants of a small community were differentiated from each other; but the same name repeated several times indicates the change from individual to family names. If several men are called Shepherd it is possible that they all were shepherds, though surprising that their names are not more varied. But if two or three men are called Reeve, for instance, it is certain that the name is inherited, for it would be most unlikely to have more than one genuine official of this sort in a village.

This kind of thing is even more definite in the case of nicknames. No village community would be so dull-witted as to call two of its inhabitants 'the Peacock' at the same time. If one sees several of such names in one village one knows they have descended from a common ancestor. In Salkeld in Cumberland, for instance, in 1296 we find Roger, John and Nicholas Clovenhead. It is not likely that they had all survived serious head wounds. The incident and the name that arose from it belong to an earlier generation.

Another indication that many surnames are hereditary by 1300 may be seen in the large number formed from Christian names that had long been out of use. The most rapid change-over from Old English to Norman or Biblical names occurred about 1200, and by the accession of Edward I the former were virtually obsolete. Looking through many hundreds of names in the first of his subsidies for seven different counties from all parts of England, I found that less than 2% of the Christian names were of the pre-Conquest type. And yet the vanished names were quite plentiful in the same lists as surnames which must have been formed when these old names were still in use at the beginning of the century or earlier. To give one example: in Stanton in Suffolk where about a hundred persons are given, not one of them has a pre-Conquest first name (John, William, Robert and Adam account for half the men), but among their surnames sixteen are derived from the old names, three from Aelfric, two from Asgar, two from Brihtwin and several more in groups of two or three.

The treatment of women's names in these medieval lists throws yet another light on the current state of surnames. From the time of the Conquest it was customary for better class ladies to use the names of their fathers, or husbands, when a second name was needed, which was not often; 'the lady Isabella' or 'Dame Margaret' being quite enough for most occasions. But by the thirteenth century when surnames were being coined freely for all, a great many working women, particularly single ones and widows earning their own living, acquired secondary names of their own in the same way as the men, such as Julia Selkwomman, who sold her silk, or perhaps embroidered with it, in London in 1319. The presence of such names shows that the idea of family names is not completely grasped, but from the early fourteenth century they become increasingly rare for the greater part of England. At this time we see the majority of women of the working class called by their husband's surnames. Often the clerk tries to make them feminine by writing such forms as Beatrice la Carpentere as if she is sawing wood herself, when she is really the carpenter's wife, widow or daughter and his trade has become the family name.

But Yorkshire, as has been said before, was always a stronghold of individuality, and women's surnames there were very late in conforming with the general usage. The Poll Tax includes many examples of all types. Sometimes a special occupation is clearly indicated as with Isabella Kerchiefwassher or Alicia Chaumbirmaydyne or Isabella Whelespynner. In the case of Alicia Sowremilke we seem to have an allusion to her nature rather than her work though both may be involved. Married women are often written down in such terms as Johanna Jackwyf, or the husband's surname may be used to produce such a form as Elena Hobsonwyf. Unmarried girls are either designated as somebody's daughter with surnames like Shephirddoghter or Robyndoghter, or as a 'maiden', which generally implies a maid-servant. The word 'girl' at this date meant only a child and was little used. We see many of these maidens in these lists, Matilda Marshalmaydyn, Agnes Marjorymayden, and so on.

Of course such surnames had no future. These girls were known by their Christian names as almost everyone still was, and when they married their children would take the father's surname, but they have a certain charm, and they serve to show us that in Yorkshire surnames for women were still a novelty in the late fourteenth century. In contrast to them similar names in the Midlands and the South were more settled a hundred years earlier. Two pairs of sisters will serve as typical examples, Cecilia and Isoude le Reve, from Sapisford, Suffolk (1283), and Katerin and Emma Shypman from the Rape of Pevensey (1296). One could only call a girl a reeve or a shipman in a community where a system of hereditary family names was accepted as a matter of course.

Of the various signs that surnames have become permanent none is more easily recognizable than the trade-name which no longer tells the truth. When we see an entry on a list like John

Carter (taylour), showing the man's occupation to be different from his name we know the latter to be firmly fixed. Surnames of this kind were a little later than some in settling down. No doubt for those who followed the family trade the names stuck as early as any, but when they were at variance with the truth the process was often delayed; so much so that when we see these contradictory forms in fair number we know we have reached a time when the hereditary principle is generally accepted.

In the rolls of Edward I occupations are seldom given, apart from surnames. If a man's surname is Baker the chances are that he is one. In the following reign contradictory entries, like that quoted above, begin to appear more frequently, and if we jump on to the Poll Tax near the end of the century we see dozens of them, even in Yorkshire and Northumberland. The Poll Tax returns have the great advantage for us that they nearly always give the occupation as well as the surname, and the very fact that this is necessary even when the surname and occupation are the same shows that the great change has taken place and that a name like Miller is no longer a guarantee that its owner is grinding corn.

Of course hundreds of men did follow in their fathers' footsteps. It must have been the normal procedure, and so in these lists we see Adam Miller (miller) side by side with Richard Miller (draper).

The extraordinary hotchpotch of languages in which the medieval rolls are written, confusing though it is, can also throw light on the date at which family names became fixed. Medieval clerks loved their Latin as a mystery or craft of which they were masters, and which the vulgar could not understand. As a modern government official likes to wrap his statements in official terminology, so the medieval clerk revelled in his Latin. But even in Domesday Book it is apparent that some of the English names defeated him. Norman Christian names nearly always appear in standard Latinized forms, Ricardus, Rogerus, Henricus and so on, but the Old English names are dealt with very inconsistently. The general rule was simply to add the suffixes '-us' for a man and '-a' for a woman, but Alwoldus in one entry is plain Alwold in the next, Torchillus and Grimmus appear elsewhere as plain Torchil and Grim (*Thirkill* and *Grimes* today), as if the scribes could hardly handle such outlandish stuff. With English surnames the scribes are hopelessly at sea. They were used to writing a patronymic in the form of 'Willielmus filius Roberti', but were sometimes caught out by the same thing spoken in English. When one of them wrote Alwinnus Dodesone, for instance, for a Saxon land-owner in Hertfordshire he probably failed to grasp that the second name was simply the equivalent of 'son of Dod' and might more properly have been rendered 'filius Doddi'.

Norman descriptive surnames are generally Latinized as 'blundus' (fair), parvus (small), and so on, but the English names, such as Aelfric Blac, are frequently left as they are, for lack of understanding. Harold's wife (or was it his mistress?) Edith the Fair, appears in many different forms and spellings, ranging from 'Eddeva Pulchra' to 'Edida faira'.

This Latinization of Christian names in all manuscripts was to continue for centuries. The clerks had the regular Latin forms for all accepted names at their finger-tips and continued to use them long after they had lapsed into French and English for surnames. Indeed even as late as the seventeenth century some old-fashioned country parsons recorded the names of their rustic parishioners in their registers as Robertus, Margareta and Johannes. But long before that date the surnames had got the upper hand of the scribes, seeming to have a life of their own which defied the intentions of would-be translators, particularly the descriptive nicknames, which were recognized as untranslatable personal names at an earlier date than the others. Both the simple type like Brun (*Brown*) and hundreds of more fanciful ones like Hwithede (*Whitehead*) or Prudfot (*Proudfoot*) had established themselves as proper names that were always written in English by 1100. They continue to appear through all types of record, giving a convincing impression of being among the earliest class of surname to become hereditary. Many of them show a hearty if unsuitable form of humour and the Latinized Christian names that accompanied them make them appear the more absurd as in such cases as Radulphus Pudding, Ricardus Wagtail and Stephanus Mug.

In the very early rolls occupations are almost always given in Latin, 'faber' for a smith, 'piscator' for a fisher and so on, which often makes it hard for us to know the exact form in which such words were spoken in English. Sometimes the Latin is very obviously made up from Norman French or English. Words like 'parcherius' for a parker, a keeper of a park reserved for hunting, and 'stirmannus' for a steersman are very bogus stuff that was never spoken in ancient Rome any more than in England. This medieval use of Latin had almost no effect on our surnames. An exception is the name *Faber* which may be a rare case of a learned Englishman deliberately choosing to express his common surname in an uncommon form, or a foreign import. In Germany, where surnames became established much later than in England, there was a definite tendency for scholarly gentlemen to Latinize their names, producing results like Sartorius and Gregorius, but this was never an English custom. *Faber* is an uncommon name, though a well-known one.

In the thirteenth-century rolls Latin begins to give way to Norman French. Instead of 'faber' and 'piscator' we have 'le fevre' and 'le pechur'. These are the forms most commonly seen in the Subsidy Rolls of Edward I and II, but there is no consistency in anything linguistic at this time, and in the same list we see Latin, French and English all mixed up together. Names like Smith and Fisher are now forcing themselves on the clerks who put up a rear-guard defence by retaining the French article 'le' and the Latinized Christian name so that the commonest way of writing a working man's name about 1300 is 'Robertus le Smythe', employing all three languages, or, as in another case where it was essential to make it clear that the man's trade was not the same as his name, 'Robertus le Barbier, Pybaker' (London 1319).

The same sort of thing occurs in place names. Someone who lived by a bridge would be at first written down as so and so 'ad pontem'. The next stage would be something like 'de la Brigge' which no human tongue ever uttered. Then the name would appear as 'Atte Brigge' ('atte' being the regular contraction of 'at the'), and finally we arrive at plain Bridge by about 1400. Once we are into the fifteenth century prepositions and articles have nearly all disappeared even in the remote North and West, and lists of names have a more modern look. This simplification is yet another sign of surnames being fixed for good and all. They have ceased to be descriptive phrases and become proper names.

In assigning any date to this change we must bear in mind that the official breed who recorded these things were always behind the times. When the upper classes were talking French their clerks wrote in Latin: when everyone was talking English the scribes clung to Norman French; by the time they came to writing names in English, prepositions and articles as parts of surnames were already old-fashioned and almost gone; by the time they brought themselves to set down the names without these adjuncts as plain Baker or Wood we may be sure that these simple forms had already been in use for generations.

It is not by any of these signs alone, but by taking them all together that we can see that surnames are well on the way to stability by 1300. The king's new legislation and wide taxation had together caused more writing down of names than the country had ever known before, and the Black Death following in 1347 hastened the process of settlement. Many survivors of this great disaster drifted into towns or other places where they were strangers and needed clearer identification than had been wanted in their native villages. This upheaval must have led to some changes of name that would never change again.

Even the North was not very far behind. The Yorkshire Poll Tax of 1379, in spite of its many peculiarities, yet shows a majority of names that seem permanent. Though the women's surnames have a very transient character, those of their husbands seem fairly well established, and it is the men's names that matter most. The Swedish scholar, G. Fransson, found that among the Freemen of the city of York in the last quarter of the century seven-eighths had the same surnames as their fathers, so we may say that Yorkshire, though behind the South in this respect, was catching up fast.

It is not to be supposed that from 1400 every family in England had a permanent surname. There were always people who in moving from one place to another would contrive to get rid of an uncomplimentary nickname; others who were known by different surnames in different places and could vacillate between them; Wales was much later than England in adopting fixed surnames and this had some influence in border counties; and right down to the nineteenth century there were vagrants, outcasts and half-wits who had no knowledge of a second name.

Then there were foundlings for whom names had to be provided and an occasional Mr Bumble did resort to invention, as in the case of 'John Found, a foundling' whose christening is recorded in an eighteenth-century Plymouth register. But by and large the great creative period of surname-making in England ended with the fourteenth century and thereafter anyone in need of a surname took one that was already long established.

One further question remains. When did surnames replace Christian names in common speech? This was another great social change comparable to that from Old English to Norman names, but being purely verbal has not been clearly recorded.

I believe that the custom of using surnames for all except the intimate circle of the family and household followed quite quickly on their general establishment and in fact accelerated it. In the Paston Letters, which run from 1440 onwards, and are as informal as we could wish, they are in regular use from the start, often both names being expressed, as 'Clement Spicer' or 'John Broom', but sometimes also as 'Master Spicer' or plain 'Broom', in fact just as it was to continue for centuries.

On the other hand, in the Poll Tax of 1381, though surnames seem to be fully developed, the Christian name alone is still used as the regular form for alluding to a person indirectly. In hundreds of villages we have the name of the principal resident, as for instance Robert de Ashfield (page 105), followed by those of his household complete with surnames and described as 'servants of the said Robert'. But these are official lists and such things tend to preserve old forms. Old fashions always seem more courteous than new ones, and at that time it must have seemed more correct and respectful to call the Lord of the Manor 'Robert' than 'Master Ashfield', in writing at least, though in conversation the latter form was rapidly coming into use.

Between the Poll Tax and the Paston Letters there is a gap of only sixty years, yet in the matter of names the one is medieval and the other modern. This was a time of rapid change and the new style of speech was one of its many manifestations. For the next five hundred years and more, surnames were to be the normal form of address. It is only in our own generation when

57

the world is changing almost beyond our comprehension, that their supremacy is being challenged in conversation, and the Christian name, so long confined to a small intimate circle, is once again coming into prominence.

Chapter 5

THE MODERN APPROACH

In the previous chapter we tried to date the fixing of surnames in England from contemporary sources. But there is another quite different line of approach by which we can check our conclusions. Let us leave the Middle Ages and consider English surnames as we know them now. After all if one wants to study Salisbury Cathedral it would be highly pedantic to concentrate on early documents relating to it. The thing to do is to look at the building itself which is still there for all to see. If there have been alterations and additions since it was built we ought to be able to recognize them as such; and the sight of the great church will tell us more about the medieval mind than anything found in archives.

So it is with our surnames; they are here all around us. Indeed the chief difficulty in studying them is that they are present in such enormous quantity that its sheer weight may overwhelm the student. The best way to reduce it to manageable proportions is to use a large directory which, though it cannot give every detail in the picture, yet gives a comprehensive view. The London Telephone Directory, containing as it does over eight hundred thousand names, provides a good quantity of material to work on, and has some very decided advantages over the medieval rolls. One is that modern names are not disguised in pseudo-Latin or Norman French. They are natural survivals of the spoken word, and are much nearer to what men were actually called in 1300 than what the clerks of that time wrote down. Their nature and the proportions in which they survive can give us direct information about the past.

It may be objected that London is not England, and that

Londoners are not representative of the whole country, but in the matter of surnames this argument does not apply. Surnames of modern Londoners were formed (if they are English) some six or seven centuries ago when the vast majority of the population lived in small villages. Ever since that time London has acted as a magnet drawing rich and poor alike from all parts of the country. Probably there is not a village in England from which some-one did not eventually find his way to London. One might try to make such a mixture by taking names from a careful selection of smaller directories, one from the North, one from the West and so on, and combining them, but it would inevitably be an artificial concoction open always to criticism, whereas the population of London is a naturally formed amalgam which probably gives as good a cross-section of the English people of the thir-teenth century as we are likely to find.

Having said so much, it must be admitted freely that many rare names are found only in special localities. Because a name is not in the London Directory we must not assume that it does not exist, we can only say it is rare. I believe there is no reason-ably common name anywhere in England of which an example will not be found in London. Conversely any name which appears in large numbers there will be found to come from many parts of England. It is as a general indicator that the book is so useful, a convenient yardstick by which we can see at a glance if a name is very common, moderately so, or rare.

Again it may be said that the hand of chance has played too large a part in the survival of families for the numbers of their surnames to be of much significance, but a study of the matter proves otherwise. Any name of which the modern numbers are at all high, over a hundred in the directory, can be found in many places in medieval records; if the modern number is over a thousand the name in question can be seen springing up every-where. Admittedly with rare names the influence of chance has been considerable. Many medieval surnames must have begun with one solitary example, and of these hundreds have failed to survive, while others have stayed the whole course and grown to moderate proportions, but no such names can compare in num-bers with the ones that sprang to life from similar causes in many places at once. I know of no name, rare in the Middle Ages, that is very common today, nor any common medieval one that cannot be found now, except a few really offensive names, like 'Cuckoo', for instance, which disappeared for special reasons that had nothing to do with chance.

On the whole the relative numbers of all the regular surnames have remained remarkably constant since they first came into use. In all that time the period of most rapid growth of population has been the last hundred years; but lists of names from different parts of the English-speaking world which have developed independently during that time, show the remarkable similarity with which the original pattern has been maintained (page 337). Therefore we may feel confident that though small variations of number signify nothing, substantial numbers are true reflections of historic fact.

Let us now take a few modern statistics from the London Telephone Directory of 1961–2 (which I have used throughout and will henceforth refer to briefly as 'the directory') and see what we can learn from them. For example, if we look at some occupational names, choosing trades which are well dated from other sources, we shall find out to what period these names really belong, and perhaps narrow down the date of their fixing a little more exactly.

Consider, for instance, the building trade. The Directory has 1,450 *Wrights*, 730 *Masons*, 280 *Carpenters*, 240 *Slaters*, 230 *Tylers*, 160 *Sawyers*, 110 workers in lead (*Plummers* and *Leadbeaters*), 80 *Thatchers* (including *Thackers* and *Thaxters*), and smaller numbers of other allied trades, but not one single Brickmaker or Bricklayer. Since Roman times no bricks were used in England until about 1420 when they began to be imported from Holland. During that century they rapidly increased in popularity, but this was too late to make surnames. There is indeed a small group of the names *Brick* and *Brickman* (about twenty each), but these must be derived from sharpened versions of the North Country *Brigg* and *Brigman*, better known as *Bridge* and *Bridgeman* in the South. In fact we can conclude that English artisans had completely fixed surnames before they began to handle bricks.

We should also note that 'wright', the Old English word for a builder, especially one who worked with wood, was still easily holding its own against 'carpenter', the French word that eventually replaced it. As for building in stone, the Normans were so much more skilled than the Saxons in this field that it is not surprising that their *Masons* (from the O.F. 'masson') far outnumber the English *Stonehewers* of whom there are just four, supported by a few *Stoniers*, *Staniers* and other contractions of the same word. Of course the simple term *Stone* must often have served as a nickname for a man who spent his life chipping away at it to build our castles and churches, but this solid, enduring Old English word is open to several interpretations as a surname. For the moment we will concentrate on undoubted names of occupation.

Let us see how the fighting forces stand. We have 820 *Knights* with 190 *Squires* to follow them and over 400 *Archers* and bowmen (*Bowman*), the two words of French and English origin running parallel. Their weapons are supplied by the *Bowyers* (80), the *Stringers* (95), the *Arrowsmiths* (38) and *Fletchers*. There are 390 of these last, but we are in a difficulty about them as they have become confused with the Fleshewers or *Fleshers*. This was the native word for 'butchers'. It lingered long in the North of England and still longer in Scotland, while the French 'boucher' or *Butcher* replaced it in the South, where the majority of fletchers were makers of arrows.

The knights' equipment was made by the armourer, generally now shortened to *Armour* (28). This name is not very numerous because until elaborate plate armour came in, such work was generally done by the smith. *Sworders* and *Helmers* may also be met with, but they too were specialists and the names are rare. There are *Pikes* in plenty, but we will not count them as the name has other possible origins and they were not all soldiers. However it was often used as a nickname for a tall, thin man, the kind of name that would arise among men-at-arms.

For anything more modern in the way of fighting men or weapons we may look in vain. The twenty-eight *Gunners* must be attributed to the Christian name Gunnor, a woman's name of Norse origin, often seen in early records. One of William the Conqueror's greatgrandmothers was Gunnor (or Gunnora) and consequently the name was fashionable among Norman ladies, as were several others with the same first syllable. One of William's daughters was Gundreda, and eventually it was from one of these same women's names, Gunhilda, that the all too familiar word 'gun' originated. A list of weapons at Windsor Castle of 1330 mentions 'una magna balista de cornu quae vocatur Domina Gunilda'. This reminds one of Mons Meg at Edinburgh, and Big Bertha on the German front. Why are big guns feminine? In any case it is certain that most of the modern *Gunners* are descended from Norman ladies of this name, and not from men who wrestled with dangerous machines. Those early mechanics who made and worked huge slings and catapults were known as 'engineers'. Their descendants are *Jenners*, and there are seventy of them in the directory.

Much the same sort of story applies to the *Musketts* of which there are only fourteen. The word meant originally the male of the sparrowhawk, much used in falconry, and just as the lady gave her name to the gun, so the bird, swift to kill in the sky, gave its name to another new weapon. In both cases the surname belongs to the earlier meaning. *Cannon* is either from an Old Irish personal name or the ecclesiastic, the use of this word as a piece of ordinance being unrecorded before the sixteenth century. In fact we are obliged to reject all forms of artillery.

There are no Soldiers in the directory, though the word was already in use in the fourteenth century. It occurs in Wycliffe's Bible and must have been well known then, but too late for surnames. On the other hand there are 360 examples of *Kemp* and more of *Camp*, both of which come from the Old English 'cempa', meaning a warrior or champion, a word that was old-fashioned by 1400 and well on its way out.

Altogether, the army we have collected has a very early look. It is not the army of Agincourt, but rather the one Edward I led into Wales and Scotland, and it could be earlier still.

It is useless to look for signs of the Renaissance or revival of learning in our list. Printing was invented far too late. The men who produced the beautiful manuscripts of the period were *Scriveners*, and with the contraction *Scriven/s* we have eighty of them. There are only four *Quillers* to supply the pens, but a bundle of goose quills was so easily come by that procuring them would scarcely make an occupation. We are now down to very small numbers, but they have a charm of their own. We have in our directory seven *Bookbinders*. Are they descended, I wonder, from Nicholas le Bokebinder who appears in the London Subsidy of 1332? I like to think so.

Creative literature is represented only by a few *Rhymers*. (With *Rimes*, both names in a variety of spellings, they total thirty-five.) There are no Poets or Playwrights. Indeed the arts as a whole come off very badly, except that of building. Pictorial art was still in the hands of monks who could found no families. (The surnames *Monk*, *Abbot* etc. will be considered in Chapter Eleven.) There are, however, fifty-four *Painters*, who were probably employed in secular work, decorating the interiors of castles and the like. Henry III, the first of our kings to show much sign of trying to live graciously, was frequently giving orders for his apartments and those of his queen to be painted with gold stars, or flowers, or heads of men and women 'in good colours', and this is just the period when the painters employed in such work might acquire the name of their craft for themselves and their progeny.

In the field of entertainment there are twenty-eight *Players*, not necessarily dramatic, thirty-six *Fiddlers*, a hundred *Pipers*, and, by far the largest contingent, over three hundred *Harpers*. Romantic writers about the Middle Ages are fond of Minstrels; no novel of the period is complete without one; but there is none in our directory. The word commonly used in the surname period was clearly 'harper', and it is clear too that they were both popular and plentiful. There is one solitary *Jester* in the list. Probably highly qualified entertainers were never very numerous. It seems from the surname evidence that a song sung to the harp was much preferred to a comedy line, however well sustained. It may be noted here that William the Conqueror had a jester whom he endowed with land. He appears in Domesday Book as 'Bardic, joculator regis', the King's joker, but the tiresome Latin prevents our knowing what exact word William used when he spoke of him; 'gestour' perhaps, or 'jongleur', but the latter has left no surname.

Enough has been said to confirm the opinion, formed from a study of the medieval sources, that English surnames were completely settled by 1400. Indeed this date is an outside one, and the general character of the mass of them belongs much earlier. In the contemporary rolls we could see names becoming established, but in the modern directory we can see the negative evidence of the later words and occupations that did not make surnames, and certainly would have if surnames were still being formed. I believe it true to say that no human activity and no word that came into England after about 1360 has produced an English surname.

It will be noted that I am careful to add the word English. In most other countries surnames developed later than in England, and these foreign names of later origin entering the country in modern times have sometimes been anglicized, slightly blurring the edges of our clear-cut picture. For instance, we have no English Shoemakers. This is one of the words that is too modern for our surnames, though common in Tudor times. But it made a common surname in Germany and is sometimes met with in anglicized spelling in America, though there are none in the London Directory.

Another piece of negative evidence comes from the complete absence of heraldic names. In some foreign countries aristocratic families have surnames derived from their coats of arms; the Scandinavian name Guildenstern, for instance, means 'gold star'. But we have no names of this kind at all. The surnames of our noble families are older than heraldry. The earliest recorded English heraldic shield is dated by Sir Anthony Wagner as 1136. By 1200 the new art was being used by all the baronial families, but their names are older than that. Occasionally a family name may appear to come from its heraldic devices, as in the case of *Bowes-Lyon*, but always it is the other way round. The name came first and the coat of arms made a pun on it.

This puts the fixing of aristocratic surnames into the Norman rather than the Plantagenet period. For the working classes it extended longer, but is still surprisingly early. The occupational names that we have been considering for dating purposes are the sort that were almost last in becoming permanent. We have seen in the last chapter how they were apt to fluctuate owing to the inadvisability of giving a false impression on matters of business. So when these trade-names were settled we may take it that all were settled.

The only surnames formed in England at a later date (apart from those of foundlings) were patronymics of immigrants from the Celtic countries, chiefly from Wales. But of truly English surnames the great mass was firmly established between the reigns of William I and Richard II. This 'surname period', as we may now call it, is earlier than many people would expect; it contains the whole Norman and early Plantagenet periods and was nearing its end before Chaucer was born. This is a long time which can be more closely defined only by dividing it into two parts. In the earlier, which extends roughly from the Conquest to 1200, the surnames of the upper classes and many of intermediate status were fixed. In the later stage (approximately 1200–1360) those of the great mass of the proletariat followed suit, the peak period being the reign of Edward I.

It is of importance to our study to fix these dates as nearly as possible, because we must look for the meaning of the word or words of which a surname is made, not in some vague and ill-defined period of history, but precisely in this 'surname period'.

Part Two

THE FOUR TYPES

Chapter 6

PROBLEMS OF CLASSIFICATION

If we were asked to identify some young man, we might answer, 'He's the chap who lives on the hill', or 'He's So-and-So's son', or 'He runs the garage', or 'He's the one with red hair'. So it always was, and nearly all writers on the subject of surnames have classified them into the four types of Locality, Relationship, Occupation and Nicknames.

However, although it is true that surnames do fall very readily into these four groups, it should be borne in mind that these neat labels have been attached by modern scholars for their own convenience and do not represent any real division of thought at the time when the names were first created. The groups merge into one another, each overlapping the next, so that, although the majority of names may be easily assigned to their proper category, there are always borderline cases on which it is hard to make a decision. For instance a *Mill* is undoubtedly a place, and yet the man who lived there was in all probability the *Miller*, or the miller's servant. A *Kitchen* is also a place (originally in a monastery) but the surname obviously implies someone who works in the kitchen, and has exactly the same meaning as *Kitchener*. On the other hand a *Church* is a place but in a village there are generally houses close to it and it is such a landmark that it is the most natural thing in the world to say a man lives 'by the Church' without implying that he is the parson or the clerk. Personally I class *Mill* and *Kitchen* as occupational and *Church* as local, but another person might arrange them differently.

Impinging closely on the occupational names is a small group which gives a man's social standing rather than his trade. A good example of this is *Freeman*, a happy name for anyone to bear, for it once expressed that glorious independence from bondage that every peasant hoped to attain; but it is hardly an occupation. Names like *Knight* and *Burgess* might be placed in this category, and perhaps *Clerk* and *Constable*, but where is one to stop? There is no clear division between status and occupation, and it is much more convenient to class them together.

The large group formed from Christian names has been given various titles by different writers. It appears to consist almost entirely of patronymics or names formed from the father's name (i.e. *Robinson* or *Robins*), but as some names in this class come from mothers (i.e. *Margetson*) or from other relations it is better to use a wider term such as 'names of relationship'.

Nicknames must inevitably be subdivided into several groups of a very varied nature showing the extraordinary liveliness and ingenuity of the human brain. C. L. Ewen, author of *The History of Surnames*, will have it that there are no such things as nicknames. Surnames which fall into this category are called by him either 'descriptive' or 'characteristic', or are explained away as being something entirely different from what they seem. Dr Reaney in his scholarly dictionary dismisses some of Ewen's theories as 'etymological moonshine', and both he and the Swedish scholars who have worked on the subject under the leadership of Professor Ekwall are content to use the old-fashioned term 'nicknames' to cover a mixed collection of surnames which vary from simple description to fanciful flights of humour and imagination.

Of the four classes that of locality is the largest, though names of relationship run very close. In any random gathering of several hundred English people it would be found that about two-thirds of them had names in these two classes fairly equally divided. The remaining third would consist of occupational names and nicknames with the former the more numerous of the two.

These are the usual proportions of English names, but in any modern group there are sure to be some names which we are unable to classify, or choose to omit for one reason or another, and before going further it is better to face these problems squarely.

To start with there are always some few names which are

totally baffling. The wonder is that there are not more. When one takes into consideration that many surnames are abbreviations or jokes spoken casually six or seven centuries ago the marvel is that so many of them can still be interpreted with confidence. It would not be so if we did not have so many medieval documents. Almost any name that is at all common now can be found somewhere in a thirteenth-century form with a preposition or article or a fuller spelling to help us; or perhaps the name will appear several times in different forms, and one of them will elucidate the problem. But there always remain at least three or four per cent about which the honest investigator can only state, 'I don't know'.

Then there are the names with only too many sources. The familiar name *Barnes*, for instance, offers several possibilities. On the one hand there is the Scandinavian personal name Biorn, often seen in early records of the old Danelaw counties, and its cognate Old English word 'beorn', meaning a warrior. Another Old Norse word 'barn' which meant a child or noble youth, still survives in the North as 'bairn'. These are ancient and heroic names that merge together in the surname period as Berne or Barne. On the other hand, in the South of England several families may have originated from Barnes in Surrey, and undoubtedly a great many people worked and slept 'in the barn'. Any of these forms could acquire a final 's' later.

Occasionally a name has a possible derivation from each of the four types. *Key, Kay, Keay* and *Keyes* have all become confused together. There was a Celtic personal name, Kay, known to us chiefly as one of King Arthur's knights, which lingered on into the surname period in Wales, Cornwall and Brittany. In the North of England 'kay' was a dialect word for a jackdaw, which could make a nickname, whereas in fourteenth-century London 'atte kay' or 'kai' meant 'at the wharf' or 'quay'. *Key* or *Keys* could also be used as a trade-name for a locksmith, and all these spellings are fairly interchangeable. Anyone with one of these difficult names who is really anxious to discover its meaning in his particular case should begin by tracing back his family as far as possible to find out what part of the country it came from. Locality can often give an indication of the likeliest meaning.

In cases of this kind an individual may seek out the origin of his own surname, with the aid of genealogy, but a student of surnames cannot classify it into one group or another. If there are two distinct solutions one can only divide the point between them, or choose the more likely, or omit it from the calculation altogether.

Another difficulty arises from the presence of foreign names among our native ones. This book sets out to be a study of English surnames, which is a large enough subject in all conscience. It cannot deal with all the languages of the world. It is true that England has been absorbing foreign names for the last thousand years, and many of them have been completely acclimatized for so long that they have become part of our heritage. Any surname, whether of English, French or Old Norse origin, that was formed in England during the Middle Ages, let us say before 1500, must unquestionably be considered English, though some few of them, like *Beauchamp*, have retained a French appearance. They are spoken as English words, have been with us for hundreds of years and cannot possibly be classed as alien. On the other hand recent additions from foreign countries are obviously not part of our subject.

The problem is where to draw the line. It is impossible to be dogmatic about it, and why should one try? My general feeling is that for a name to be accepted as English it should be at least partly anglicized and have been in use in this country for at least two hundred and fifty years. This will just include the large number of Huguenot refugees who came into England in the late seventeenth century, many of whose names are well known and greatly respected. As they were largely French, their names in any case cannot always be distinguished from Norman ones that came in centuries earlier, and nearly all are anglicized in spelling or pronunciation or both. *Bosanquet* and *Courtauld*, for instance, have retained their French spelling but are pronounced as if they were English; others, like *Pertwee*, in which the French spelling (Pertuis) has been lost, have kept much nearer to the original sound; still others, like *Garrick* (French 'garigue' meaning 'a heath'), are completely English in sound and appearance. But though I am prepared to class such names as English, I cannot go deeply into their origins, preferring to concentrate on truly home-grown products.

A much more complicated question is presented by our own

Celtic neighbours. In most senses they are more closely allied to us than any of the continental countries, but linguistically they are far more remote, and the size and scope of this book will not admit excursions into Gaelic, Old Irish and Welsh etymology. Of the three the Irish problem is, for once, the most easily settled. There was no great flow of immigration from Ireland into England before the late eighteenth century, and most of it belongs to the last hundred and fifty years. Therefore I make no attempt to deal with the Gallaghers, Callaghans, O'Reillys, Murphys and so forth who are met with on all sides today, but whose names are quite unrelated to English. Of course many Irish families have English or Anglo-Norman surnames such as *Butler, Moore* and *Fitzgerald*. They belong to our own history and cannot be separated from it.

It is rather more difficult to decide how to treat Scottish names, but here again the most logical division one can make is between those of English and Gaelic origin. Linguistically the Lowlands of Scotland are much more closely united with England than with the Highlands. Indeed it may be said that they speak a purer and more ancient form of English than we in the South. Their surnames are very much the same as our own, with the difference that they became hereditary at a rather later date, and consequently include some names not found in England, and some distinctive forms. But a *Smith* or *Wilson* from Edinburgh is indistinguishable on paper from one of the same name from London, and there would be no sense in trying to differentiate them.

But the Highlanders are another matter altogether. Most of their surnames belong, not only to another language group, but also to a background and usage, arising from the clan system, that is entirely different from ours. A clan surname signified allegiance to a chieftain rather than blood relationship, and could be multiplied by hundreds of new adherents out of all proportion to the numbers of English family names, which increased only by lineal descent. Few Highlanders came into England before the union of the crowns, and it was not until after the stormy troubles of the eighteenth century that they came in any numbers. After the Forty Five several of the clans were forbidden to use their traditional names, in an ill-judged attempt on the part of the Government to break their spirit. In

the hard times that followed many Highlanders drifted south-
wards adopting names of English type. Some took patronymics
like *Johnson* that were common in the North of England, or
called themselves *Donaldson* instead of *Macdonald*. Many kept
their clan names in spite of authority. We are now familiar with
Macleods and *Macmillans* on every side, even in the highest
places, but the Highland invasion, like the Irish, is comparatively modern. In a thousand names taken at random from
seven London parish registers between 1540 and 1560 I found
only one name beginning with Mac- and no other name that was
recognizably Scottish.

Welsh names present yet another problem and one that forces
itself upon our attention by the high numbers concerned. Wales
was united to England more than three hundred years earlier
than Scotland, just at the period when English surnames were
taking their permanent form. From that time onwards the influx
of Welsh into England, which had never been negligible, increased greatly. The Welsh have always been first-class fighting
men, and after the conquest of their country by Edward I and
the peaceable settlement that followed it, many of their young
men, lacking their traditional pastime of warlike sallies into
England, enlisted in the armies of the English kings. Shakespeare's Fluellen (an Englishman's jocular version of *Llewellyn*)
was typical of hundreds of Welshmen who fought side by side
with the English from Crecy to Agincourt and many of these,
returning from the wars, settled in England.

In their own country the Welsh did not adopt fixed surnames
until about three hundred years after the English had done so.
Their own system was not so much a matter of single surnames
as of whole genealogies. They proudly remembered their forbears, calling themselves Ap- (son of) Hugh-ap-Owen-ap-David
and so on. This seems rather cumbersome, but we must remember that, as in medieval England, Christian names sufficed for
daily use. It was only on special occasions that these genealogical effusions were necessary. But a Welshman who settled in
England soon complied with the customary usage around him
and became known by a single surname instead of a whole
family tree, generally by the name of his father.

Thus from the Norman period onwards we find Welsh surnames in England, especially in the western counties. Some

families with names like *Maddox* (Madoc's), or *Craddock* (Caradoc, a particularly ancient and historic Welsh name), or *Griffiths* with its Norman version *Griffin*, have been settled in England for so long, six or seven hundred years, that they cannot possibly be excluded as foreigners or latecomers.

The trickle of Welshmen into England, which had continued all through the Middle Ages, turned into a regular flood when the Welsh Henry Tudor ascended the throne in 1485. (His name is a typical Welsh patronymic, ap-Tudor, the son of Theodore.) Many of the Welsh gentry flocked to court, and even those who stayed at home began from that time adopting English manners and customs and using English-style names. Both Henry VII and Henry VIII urged them to take fixed surnames, but it was not until the seventeenth century that most Welsh families did so. Then almost all took the name of their father and contented themselves with that one unchanging patronymic. A few old nicknames also became permanent in this way (page 331).

If they had remained faithful to their ancient, native Christian names such as Owain, Hywel, Rhys (*Owen, Howell, Rees* or *Rice*), and *Morgan*, all of them princely names as may be seen in the endpapers, we should always be able to recognize them and treat them separately in our calculations if we so wished. But, unfortunately for the student of surnames, they had by this time adopted the very Christian names that were most popular in England, and consequently there has flowed into England ever since a stream of Welsh families with names like *Williams* and *Thomas* which are indistinguishable from the same names formed in England. When the Christian name began with an 'R' or an 'H', the 'p' from 'Ap' sometimes stuck on to it, as in *Probert, Pritchard, Probyn, Prodger, Pugh, Parry, Price* and several others, or if the name began with a vowel the 'p' would turn to a 'B', giving *Bevan, Bowen, Bedward* and so forth. These, like the old Welsh Christian names, may be readily distinguished, but far more often the 'Ap' was dropped altogether and a genitive final '-s' added instead.

The result is that we cannot distinguish a Welsh *Williams* from an English one any more than we can pick out a Scottish *Wilson*; but whereas Lowland Scots have names of all four kinds like the English, Welsh surnames, being almost all concentrated on the one type, have much more effect on the proportions of

75

English surnames. And although we can easily recognize the old native Welsh names like *Griffiths* or *Morgan*, these are in many cases the very ones that have been longest in England. It would be illogical to exclude them from our classification while admitting others that came into England much later.

One more alien group must be mentioned briefly, the Jews. Their names have not been mingled with ours for any great length of time, because in 1290 Edward I expelled them all from England, and it seems that, except for a few converts, they really went. It was Oliver Cromwell who first allowed a few to return, but it was not until the late eighteenth century that they began to come in large numbers. The surnames they brought with them, if not Hebrew, belonged to the various European countries where they had been living, and are mostly so obviously foreign that they need not concern us. The two commonest Jewish surnames in London at the present time are *Cohen* and *Levy*, both very distinctive. However, some English Jews have anglicized their names, turning Levi, for instance, into *Lever* or *Lewis*, and such names must then be accepted at their face value. When a foreigner takes an English name it remains an English name. But the numbers concerned in such arrangements are not great enough to affect any general conclusions about groups of names. The number of Jews in Greater London is only 3% of the total population, and much less in the rest of the country. As the majority of them have obviously alien surnames, those that might be confused with the English cannot be more than one per cent. However in some particular cases the Jewish influence should be borne in mind.

In view of all these problems, if I am to try to classify a list of surnames into their separate types, I begin by sorting out the unknown, the obviously foreign, the Gaelic and the Irish, and I note the distinctively Welsh names as a matter of interest and as an indication of the total amount of the Welsh element in the group, but eventually include them with the English.

If we are now to make some statistics on these lines, we must look for a mixed group of ordinary people whose ancestors are likely to have come from all parts of the country and from all sorts of backgrounds. My usual standby, the London Directory, will not serve here, as the whole book, with nearly a million names, is too large, and to take one letter only might not offer a proper assortment. 'S' would be overweighted with Smiths; 'W', containing all the Williamses and Wilsons, would score too heavily on Christian names. For the particular purpose of classifying the names into their distinctive types we need the whole range of the alphabet.

What body of people could be more truly representative of the country as a whole than the members of the House of Commons? Taking the English boroughs and counties only, we have 511 members. Of those elected in 1964 twenty-nine have double-barrelled names, a modern phenomenon which simply implies two surnames instead of one. We may as well accept this bonus as further grist for the mill, bringing our total to 540. A preliminary sorting produces the following result:

	Number	%	Total
English names of known origin	439	81	81%
Old Welsh	21	4	
Gaelic	16	4	
Irish	20	3	19%
Foreign (including Jewish)	27	5	
Of unknown origin	17	3	
	540	100	

In this list the number of alien names is higher than would be found in many English communities. Obviously this is a matter which varies from one group to another. But it is the English names that concern us, and our next step, after adding in the Welsh numbers for reasons explained above, is to make our detailed analysis as follows: Locality 36·5%; Relationship 33%; Occupation 17·5%; Nicknames 13%.

These proportions are very average and typical. In order to obtain more reliable statistics I have classified much larger groups, always with much the same result. From old school lists of Haileybury College, a boarding school near London that draws boys from all parts of the British Isles and from English families overseas, I analysed three thousand surnames, and the resulting figures are so nearly the same as those given for the House of Commons that it is not worth repeating them. The slight range of variation is no more than could be accounted for by the decisions on doubtful cases and the size of the Welsh contingent. A similar school on the Welsh border, Shrewsbury, for instance, would be bound to have a higher percentage for the Relationship group, while one in Devonshire would have a more definite majority for local names, because among the Cornish – unlike their Welsh cousins – the majority of surnames come from places. This subject of local variation is a large one which can only be touched on lightly in a book of this size.

The kind of community that provides an excellent mixture of genuine English names may often be found far from England. For instance in Christchurch, New Zealand, the most English city of the most English dominion, the proportion of foreign names is far lower than that found in most English towns. The Scottish percentage is about the same, but the Welsh and Irish are lower. I found that an analysis of a school list there of over a thousand names gave the following result: Locality 38%; Relationship 33%; Occupation 16%; Nicknames 13%. These figures are not important in themselves, but some sort of analysis is necessary to an understanding of the subject.

As we have already had occasion to look closely at some of the names of occupation, it is convenient to concentrate first on them. I shall then turn to nicknames, because our oldest names are probably among them, and come finally to the two larger groups.

I. Occupational Names

Chapter 7

HIGH SCORES

Although names of occupation amount to only about 16% of English surnames, this group has the honour of including the most numerous and familiar of all, *Smith*. In its group it stands alone, having more than twice as many examples in the London Telephone Directory (5,750) as any of the others. I forbear calling it the commonest English name because there was nothing common about a smith in the Middle Ages. The reason for the multiplicity of the name is not so much that workers in metal were so numerous as that they were important and widespread. On the skill of the smith everyone, rich and poor, depended for the most essential things of life, the tools of husbandry and the weapons of hunting and war. Every community in the land must have a smith, every castle, every manor. But in most communities there would be only one, an outstanding man in his little world, known to all by his trade.

Another point that makes this name so numerous is that its predominance among craftsmen continued throughout the whole surname period, from the most ancient times right through the later Middle Ages when the last stragglers were getting their names, and it has always had the one simple form used in all parts of the country. The earliest recorded example of its use as a surname is in a charter of the year 975 (in the reign of Edgar), where one Ecceard Smith appears as a witness. At this date it was customary for the names of witnesses to be followed by another word indicating their rank or status, most frequently bishop, abbot, priest or thane. Ecceard must have been a well-respected person to be in such company. There was of course no idea at that time of such designations ever being permanent, but as in time they did become so, Ecceard is worth mentioning. But this example of a written name that has survived a thousand years does not imply that there was anything new about calling a man 'Smith' in that way at that time. There had been 'smiths' in England ever since the first Angles and Saxons invaded our shores, and no doubt the word had often been added to a personal name.

That the Normans used this familiar craft as a surname in the same way is shown in the Chronicle of Battle Abbey, which gives a vivid account from the Norman point of view of Duke William's landing at Pevensey. When the Conqueror leapt from his ship on to the English shore, he unfortunately slipped and fell on his nose which began to bleed profusely. His knights and barons who crowded round ready to acclaim him at this historic moment were much embarrassed at this dreadful portent, all except one William Smith who was clearly a man of resource. He at once stepped forward and exclaimed that it was a wonderful omen of success that the Duke should thus take possession of the land by sprinkling it with his blood. Thereafter William Smith was in high favour with the Conqueror and went on to further successes.

As the Chronicle of Battle Abbey is written in Latin, William Smith appears as 'Willielmus Faber'. His Norman companions would have called him 'le fevre' or 'le ferour', which words have given rise to a variety of surnames, *Feaver* (not common), *Ferrar*, *Farrar/er* and even *Farrow*. No doubt *Ferrier* is also sometimes from the same source, but there were many ferries on the unbridged rivers of the Middle Ages and the man in charge was a 'ferrier'. Another complication is that at least two baronial families came from Norman villages called Ferrières, and were known in England as de Ferrers; so that altogether the Norman version of this trade-name is as confused as the English is simple. But even if all the possible French forms were added together they would not amount to one-twentieth of the numbers of Smith.

Many people think that trade-names of this sort are so straightforward that there can be little to say about them, but this is not so. For one thing the comparative numbers in which they survive (some of which can be seen on page 327) are full of significance. In a previous section (page 61) we considered the building trade and the fighting forces of the Middle Ages as represented in the London Telephone Directory of today. Let us now take this same useful yardstick of comparative numbers, follow the names with the highest scores, and see what we find. The high-lights of medieval life are there for us, if only we can see them.

Everyone knows that *Smith* is the most numerous English surname, but how many could name the second among names of occupation? Two run very close together, *Clark* and *Taylor*, the former being very slightly ahead with 2,740 examples as against 2,570. It is not at all surprising that the clerk stands so high on the list. Like the smith he had a skill that was greatly in demand, and rare enough to be valued; in an unlettered age he could read and write. He represented learning; and a very little of it was enough to earn him the name; for it included a wide variety of persons from the highly intelligent secretaries of great men who often managed their affairs, to the humble parish clerks who chanted the responses in church, or poor students at the newly founded universities. While the smith's handiwork controlled the physical world, the clerk's abilities stood for intellectual power, and Norman rulers, while using the sword vigorously, were finding more and more use for the pen.

The higher orders of the Church were supposed by ecclesiastical law to be celibate and therefore unable to found families. If it were not so, *Parson* would be almost as common as *Smith*, for there was one in every village. Even as it is there are quite a number of names derived from Parson, which will be referred to again. But the proscription did not include the minor orders, as the large numbers of *Clarks* in our directory attest.

Before we go further down our list of names with large numbers, a point should be made about spelling. Sometimes the difference of a single letter may be significant, but there are certain regular variations which do not make a button of difference to the sense or origin. 'Er' and 'ar' are often interchangeable, and whether a name is spelt with an 'i' or a 'y', or whether it has or has not a final 'e' is entirely a matter of custom and family preference. In old manuscripts proper names like other words are found in many spellings. By the eighteenth century almost all had settled down to a regular form. It often happened that the ordinary noun like 'clerk' became fixed in one form (in that case pedantically influenced by its derivation from the Latin 'clericus'), and the surname in another. In many cases the surname preserves the older spelling or pronunciation of the two (*Smythe* and *Taylor* are both old spellings), or survives in several different forms, all derived from the same word. Consequently when I refer to a name by its most usual spelling it may be assumed that these slight and obvious variations are included.

The multiplicity of *Clarks* in the directory is easily explained. The almost equally large number of *Taylors* is more surprising. One would have thought that tailoring was a luxury trade employed chiefly by the rich, while ordinary folk had their clothes made by their wives and daughters. One would also expect to find more shoemakers than tailors, for footwear is more important to working people than fine clothes and more difficult to make, but there is not one in our list. Nor are there any 'cobblers', and a search for alternatives produces very little. When we turn to the medieval rolls we very often see the Latin word 'sutor' which is always translated 'shoemaker' and represents the Old English 'sutere', itself of Latin origin. This old word which lingered on in Scotland and the North Country long after it was forgotten in the South, has given us the surnames *Souter*, *Suter* and *Sowter* with one or two other variations of spelling, but altogether they add up to barely seventy. We also see a certain number of 'Cordwainers', particularly in the fourteenth-century rolls of the towns. They made fine shoes of Cordova leather for the élite, and were very prosperous, but their only descendants in our London Directory are four *Cordners* and two *Cordiners*. There is also the name *Boot/s* with thirty examples, but this is much more likely to have been a jocular name for a wearer of unusual boots or someone with large feet than a name for the maker. These small groups will not suffice to cover the feet of a nation. The problem remains. What has become of the shoemakers and why so many tailors? Clearly the answer to one question will also solve the other. The tailors during the surname period made shoes as well as clothes, indeed they must have made everything that was needed in the way of clothing, for headgear is as poorly represented in our surnames as shoes (10 *Hatters*, 28 *Cappers* and 30 *Hodders* or hood makers).

If we are to find the true significance of the name *Taylor* when it became attached to so many families, we must begin by getting rid of the vague idea of a tailor sitting cross-legged in his shop stitching away, and look more precisely at the life of the twelfth and thirteenth centuries. To start with 'tailor' is a French word, which is very unusual among trade-names with high numbers. (A name like *Smith* stood as firm as a rock. *Clark*, though derived from Latin, was in use in England long before the Conquest.) This suggests that the occupation was a new development of older crafts, for which a new name was useful. It might be said that it is natural for the word to be French since the Normans wore the finest clothes, but the high numbers in which the name survives show that it rapidly became an ordinary word used by everyone. The Cordwainers, for instance, made fashionable shoes and their total score is six.

The literal meaning of 'tailor' is cutter, and the Old English word which it displaced in this sense is *Shearer* or *Shearman*, both of which survive in small numbers. *Cutter*, a word of uncertain origin, appears later. We must think also in this connection of *Shears*, which must have been a nickname for the man who possessed or wielded this valuable tool. This two-bladed cutting instrument, which was evolved very early in the history of civilization, was really essential, first for shearing sheep, and later for finishing off newly woven cloth and cutting both cloth and leather neatly to make clothing. Every small community in the early Middle Ages must have possessed a pair of shears, but if the village was small there might be only one pair and one expert shearman to use them for anything that needed cutting in the village. Sewing was generally women's work, but in large groups where there was much hard stitching to be done the man who specialized in it was known as the 'souter', and what he made was chiefly shoes.

If we look at the fashions of this period, portrayed in illuminated manuscripts and carved figures in our churches, we see that clothes were so simple and loose fitting that they required very little shaping or what we should call tailoring at all. The criterion of the well-dressed man was a wealth of folds and drapery, embellished by heavy jewellery and elaborate embroidery contributed by his womenfolk. His headgear was that simplest of all garments, the hood. The only part of his attire

83

that required skilled cutting and workmanship was his foot- and leg-wear, and there seems to have been little distinction between them. The shoes of the period look more like soft slippers or socks than the hard-soled shoes that we are used to. The leggings, breeches or hose – whatever we choose to call them – were often made of leather too, and it would be natural for the same man to make both. Indeed as time went on they were often all in one piece. Leather was plentiful and nether garments must have worn out quickly and needed frequent replacement as compared with a tunic and cloak which, made of strong cloth and richly embroidered, would outlast very many pairs of leggings. Therefore it is quite natural that the Anglo-Saxons seem to have had no word corresponding to 'tailor'. The shearman trimmed and cut the cloth for the women to sew, and the souter made up whatever was needed, but nine-tenths of his output must have been for the legs and feet.

However by the twelfth century fashions were changing fast. Better fitting hose for the men's legs and well-fitting gowns for the ladies were becoming matters of high importance. Some Normans probably brought their own tailors with them. In any case it was their word that provided a name for the craftsman who now began to make whole outfits for those who could afford it. The older words receded into the background, their meanings narrowed. *Shearer* was left for dealings with sheep; *Shearman* (or *Sherman* or *Sharman*) for the trimming of cloth in the weaving trade, while *Souter*, having sunk by the fifteenth century to an old-fashioned word for a low-class shoemaker, dropped out altogether except in the Lowlands of Scotland, that last refuge of many a good old English word.

It should however be noted that there are 230 *Glovers*, not a large number perhaps but high for a luxury article. Gloves, often elaborately embroidered, were worn for the popular sport of falconry and by all the better class people for riding. Making them demanded a particular skill, and our statistics show that this provision for the hands became a widespread craft long before there was any similar specialization on shoes.

Thus our three most numerous occupational names supplied our ancestors with weapons and tools, a little learning and clothes from head to foot. It is not surprising that the *Miller* and *Baker* are next on the list to provide them with food. It may seem strange that those who toiled to grow the wheat in the first place are so poorly represented (the *Plowman* scores only forty-eight), but mere labour was not of much account in the surname period. It was special skill and equipment that gave a man importance. The smith who forged the plowshare was far more distinguished than the yokel who plodded in the mud directing it.

'Miller' is one of those words which have survived in several forms with identical meanings that should reasonably be taken together for a just comparison. The Old English word for a mill was 'mylen' which became in Early Middle English *Milne* or 'mulne', and was then naturally simplified to *Mill*. Thus the man whose work was inseparable from this building was first the *Milner* or *Mulliner* and then the *Miller*, while in some places, particularly in the South, he was known as the *Millward* (or keeper of the mill) which often became *Millard*, *Millyard* or *Millar*, which might again become *Miller*. If we add all these together and also *Mills*, in which the final 's' seems to add a genitive rather than a plural sense (for this final 's' see page 274), then the whole milling business produces about 2,570 names, putting it practically equal with tailoring.

At the first thought one might be surprised to see *Baker* so high on the list (1,790). But if we suppose that in the surname period every housewife baked for her own family we are not letting our imaginations carry us far enough back. That kind of *ménage* belongs to a later and more civilized time where every farmhouse had a properly built fireplace with a solid chimney and brick ovens. In the days when our surnames were formed, peasants cooked over central fires on the floor. Dough cakes could be laid out on a griddle or hot stones, as they were for King Alfred to watch, but the important loaf of bread, the mainstay of the family, or anything else that needed baking, was taken to the communal oven or bakehouse. A castle would have its own oven and baker, but humble villagers shared in this important institution, as the large numbers of the surname attest. It survives in two regular forms, *Baker* and *Baxter*. The latter, originally 'bakester', was a feminine form of the same word, but it seems that at an early date the sense of different gender was lost and the word used indiscriminately for either sex. There are several of these pairs, *Brewer* and *Brewster*, *Spinner* and

85

Spinster are typical examples. In the former case both forms seem regularly to have been used for men; in the latter the second has remained very definitely feminine. In fact these pairs behave erratically. All we need note is that *Baxter* is simply another form of *Baker* and that the building, which (like the *Mill*) is inseparable from the occupation, is represented by forty examples of *Backhouse* and fourteen of the glorified version *Bacchus*.

Next on our list comes *Webb*, a very old word for one skilled in the ancient craft of weaving. It also had a feminine form, *Webster*, but as with *Baker* and *Baxter* the distinction seems to have been lost at an early date. *Webber* and *Weaver* are later variants of the original root word (O.E. 'webba', a weaver). These four total just over 1,600. But they mark only the starting point for the woollen industry for which England became famous in the fourteenth century, an industry second only to agriculture as a national occupation. Our directory also contains 1,250 *Walkers*, and they did not get their names for progressing on their feet. After the cloth was woven it had to be trampled on, or beaten in water for hours to soften and cleanse it before it was fit for use. 'Walker' is the old word for the man who performed this task in the simplest way. It is found chiefly in the North and Midlands, while in the South-East the same worker was generally called a *Fuller* and in the South-West a *Tucker*. The last two names represent newer and improved methods, but the three are identical in purpose. Together they add up to over two thousand.

A great many more surnames belong to this important business of producing cloth. The *Carder* and *Comber* (or *Comer*) prepared the wool; the *Tozer* teased it; the *Lister* was a *Dyer*; the *Burler* made a coarse cloth in very common use called *Burrell*; and the *Challoner* made blankets of a kind known as *Challen* which took their name from the French weaving town of Chalons. None of these specialist names exist in large numbers. They belong to the latter end of our period when the business was being organized on a national scale with weavers' guilds in all the principal towns. The high numbers of the two principal craftsmen involved – the weaver and walker – and the varied and early verbal forms of the former (the earliest form, *Webb*, being the commonest) show us that long before that time they

86

had been producing homespun cloth in scattered villages and little market towns all over the country.

We have strayed a little from the numerical order to take the best-known surnames from the clothmaking industry together. The next name on the list after *Webb* is *Wright*, a builder, about which something has already been said (page 61).

We therefore pass on to *Turner* with 1,360 examples. We tend now to think of a turner as one who works in wood, but those early turners used their wheels or lathes to round objects in many materials, wood, metal, bone and even clay. The earliest example of the word given by the New English Dictionary is from a metrical romance dated about 1400 which alludes to 'turners of vesselles', but many examples of the word used as a surname can be found two hundred years earlier than this, for example Warner le Turner from the Pipe Roll of 1180. In fact it frequently happens that surnames prove the existence of a word long before the dictionary has evidence of it.

We are inclined nowadays to think of bowls, cups and dishes as being made by *Potters*, and this word was certainly in use from early times in this sense; but their number is only 360, supported by eighty *Crockers* (and *Crokers*) who also made earthenware, which seems an insufficient total for such a basic craft. But the deficiency is made up when we realize that the *Turners* with their wheels were producing the same articles.

The *Coopers* (including the variant spelling *Cowper*) have almost the same numbers as the *Turners* and served a very similar purpose, but on a larger scale. They made barrels, tubs and wooden buckets, articles that were absolutely essential to primitive communities, for fetching and storing water, milk and other fluids. Most people will agree that the brewing of ale, mead and other beverages is a fundamental craft, but the making of the utensils to contain them was the most skilled part of the business. There are only 240 *Brewers* in our list (including *Brewsters* and *Brosters*) to 1,350 *Coopers*, to whom might be added 260 *Hoopers* who were contributing to the same product. Brewing was comparatively easy and was frequently done by the women, but the large containers for the liquid had to be professionally made.

Next on our list comes *Cook/e* with 1,230 examples, including *Coke* which is an early spelling variant. Here is a different type of name, a household servant rather than a craftsman, but a very important one. Later on we will take a look at a typical large household with servants of many kinds. We need not wonder that *Cook* is by far the most numerous of them, for every establishment of any size from a royal castle to the smallest manor house or inn, even a camp of outlaws in the forest, had a cook. There were many cooks in Duke William's army when he sailed from Normandy. We see them in the Bayeux tapestry busily roasting small birds over spits at very neat looking camp kitchens. His own special cooks were much favoured and given English manors to reward them for the tasty dishes he had enjoyed. No one need think that because methods of cooking at that time were somewhat crude beside our own, cooks were the less skilled. On the contrary they were probably more so. Human ingenuity is generally more inspired by difficult circumstances than by ease. The country produced an abundance of edible wild life, and the cooks used every possible herb and spice for sauces and flavouring.

After the cook it is natural to think of the huntsman who brought in so much of the food, especially in royal and noble households. *Hunt* and *Hunter* must be taken together for they are the same word, the former being the truer representative of the Old English 'hunta', whose normal development was to drop its final vowel and come down to us as one syllable only. Most of the French nouns, and some of the English ones, that expressed the idea of an agent ended in '-our' or '-er' with the result that this suffix of agency was sometimes applied by analogy to other words where it did not rightfully belong. Thus the Middle English 'hunte' became 'hunter' in ordinary speech, but in our surnames, as so often happens, the older form is preserved as well and is the commoner of the two. Together they total 1,080.

When one considers how strictly all hunting was controlled by the king for the benefit of himself and his most highly favoured barons, it is remarkable that this Anglo-Saxon word should have survived to the almost complete exclusion of the corresponding French 'chasseur' and 'veneur'. Since the Normans had a monopoly of hunting we might reasonably expect to find hundreds of modern Chasers and *Venners*, but there are none of the former in our list and less than twenty *Venners*, some of whom are *Fenners* or fen men in disguise.

However the men who policed the great royal forests enforc-
ing the king's cruel laws that excluded the English from their
own traditional hunting grounds were called by a French word,
as one would expect, *Foresters*. Even Norman barons were not
allowed to hunt in the forests without the king's authority.
Consequently they enclosed large tracts of land around their
new castles for their own private sport, their 'parks' they called
them, from which the English peasantry were also excluded by
the *Parkers*, another French word for another unpopular official.
(I do not know how old the term 'nosey Parker' is, but it was
certainly the business of the parker from the eleventh century
onwards to nose out poachers.) There are 860 *Parkers* in our
directory, and *Parke*, which probably has the same meaning,
though it may overlap with a pet-name for Peter (page 228),
would bring it to nearly 900. *Forester* is harder to compute
accurately. It was generally shortened to *Forster* and often to
Foster, but some few of the latter name might have been genuine
foster brothers or parents.

With so many Norman officials about, it is pleasing to know
that the man with the dogs and the bugle horn, the man who
was employed because he best knew the woods, was English, and
that he had with him English companions and assistants who
called him by the old name *Hunt* so steadily that in time even
their proud masters took it up and forgot the Norman word.

Chapter 8

FOLLOWING THE NUMBERS

In the last chapter we looked at the twelve most numerous occupational names, and some others closely linked with them for comparison. Already we can see a picture of medieval life appearing like the first shadows on a photographic print. If we follow the numbers a little further details emerge more clearly.

The next surname in order, still well over the thousand mark, is *Bailey*, which gives the first sign of authority on our list. It comes from the Old French 'bailis' (Latin 'balivus') and occurs in a great variety of spellings, *Baillie*, *Bayley* and *Bayliss* being just a few. To write a full account of this word in all its diversity of forms and functions would involve one in a treatise on early methods of government. It is enough to say now that the bailiff represented law and order. He was an official who presided at local courts of justice, often taking charge of a Manor Court and all the affairs of a village in the absence of its lord.

As we look through the Subsidy Rolls, in almost every village the first name on the list is either that of its lord (preceded by 'Dominus' or followed by 'armiger' or some other Latin word indicating knightly or noble status), or if there is no such gentleman resident at the hall, we have a name followed by 'balivus' or 'praepositus', in fact the bailiff. The English word for this same person was 'reeve', and we cannot tell by looking at the medieval list which word the villagers were actually using – certainly not a Latin one. But our surname statistics show us clearly that *Bailey* and *Reeve* were running neck and neck with the former slightly in the ascendant. (They also tell us its old pronunciation before a pedantic knowledge of its Latin derivation added the final 'f'.)

'Reeve' died hard. It comes from the Old English 'gerefa' and in many cases the initial 'g' lingered on, producing *Grieve*, *Greaves* and sometimes *Graves* (*Graveson* is certainly 'the reeve's son', and probably *Grayson* too). If we add these variations to *Reeve/s* we have approximately 680 names as against 1,070 *Baileys* etc. Chaucer, of course, has a reeve among his pilgrims, but in his day the word was already old-fashioned and confined to village use, while 'bailiff' was used in Government circles.

Before we leave the subject of the reeve or bailiff we should give some thought to another surname, very close to them in meaning, and so numerous that it deserves careful attention. This is *Hall* (1,230), which sounds like a local name and is so literally, but which, like *Mill*, is really a borderline case referring more to the owner's livelihood than to his place of residence. The many men whom one sees in the Subsidy Rolls referred to as 'of the Hall' or, in dog-Latin, 'del Aula' were employed in some useful way in the principal house of the village.

One thing is certain. The name does not refer to the lord of the manor himself. It is too parochial in its outlook for that. It is a word used in the village by people to whom 'the Hall' has only one meaning, 'the big house' that, with the church, is the centre of their small world. The knight who owned the village or held it from a greater lord belonged to a wider sphere. He might be resident in the Hall, but he sometimes rode away to the Hundred Court, or to the Shire Court, or followed some baron even farther afield. He frequently mingled with others of his own standing who had halls of their own in other places, and among them he was naturally called by the proper name of his village which might easily be unique, or by some other more personal surname.

But the man 'at the Hall' could easily be the steward who managed the place for this knightly owner, the person in charge in his absence, and even, in many cases where the owner was never resident at all, the permanent occupier. Looking through many of the early Edwardian Subsidy Rolls, I have noticed how the name occurs most often in villages where there is no recognizable member of the gentry, and that the tax he pays is often the highest in the village. In these cases *Hall* is just another name for *Reeve* or *Bailey*. In other cases where 'John at the Hall' pays only a groat near the bottom of the list, the term is distinguishing a humble man who works and sleeps at the Hall from one who lives in his own hut.

The last occupational name to pass the thousand mark is *Ward*, a simple Old English monosyllable meaning a guardian, keeper or watchman, a person so obviously useful and important that little more need be said about his function. This word (O.E. weard) was a favourite among the Anglo-Saxons for forming their Christian names, as in Edward and Hereward, and was used in many compounds. The title 'lord' originated as the 'hlaf-weard', the guardian of the loaf, but this is going a long way back. Our surnames still echo the lesser titles of the *Durward* (Door-keeper, largely superseded by *Porter*), the *Hallward*, the *Woodward* (later the forester), and the *Churchward*, now become the Churchwarden. The best known of these compounds was the *Hayward*, a familiar figure in most villages from early times. His task was to guard – not the hay as one might easily think, but the enclosures. (The word comes from O.E. 'haga', a hedge.) The great fields shared out in strips and cultivated communally by the villagers were protected by moveable hurdles, and it was the responsibility of the hayward to see that all was well and no animals strayed on to the precious crops. If they did he might impound them. Custom varied from one place to another, but in many villages there was a certain authority as well as useful perquisites attached to the office of hayward which made it well worth holding. There are about 280 *Haywards* in our directory, and most of the *Haywoods* and *Heywoods* probably spring from the same source, bringing the total to over four hundred.

The name with the next highest number after *Ward* is *Parker* which has already been mentioned in connection with preserves for hunting (page 89). Following on, we come to what might be called the travel section. *Carter* scores 900 on our list. There were few vehicles in England in our period by modern standards, but those few were very important. On every manor of any size there would have to be a cart of some kind, a primitive affair but valuable for drawing heavy farm produce or casks of ale slowly over the muddy lanes. Great lords and barons, who frequently moved from one castle to another with a vast amount of paraphernalia, had carts as well as pack horses to bring their baggage.

It is almost incredible how kings and princes with great retinues of attendants got about so much from the earliest times. There is a cart depicted on the Bayeux tapestry bringing Duke William's gear down to his ship. Henry II rushed about all over France and England with a great following of barons, priests, soldiers, courtiers and servants, and baggage for all of them. In such a world the carter, managing his team of horses or oxen in conditions that we would think impassable, was at least a well-known character.

An alternative word for a wheeled vehicle was *Wain* or *Wayne*, driven by a *Wainer* or *Wainman* (which might be slurred into *Wenman* or *Weyman*). These names provide another hundred with the same meaning as Carter. Both words, 'cart' and 'wain', are of pre-Conquest origin, but 'waggon' is too late for surnames.

While on this subject we must give a thought to the skilled men who built these vehicles, the *Cartwrights* and *Wainwrights* who together number nearly two hundred. This brings to mind the *Wheelers* who were clearly important for they number five hundred. It is unlikely, however, that they made cart wheels only. For every cart in England there must have been at least a dozen spinning wheels which required a special craft to make, though using them was a common ability among the women. I believe that spinning wheels formed the chief preoccupation of the Wheelers.

But to return to travel, the normal way of getting about for the more prosperous was on horseback, and the man who looked after the horses in Norman and Plantagenet times was called the *Marshall*. This word has risen so high in the world that it is hard to realize that at that time it simply meant a farrier, groom or horse dealer. His work overlapped the smith's only in the matter of shoeing horses, and he cared for them and their welfare in all other ways.

Horses were so important for fighting and hunting and as a status symbol from the earliest recorded times that in royal circles the care of the stables was an honour given to one of the king's most trusted men. In the Anglo-Saxon period the word for this important position was 'horse thegn', but after the Conquest this English title was replaced by the Old French 'mareschal' (the horse servant). The word then developed along two very different paths. At court and in the households of great men it continued to rise in status, until it reached the dizzy height of the premier Earldom. But it did not stop there. In modern times it has out-grown the exclusive circle of the court where the Master of the Horse has inherited some of its honours, gone on to the highest rank of the Army, and finally taken flight and soared into the air. Who would have thought that 'servant who looked after the horses' would one day command hundreds of aeroplanes? But in the twelfth and thirteenth centuries, although already a high official at court and a kind of superior usher in the households of great men, the ordinary marshal also continued in a workmanlike way tending horses and doctoring their ailments in villages all over England. There are about 860 *Marshalls* in our directory, including a few *Mascalls* and *Maskells* (variants of the same word), and it is only too plain that most of them got their name from this useful occupation, and only a few from the stately officials who marshalled the élite at banquets, processions, tournaments and other state occasions.

The *Groom* on the other hand, of whom there are only seventy-five, was originally a very general sort of servant, and it is only in comparatively modern times that his services have been narrowed down to attendance on horses and brides.

We come now to the *Knight* who has 820 representatives in the directory. Of this well-known and typically medieval figure something will be said later (page 132). It is enough to note now that, though in time the word came to be little more than an honourable title conferring a certain status, in the years after the Conquest it was a very definite occupation, that of a mounted soldier bound in loyalty to fight for his feudal lord. It is fitting that he should be next in sequence to the *Marshall*, for without a horse he could not be a knight.

After the knight the *Fisher* seems a humble character, but he was extremely important in the national economy. When hunting was so much restricted and domestic animals so precious, fish played a large part in the national diet, encouraged by the Church. As only a small proportion of the population lived near enough to the coast to eat sea fish, and every district had to be almost self-supporting in the way of food, there were elaborate systems of weirs, nets and fish traps on all the rivers, ponds and fens. England was an even wetter land then than it is now.

Hundreds of ponds have been drained, marshes reclaimed and streams put neatly underground since the thirteenth century. In those days the land abounded with water, and the water with fish, and we must imagine the *Fisher*, not as an amateur enjoying himself, but as an expert employed as such on the manor where he lived, spending his days by the water's edge, almost amphibious, tanned by sun and rain, returning to his village with basketfuls of pike, perch, mullet, minnows, freshwater crayfish or anything he could get, particularly eels, which were highly popular, and on a good day that delicacy, beloved of kings, lampreys.

The *Fisher* brings to mind the *Fowler*, whose numbers are much lower. This is probably because the former worked on the sea as well as land and is to be found in every seaport and coastal village; but when one reads, for instance, in *The Boke of Nurture*, written by one of the household of Duke Humphrey of Gloucester, brother of Henry V, instructions for serving

> Goose, teal, mallard, osprey and swan,
> Woodcock, bittern, egret, snipe and curlew,
> Peacock, stork, bustard and shoveller,
> Quail, sparrow, lark and the little martinet,
> Pigeon, swallow, thrush and ousel ye not forget

then one understands that the *Fowler* had plenty to do.

The next name on our list is *Chapman* (770). This is the English word for one who bought and sold, a dealer of any kind, gradually superseded by the French 'marchand' which has given us *Marchant* and *Merchant*. As this new word was used by the wealthier people and those with continental connections, so 'chapman' went down in the world, narrowing in meaning until it came to signify nothing more than a *Peddler* or *Packman* and finally dropped out of use altogether. But it lives on still in numerous local names, such as 'Cheapside', and in the colloquial term 'chap', while its large score as a surname, far exceeding that of *Merchant*, shows its importance in the surname period as the regular word for a dealer of any kind. In numerical order the *Chapman* is twentieth on our list, and the first representative of commerce. The other nineteen belong primarily to the country, and if they sold anything it was what they had made themselves.

As we descend to lower numbers the names come thicker and faster. The *Mason* has already been mentioned elsewhere. If we take one more for special attention we shall have included all those with over seven hundred examples. The last one to reach this score is that most endearing of all English medieval figures, the *Shepherd*, familiar to us through many early church carvings and illuminated manuscripts with his crook and rough, homespun cloak and hood.

After the Black Death when farmland lay uncultivated for lack of men, the keeping of sheep increased enormously, and the weaving of cloth for export was encouraged by the king on a nation-wide scale; but wool had been the wealth of England long before that, known and valued all over Europe, and every manor had its flock. As one looks through the Subsidy Rolls of Edward I, one sees the name Shepherd again and again, particularly in hilly districts, the South Downs, the Cotswolds and the northern counties. In the Cumberland rolls of 1293 *Shepherd* is the commonest surname of all. The only reason why its number was not ultimately so large as some lies in this very proliferation. Where too many men were shepherds the unconscious urge for variety produced different names for many of them.

Before we leave the shepherd with his flocks and the marshal who cared for horses, we may take the occasion to glance at some of the other men who tended these same animals in a specialized way. We have, for instance, *Ewart* (ewe-herd), and there is no doubt that some of the *Lamberts* were originally lamb-herds. As regards horses, there are *Stoddarts* and *Studdarts*, who looked after the stud horses or steeds (these words are all related). *Steedman* also means the same thing. Then there is the *Coltard* or *Coltman* and the *Runciman* who cared for the rouncys or nags, and, a rather surprising survival, the *Palfreyman*. There are ten examples of this picturesque name in four different spellings in our directory as well as ten simply of *Palfrey* and three of *Parfrey*. A palfrey was a small saddle horse, particularly suitable to a lady or cleric as compared to the great 'steed' necessary for the armoured knight.

As for other domestic animals, the care of cattle has given us some surnames, but none in great number. There are about sixty *Cowards*, a very misleading contraction of 'cow-herds', rather more *Calverts* and *Calvers* and a few examples each of

Bullard, Buller, Bullman and *Oxer*, less than two hundred in all.

Pigs must have played a large part in medieval life, and one would expect to find the swineherd well represented as *Swinnard* or something of the sort, but though the name exists there are none in our directory. A much less recognizable word with this same meaning is *Forward* from the obsolete Old English word 'for', meaning a pig, and 'ward', a guardian. There was also a hog-ward or -herd, which has given *Hogger, Hoggard* and *Hogarth*, but none of these are numerous. Pigs were generally turned into the woods to fend for themselves with only children set to watch or drive them. It seems to have been considered unskilled work and hardly sufficient to make a complete occupation for a man.

On the whole the care of domestic animals kept only for food has not produced any specialist name in large numbers, comparable to that of the marshal or hunter with their horses and dogs, or the shepherd whose woolly flocks meant wealth for their owner. Tending the other animals was a more ordinary task expressed most often in the general term *Herd* (*Heard, Hird, Hurd* or *Herder*). *Driver*, too, nearly always means a driver of herds or flocks. I have seen 'Le Sheepdriver' as a frequent name in thirteenth-century Hertfordshire records, and this would naturally be simplified in time.

When we come to consider nicknames we shall find that the farmyard animals have indeed made their mark on surnames, and men who spent their lives among them were apt to describe each other in farmyard terms. This brings us to a point where one class of name overlaps another, and it is best to keep now to those surnames that are strictly occupational in form. However I will give one example to show how closely the different types interlock. The name *Best*, sounding so superlative, is really 'beast' which was not at all 'beastly' in the Middle Ages but just the ordinary word for an 'animal' (a high-class, intellectual word that came in the Renaissance). The *Bester* tended the animals, but the name is more common in the shorter form. In the Dorset Subsidy of 1327 I find John Nuxethebeste, or 'Next the beasts', which must have been where he slept, a nice warm place for a winter's night. We need not ask what his occupation was.

Since so many of our occupational names are concerned with

97

what we should now call 'farming', it may be asked, how does the name *Farmer* stand, and why are there not more of them? There are only 190. It might easily be answered that when everyone farmed there was no distinction in it, but there is quite another reason. It is a word of French origin, 'fermier', which entered the language rather late with an entirely different meaning from its present one. It meant, at first, an agent who 'farmed out' the land and collected the rents from it. It is one of the vagaries of our language that this word, which began as a foreign-sounding rent collector, should have climbed into such an unassailable, solid, popular, John Bullish sort of niche as the one it now occupies.

Chapter 9

THE HOUSEHOLD

By following the surnames with the highest numbers we have so far been confined to village life, but if we turn from the village to the castle we shall find another community, typical of its age but now completely gone. The nearest approach we have to such a thing, apart from the rare stately home that can still keep an enormous staff, is the big boarding school or University College, but there are many differences. The modern institution, however wealthy and well equipped, does not have unlimited manpower; it is not prepared to defend itself against attack; nor does it periodically take to the roads and move on with all its paraphernalia to another place. Perhaps a millionaire with a retinue of secretaries, valets, private detectives and chauffeurs would come nearer to the mark; but in truth the phenomenon of the great medieval household is gone, though if we look we can still find it in the directory.

It goes without saying that the great household would contain many of the people who have already featured prominently in our list. Like the village it was a self-sufficient community with its own smith, wright, tailor, clerk and so forth; probably, if the lord were a great enough man, several of each, and certainly a good number of armed retainers, but there are certain functionaries who belong particularly to this kind of *ménage*.

There are, for instance, the *Chamberlain*, the *Page*, the *Butler* and the *Spencer* (or dispenser), who all score round about six hundred in the directory. Of these the most numerous is the *Chamberlain*, if we take into account the more familiar form *Chambers* and the northern version *Chalmers*. His task was to look after the private room or chamber where his lord slept;

99

to help him dress, to bring him water for washing, to comb his hair, make his bed, strew fresh herbs and rushes on the floor and in fact combine the duties of a valet and a housemaid. No wonder the royal chamberlain became such an influential person in remote times when his duties brought him into such close contact with the king. The title has always remained a high honour at court, though the Lord Chamberlain no longer combs the sovereign's hair. But the surname could not be so numerous if the office were confined to the households of the very great. Inns had their chamberlains too, to look after the sleeping accommodation; and the last survival of this word in the ordinary workaday world is in the feminine form, 'chambermaid'.

The next in this group is the *Page*, which is perhaps surprising. The name seems to lack that quality of singularity within its own community that would make it sufficiently distinctive. One might have thought that in a large household there would be several young pages who would rise to other titles or appointments when they were older, and so not retain the name all their lives. But there it is; there are just six hundred *Pages* (with *Paige*), so there must have been many households where a faithful attendant was known all his adult life by this name, and passed it on to his son.

The importance of the *Butler* can be easily understood. He was in charge of the drink and served his master with wine at table, the derivation of the word being close to the 'bottle'. Again at court such personal attendance on the king was an honour, and the name has been proudly held by noble families; but at the same time in lesser households butlers have performed much the same tasks from Norman times to the present day. The *Spencer* was the dispenser of stores, an important post in a great household where supplies of the more costly foodstuffs like spices had to be carefully controlled. The place where he presided was called the *Spence*, and anyone who worked there with him might earn this name.

In many households the man in charge of the supplies in general was called the *Steward*, but the numbers of this surname are hard to compute because the Scottish clan, *Stewart*, has confused the issue. Its name is the same in origin as the English word, but the multiplication of its numbers under the clan system is out of proportion with the natural English development. It is sometimes stated that the original meaning was sty-ward, or guardian of the pig sty, but the New English Dictionary will not commit itself on the exact Old English meaning of 'sty'. It was some kind of building but not originally confined to pigs. However this is delving further into the past than we need go. At the time that surnames were being formed the word already meant a responsible member of a household who might take charge of it, or even, like the marshal, a high officer of state. When Walter, the Steward of Scotland, married the daughter of Robert Bruce in 1316 he was himself of royal blood and his name a distinguished title. Since then it has had a chequered career, climbing to the supreme height of the thrones of Scotland and England, but simultaneously continuing in several other humble capacities, always narrowing in function so that it is now applied chiefly to caterers in colleges, organizers of race meetings, and servants on merchant ships. Of the English form of the name, *Steward*, there are only about eighty on our list.

We may picture our great lord – an earl or baron, shall we say – sitting at table with his *Butler* and *Steward* to serve him, his favourite *Page* behind his chair, his *Chaplin* at hand to say grace, and his *Leech* (the doctor) in case he should eat unwisely. His *Napier* may be hovering with a supply of napkins, but as we have only about fifty of these it is clear that this refinement did not often require a special attendant. His *Chamberlain* is probably well placed at table, his *Barber* rather lower down, though he too may be a favourite. There may be some *Guests* of course, but we will speak of them elsewhere.

The lower tables in the great hall are thronged with the baron's armed retainers, his *Knights* with their *Squires* to wait on them, his *Archers* and other men-at-arms. There may also be a few *Tennants* from his estates and a *Messenger* or two ready to gallop off at his pleasure.

There are *Ushers* to see that all are seated in proper order; the *Porter* is at the door, and the *Wards* on guard outside. The *Bailey* of the village belonging to the castle is in the hall hoping to have a word on business, but the great man is more intent on pleasure at the moment, more inclined to chat with his *Hunter* and *Parker* and *Falconer* about the next day's sport.

What else is missing? Of course there is music in the room.

We know from figures given before (page 64) that the *Harper* was by far the favourite performer, but there might also be *Pipers* or *Fiddlers* or even musicians with a curious kind of portable *Organ* which can be seen in illuminated manuscripts of the period. There are twenty of them in our directory. And there might be *Singers*, *Players* and even *Dancers*, though all of these are in rather short supply.

And of course down at the end of the hall behind the screens is the red faced *Cook* presiding in all his glory over the fiery furnace with its spits and cauldrons. He has several lads running at his command, but very few of them gained surnames from this kind of task. There were too many of them at it, and the work was too undistinguished. There is just one *Scullion* in our directory, and a few more *Skillins* and *Skillings*, which are the same thing. These boys rose in time to more important work or were called by names of other types. How different from the *Cook*, whose name continued to be used as a personal title right down into this century!

I have said nothing about the ladies present because we are thinking now of occupations and official duties which did not concern them. Nearly all the servants in a household of this kind were men. There was even a *Maidman* (now more often *Maidment*) to wait on the maidens, not particularly at table but for any service they might require.

In any case comparatively few surnames have come from women. But there was one essentially feminine task that was so important that it has left some examples. If our baron was a family man the *Nurse* (or *Nourse*) was certainly at the table, and her own son as he grew up must sometimes have carried the name with him for life and passed it on. As a personal link with the young lord it was not to be despised. The French form 'nourrice' has been absorbed by *Norris* (page 299), so the numbers of this occupation are larger than they seem.

Another form of work that was often done by women was the washing of clothes. *Launder*, *Lander* and *Lavender* are all derived from the French 'lavandier' or 'lavandiere', and could be of either sex. There are just over a hundred of them, whereas the only English equivalent, *Washer*, scores only seven. From this contrast we should not necessarily conclude that the English washed that much less than the Normans, but rather that it was only in the grand establishments of the ruling class that a special person was appointed for the purpose.

Although *Lavender* does not signify the herb of that name, or very rarely so, sweet-smelling herbs were much used in great households, and one of them, which is little known in modern times, scores over sixty in the directory. This is *Woodruffe*, a small, inconspicuous plant that grows freely in our woods. The reason why so much importance was once attached to it is that it lasted well when dried, retaining its pleasant fragrance, which made it particularly suitable for strewing in bed-chambers, or even stuffing mattresses. The part it played in the domestic economy is plainly indicated by the fact that the genus to which it belongs is called 'Bedstraw'. Rich people had feather beds, but even they may sometimes have preferred something cooler and sweeter in hot weather, and liked the scent of it in their rooms to counteract the lack of sanitation. While the man responsible for providing the rushes for the floor of the great hall was sometimes called *Rush* or *Rushman*, the nickname *Woodruffe* (now spelt in various ways) must have been given to someone concerned with the more delicate and fragrant 'bedstraw' for the sleeping chambers.

Every castle had a host of outside workers, the permanent residents of the countryside who worked hard to produce much provender when the lord was in residence. Among them a special mention is due to the *Gardiner* (or *Gardner*). There are 660 of them, more than the *Butchers* and *Brewers* put together. This may be somewhat unexpected. A gardener seems such a civilized person for that fierce age, but looking again at all that company to be fed, one realizes that every castle and manor house must have a garden, not so much for beauty, though the ladies loved lilies and roses as they do still, but for fruit in season and herbs at all times, fresh or dried. The author of *The Boke of Nurture* (see page 95) instructs his readers to:

> Serve fastyng plommys, damsons, cheries and grapes
> to plese,
> After mete, peeres, nottys, strawberries, wyneberries
> and hard chese,
> Also blawnderelles, pipyns, caraway in comfyte.
> Compostes ar like to these.

> Aftur sopper, rosted apples, peres, blaunche powder
> your stomak for to ese.

When he instructs a chamberlain how to make 'a medicinable
bath' for his lord, he begins by telling him to boil together no
less than twenty herbs and flowers, beginning,

> Hollyhock, yardehock, peritory and fennel,
> Wall wort, herb St John, centaury and camomel,

and finally to 'set his lord in it . . . as hot as he may abide'. It
sounds more like a thick soup than a bath, and could only be
done with the aid of a good gardener.

We are flying rather high with such a luxurious household.
For every royal prince or nobleman who lived in this state there
were hundreds of simple knights and younger sons of noble
families who lived, not in great castles, but in primitive stone
keeps or manor houses that to our eyes would seem no better
than barns. Each would consist only of a large, high-raftered,
smoky hall with a single more private chamber divided off for
the lord of the manor and his wife, and perhaps some other cur-
tained recess for the attendant women. And yet the gentry
living in such places were waited on by hordes of servants far
beyond the means of most of us today. Any manorial lord, however small and poor his estate and few his acres, would have at
least one body servant in constant personal attendance who
would be called (so our statistics tell us) either his *Page* or his
Squire or just his *Man*, several other men and women to brew
and bake and cook for him, and a number of villagers outside
his doors who were more or less his dependants, to be called on
for various duties.

The only indoor servant not yet mentioned, whose name survives in large numbers though quite unknown to most, is the
'dey' or *Day*, a word that, though now completely obsolete, was
in common use in the Middle Ages as a household worker. In
Old English it meant first a kneader of bread and gave us the
second syllable of 'lady' which was originally the 'Hlaef dige' or
loaf-kneader (while her lord was the loaf-ward). Then as 'dey' it
passed on to being a servant of either sex who prepared food,
especially cheese and butter, in the dey-ery or dairy. There are
570 *Days* in our directory and though some of them might be

abbreviations for the name David used as patronymics, the great majority refer to those skilled dairymen and maids who worked, both in castles and manor houses, in the Middle Ages. The New English Dictionary gives the meaning as 'a female dairy worker', but the many cases in the Subsidy Rolls of such forms as 'Roger le Deye' and 'Walter le Deye' prove otherwise.

It is time that we looked at a real medieval household in the setting of a real village instead of dealing in generalizations, and this can be done with the aid of the Poll Tax of Richard II. It comes at the very end of our period; surnames have already been fixed for a generation or two, but it has the advantage of giving more detail than any other of the taxation lists, and including – or at least so it was supposed – the whole population over the age of fourteen. The village I have chosen is Stowe Langtoft in Suffolk, not because it is in any way remarkable, but because it has a resident lord of the manor, is not too large and is more detailed than most, giving the names very conveniently grouped according to their place of residence. The date is 1381, so that anyone in it over the age of thirty-two has survived the Black Death, which perhaps accounts for the number of people who seem to be the only one of their family.

Seventy-three people are given in the list with forty-one different surnames. Of course they are not all called by their occupations like the staff of my imaginary castle. They have names of all types, but thirteen are occupational, a higher percentage than for the country as a whole. With the exception of the lord of the manor they have all lost the prepositions ('de' and 'le' and 'atte') that their names would have had a century earlier. In fact the list has quite a modern look, except that everyone's actual occupation, as distinct from his surname, is given in Latin.

The lord of the manor is Robert de *Ashfield*. He has a wife, Margaret, who has a waiting gentlewoman who in turn has a maid of her own. There are three more women servants at the hall and fifteen men, none of them married. At this date the serving men slept in the hall where everybody ate and lived, and it is perfectly plain from this list that when any of the servants married they moved into cottages of their own close by. Of the eighteen servants living at the hall we are not told the detailed occupations. They are only 'servientes Roberti', but their surnames show very well the kind of tasks that their fathers and grandfathers have been doing. They include *Cook*, *Baxter* (baker), *Butler*, *Carter*, *Waller* (who repaired the walls) and the nickname *Bacon*. Two of the servants have the surname *Butler*, clearly a family inheritance, for no one would have two butlers.

The rest of the village consists of nineteen habitations. In one the parson seems to be very comfortably settled with five servants, a married couple and three young men. The tax-collector has forgotten to put down the surname of the couple, they are just Robert and Isolde; but as the three serving boys are all called John he has written down their names in full. One of them is *Mason*; perhaps his grandfather built the church.

There is also a chaplain, John *Pope*, with a widow to keep house for him. He may be just the household chaplain, but more likely he is a chantry priest appointed to say masses at some special chapel that Robert has added to his church.

An unexpected character in the village is a 'scrivenor'. This is the Latin explanation, not his surname which is *Kentford* and only tells us that his forbears had come from the Wiltshire village of that name. He might be the parish clerk, but that office is nearly always described as 'clericus'. 'Scrivenor' is a much more unusual word, giving few surnames, and generally used only for an expert writer, a professional copyist of manuscripts. Did Robert of Ashfield aspire to possess a book of his own, a missal or a psalter perhaps? We shall never know.

The rest of the inhabitants are entirely typical of any village. Three men described as 'agricolae' are probably freemen or nearly so, cultivating their own land with only a small money payment and the duty of attending the Manor Court to bind them to their lord, Robert. They are probably increasing in prosperity; two have men-servants, one each, and all three some female dependants, some of whom are described as 'brewsters' and 'spinsters'. There are also a smith, a miller, a marshal (the Latin word given here is 'coursour' or horse dealer), and a thatcher each with one servant, three shepherds, a carter ('tentator carucam'), three men described as labourers and three as threshers. The last six all pay the lowest tax (fourpence), as do the servants at the hall. They seem to differ from the latter only in being married and therefore are taken separately by the assessors, but they are probably just as much Robert's servants as those who sleep in the hall.

Of these villagers the *Smith, Miller, Marshall, Thatcher* and one *Shepherd* (out of three) have these same words for their surnames. But this need not imply that they are not hereditary, only that the men have followed their fathers' trades. Often a family's occupation coincided with its surname for centuries. But side by side with these we see the other development, the contradictory names. One of the threshers is called *Brewster*; John *Carter* is not the man in charge of the cart; John *Mason* is only the parson's serving boy.

In fact we see in this small village that the most important of the craftsmen have been spoken of regularly by their trade-names so that they have stuck as surnames, but that the less important people and those who do the more general kind of work such as agriculture have developed names of other types. Nearly all these men must have had their strips in the common fields and been used to ploughing but there is no reference to this universal task in any of their names.

We may also note in passing that of the forty-two men in this village nineteen have been christened John. No wonder they needed surnames.

Chapter 10

LONDON

The surnames of modern Londoners, having descended to them from all parts of England, form very much the same mixture as one would find in any large group of Englishmen anywhere. But in the days when surnames were being formed, those of London had a special character of their own, similar perhaps to what one might find in the other principal cities such as York, Bristol, Lincoln and Norwich, but quite different from the small country towns and villages.

When first I looked at the London Subsidy Rolls from the reigns of the first three Edwards, I expected to see the leading occupational names in great number giving a picture of smiths hammering, tailors stitching, millers grinding, wrights building and so forth, more than anywhere else. But it was not so. The important names are there indeed, but in very moderate numbers.

The first thing that strikes one about these London rolls is that it was a city of specialists. Whereas in the country the smith dealt with all kinds of metal work, in London it was divided among many crafts. There were locksmiths, who have given us the names *Locker* and *Lockyer*; knife-smiths, now *Naismiths* or *Cutlers*; nail makers (*Naylors*) and so on; and while the general smith in the country could make and repair chain-mail it is clear that a knight or baron who wished to be well-turned out for the campaign against Scotland would go to a city expert. There were many armourers in the London of Edward II, doing extremely well judging by the taxes they paid, but the resulting surnames *Armour* and *Larmer* ('le armurer'), amount now to only thirty, showing that such specialists, though numerous in a city, were rare in the country as a whole. More plentiful were the *Furbers* or *Frobishers* who repaired or furbished up old armour, like the mechanics who now repair our cars, a very necessary service for economically minded knights, to whom rust was a constant problem.

The same theme is repeated when we look at clothing. There are indeed quite a number of tailors, as we would expect, but whereas in the villages they would dress you completely from top to toe, if you wished it, in cloth or leather, here in London every garment seems to have its special craftsman. We see prosperous cordwainers (see page 82) making the shoes which in the country would still be a large part of the tailor's art, and there are *Hatters, Cappers, Mantlers* and *Chaucers*. We cannot help feeling a particular interest in these last, for the sake of the poet, whose forbears must have belonged to this craft, though not within his memory. Chaucers made the long hose which we now call tights, but as they had no finely stretching materials as we have for the purpose, they had to be particularly skilful in the cutting and making to ensure the best possible fit while admitting the passage of the foot. The word 'chausses' seems to have covered fashionable leg-wear in all materials from leather to velvet, but eventually it gave place to the more homely English word 'hose', and the craftsman in question became known as the *Hozier*, a name that has never been common but has produced at least one distinguished modern example.

The makers of dress accessories include *Girdlers*, who made girdles often of silver and gold and set with precious stones; button-makers (surviving now as *Butner* and *Button*); *Bucklers*, who made buckles, much used for strapping leather belts and harness, and *Pursers* or pouchmakers. All these are rare surnames, but all are in the directory.

Then there are the rich merchants or *Marchants* who supplied the materials for clothing, *Drapers* who dealt in cloth of all sorts, and *Mercers* who specialized in rich silk fabrics from the Continent, making London the fashion centre of England. Margaret Paston, writing to her husband or son in London, often gives instructions about buying lengths of velvet or sarcenet ('of a goodly blue, or a bright sanguine'). The local tailor would make it up at home, but the stuff must be got in the city. There is little sign of weaving. That ancient craft belonged to the country near to the flocks of sheep where there was plentiful clear water for washing and dyeing. In the course of time some of the cities, as for instance Lincoln, developed great weaving industries, but in our period names like *Webster* are found far more in villages than cities.

Another supplier of clothing materials was the *Skinner*, who provided the furs that were much in demand for trimming and lining, and no wonder, considering the chilly conditions of damp and draughty castles. Skins were used for parchment as well as for clothes, and leather was such an important commodity that it may seem surprising that the trade concerned with it does not feature among the top twenty names. So it might have done if one comprehensive word had covered the whole business. The word we know best for one who prepares leather is *Tanner*, but the term more commonly used in Middle English was *Barker* (the bark of oak trees being used in the process), and these are three times as numerous. These two terms are fairly widespread, but *Skinners* were dealers found mostly in large towns.

This was the great age of Gothic building. Castles, halls and churches, with towers and spires, traceried windows, moulded columns and carved figures, were rising everywhere, making London one of the finest cities in Europe. No wonder there were many *Masons* and many specialized craftsmen working on the details of building, such as Nicholas le Glaswrighte (now *Glaser*, *Glaisher*, *Glassman* or *Glass*), Peter le Peyntour (*Painter*) who decorated interior walls, and Patrick le Ymager, all from the roll of 1319. The last of the three is represented now by just two examples of *Image*, perhaps descended from that very Londoner who carved figures of saints and angels six and a half centuries ago. But there are hardly any *Wrights* in the London rolls. The old name for the general builder which makes such a tremendous block in our directory was outmoded in the city by 1300, though still in use in countless villages.

When we look at food supplies, the variety of articles whose sale seemed to provide a complete occupation is amazing. There were no 'general stores' in those days. The *Spicer* was a very important tradesman who would be found in many market towns as well as cities, for he provided the only part of the national diet besides wine that was regularly imported. As so much salt meat and fish had to be eaten during the winter months English people dearly loved spices to give it variety. *Salt* was of course a very important commodity produced in various places in England (the distribution of *Salters* in the thirteenth century would make an interesting study), but *Pepper* came from overseas and a special trade or craft dealt in it. In 1345 the Pepperers and Spicers were amalgamated to make the city company known thereafter as the Grocers, but this name which had not been in use before was too late to make many surnames. There are 120 *Spicers* in the London directory today, 85 *Peppers* ('Pepperer' ending with a double '-er' would naturally lose one of them; cf Armour/er), and only three *Grosers* to represent the new word that was to swallow up so many others. Pepper was a popular commodity which has given us many nicknames. *Pepperell* is the English version of the French *Peverell* which means 'little peppercorn' and occurs as a nickname in Domesday Book. *Culpepper* and *Peppercorn* sound like nicknames for those in the pepper trade. The *Pepperman* undoubtedly sold it, but how many of the *Peppers* were tradesmen and how many had hot tempers we cannot now say.

Ginger is another spice that might be sold by the spicer or by its special dealer 'le gengere', the Ginger-er. Like pepper it could also be used as a nickname. Both commodities were used in England before the Conquest, which shows not only the Englishman's inherent love of spice but also his aptitude for adventurous trade. Ginger makes one think of *Pickles*, but that surname has an entirely different origin (page 274).

It seems strange that anyone could make a living – and a good one – by selling only *Mustard* or *Garlick*, but the London list of 1292 contains both 'mustarder' and 'garlickmonger', and both still exist in the above shortened forms. I cannot help feeling that they must really have sold an assortment of garden produce and become known by those of which they had a specially good supply. A description of London, written in the twelfth century by William Fitz Stephen, speaks of the beautiful gardens outside the city walls on the north side. Probably some of these supplied fruit and herbs to the inhabitants. By modern standards very few vegetables were eaten. We can imagine the *Gardiners*, of whom there are several in the London rolls, passing through the crowded streets with their laden baskets – perhaps already uttering those typical cries which lasted well into the nineteenth century, while the law of differentiation, to which no one gave a thought, came into play automatically, causing some to be known by the name of one commodity and some by another.

Other foodstuffs that are well represented are fish and cheese, and to a lesser degree honey, butter and cream (*Honeyman, Butters* and *Creamer*). Milk hardly appears at all.

Apart from the specialization of trades, the feature of these London rolls which makes the strongest contrast with those of the country is, just as one would expect, the large amount of buying and selling. We have already noticed merchants of various kinds, and besides these we see numbers of people, like the garlickmonger, whose surnames consist of the native word for a dealer, *Monger*, tacked on to some commodity with the implication that they are selling it. In ordinary speech this has survived only in the case of fish, cheese and iron, and among surnames the *Iremonger* is the only one to preserve 'monger' in full. In general it became 'man' or was dropped altogether. Thus for 'fishmonger' and many more of the sort we have *Fishman, Cheeseman, Woolman, Hayman*, or just *Fish, Cheese, Wool* and *Hay*. The last name has several other origins, mostly of a local sort, but a good deal of hay was sold in London. Horses had to eat as well as men, and there must have been hundreds of them stabled in the strong-smelling alleys of medieval London.

There is a clear distinction to be observed between the *Cheese(w)right* who made cheese and the *Cheeseman* who sold it, and between the *Fisher* toiling with his nets in the river and the *Fishman* who sold his produce. In each case the dealer originated in a large town. The rolls set out the names arranged in order of the city wards or divisions, and in Billingsgate the names are decidedly fishy. A number of citizens are described as 'stockfishmongers' which means that they sold salt fish to be kept 'in stock' for fast days. Some of them have this ponderous word as a surname, and the three examples of *Stockfish* in the modern directory may be their descendants, but fishmongers' names are varied like all others. Some are called by topical nicknames like *Herring* or *Pikeman*. The latter sounds like a soldier, but as he is described as a fishmonger we may suspect that the pike is a fish.

Even water was a saleable commodity in those crowded streets, clean fresh water from the wells of the pretty villages outside the walls, Clerkenwell and St Clement's being especially recommended. One of my favourite characters in all this throng of busy people is 'Lavinia la Waterladestre', but whether she herself ladled out the water with which she was laden, or was only the wife or widow of a waterlader is impossible to say. Two examples of *Lader*, five of *Laderman* and possibly some of the eighty *Leaders* must represent this profession.

The name with the highest number of all in these early Edwardian London rolls is *Chaundler*. In fact it is due to the number of chandlers or candlemakers that one of the city wards or divisions was known as Candlewick. This surname was not at all common in villages at that time, presumably because country people rose and went to bed with the sun, and if they needed a light were well able to make their own. But the city was more dissipated. Indeed, as we glance down the London lists we have a great sense of conviviality. There are plenty of *Cooks*, *Butchers*, *Brewers* and *Bakers*, the last frequently particularized as Pye-bakers, showing that this most typical English dish, the pie, has been well to the forefront of our diet for over six hundred years, and there is no reason at all to think it was a novelty then. Walking through London streets in the 1960's and seeing pre-fabricated meat pies stacked neatly in the shop windows, I often think how constant we are to our old traditions. As a surname the word was eventually simplified to *Pye* or *Baker*, but the former name could also be a nickname from the bird.

In fact there were so many butchers and bakers that, as with other crowded trades, specialized nicknames developed to make variety, nicely suited to each case. We have noticed already some nicknames of spicers and fishmongers; in the 1317 roll two of the butchers have the surnames Piggsflesh and *Blood*. The latter has made a highly respected modern family name; the former, which was still extant in Sussex in the last century, seems now to have disappeared, which is not surprising. The bakers' regular nicknames, *Whitebread*, *Cakebread* and *Pye*, are much pleasanter.

There were also a good many *Taverners, Ostlers, Hostlers* (the last two representing the 'host', not a groom), or occasionally an *Inman*. We catch glimpses of some of these early inns in the rolls, and see that they could occasionally originate surnames. John at the *Bell* and Adam at the *Rose* are probably innkeepers, but in each case the name has other sources. Some of the taverns were situated on the river bank where there was also a famous Cook-shop, praised by William Fitz Stephen who described London in the reign of Henry II. Here too the vintners (now *Vinters*) had their cellars, conveniently placed for the unloading of casks of wine directly from the ships that had brought them from France. How pleasant it all must have been, quaffing one's wine and eating one's pie beside the river with the barrels stacked nearby in the *Wynyard* and the masts of the ships bobbing on the water, and the ship-boys calling.

Here I must make a digression to consider these Ships. Seagoing is an aspect of English life very poorly represented in our surnames. That there are no shipmen in the London Subsidy Rolls is not surprising, for they list only the regular tax-paying citizens and these seamen coming and going and living on their ships must have been experts at tax evasion. But our modern directory gives us a sample of all the names for the whole country, rich and poor, and it shows remarkably few from this great profession. The word *Seaman* was used as a Christian name by the Anglo-Saxons, and its forty examples should therefore not all be taken as indicating occupation. There are only two *Sailors* (and two more *Seylers*, which are just the same). The word is too modern. The name we would expect to find most of is *Shipman*, but there are only thirty-three of them, including the contracted form *Shippam*. (*Shippard*, of whom there are very few, must be a variant of *Sheppard* or *Shepherd*.) We must add to this small collection sixteen *Mar(r)iners* and ten *Marners*, but when all are put together we have barely a hundred names, a meagre quantity for a seafaring nation. It is probably true to say that the English tendency towards seafaring was somewhat in abeyance at this period. The travelling tendencies of the upper classes were fully absorbed by wars and crusades on the Continent; the native population had little chance of moving about much, except in the retinues of their rulers. The thousands of men who did venture on the seas all round our coasts in their small ships were valued mostly for the fish they brought back, and probably a good number of the numerous *Fishers* must have worked on the sea. But those who made great journeys like Chaucer's Shipman must have been comparatively rare. In any case they would be found in groups together in coastal places and not distributed widely over the land. *Shipwrights* are even more lacking in our modern list – only two of them: but they would be even more congregated together and must have called each other by any name except the trade they had in common. We know they were there in early Plantagenet London, down on the wharfs by Tower Bridge, but their trade made very few distinctive surnames.

In early chapters we have looked at the commonest trade-names, and in this one largely the specialists originating in cities only. In between these come a large number of what we might call 'intermediate class' names, of craftsmen performing useful tasks of an obvious nature, who would be found in many country towns as well as the principal cities, men like the *Ropers* and *Sopers*, *Bowlers* and *Spooners*, and the *Horners* who fashioned objects out of horn, from bugles and drinking 'tumblers' to combs.

Then there are the *Saddlers* and *Lorimers* who specialized in harness. It is said by several authorities that *Seller* signifies a saddler because 'le seler' was Norman French for that word. But I cannot think this likely. Although we see many French occupational words of this kind in writing, none of them has become an English surname unless it has also been adopted for use in ordinary speech. 'Taylor' and 'butcher', for instance, are French in origin, but they became part of our language and survived in common speech. But the English 'saddler' held its own against 'seler', and the familiar meaning of the word with this sound was that of a 'cellar' where the wine was kept. All inns had cellars (or *Sellars*), and these make the likeliest origin of the name.

One typical city craftsman who must not be forgotten is the *Goldsmith*. Found in all the great cities and in the households of great lords, favoured of kings, always growing richer, he has stood out as a prince among craftsmen from the time of Edward the Confessor when Theodoric the Goldsmith became a wealthy landowner. There were many goldsmiths in London in our period and we have about 260 in the directory, but there are no Silversmiths. *Silver* may often have this meaning, but it can also be a nickname for one with silvery hair. *Silverman* is generally foreign.

Gold and silver bring us to money. In Saxon times every borough had its own mint. Norman kings gradually reduced the number of places that had this right, but in the reign of Henry I there were still thirty towns with mints where skilled 'moneyers' produced coins bearing their own names as well as the head of the king. We do not meet any of these men in the subsidies, as they had exemption from taxation, but our modern directory, which has no such reservations, has forty *Minters* and forty-five *Moneys*. It must have been a profitable business or few would have adopted it, seeing the occupational hazards incurred. When Henry I realized that the coinage was below standard he summoned all the moneyers in England to Winchester and had their right hands struck off without any further inquiry.

It is impossible to write of names in medieval London without paying tribute to the work of Professor Ekwall in this field. He has not only published the subsidies of Edward I and II, with detailed notes, but also devoted years to researches into their background, using wills, legal deeds and any other contemporary records that can throw light on the lives of those whose names are recorded in them.

From the family details that he has reconstructed we see that the majority of Londoners had fixed surnames by the accession of Edward I; but it is also apparent that a constant stream of new arrivals from the country were liable to suffer a change of surname, though this was unplanned and just happened in the natural course of events. He shows also that in many cases a young apprentice came to be known by his master's name. One can easily see how it would happen. The master stood in the position of a father to him. The boy might have been Tom Wright in his native village, but in London where his family was unknown he would be spoken of as Master Draper's boy, and soon come to answer to the name of Tom Draper. In Ekwall's studies of London we can catch glimpses of several London families whose surnames increase gradually, both from natural causes and by the occasional adoption of an apprentice into the family circle.

We also see that many men put down in the rolls with a surname denoting one trade are really following another, as in the case of Alan Taverner, who is really a chaucer, but is sometimes called Alan of Suffolk, presumably to avoid this complication; and Luke the Garlickmonger, stockfishmonger.

The slight fluidity among the surnames of young newcomers to the city, moving always towards more diversity, produced a gradual change in the composition of London surnames in the early fourteenth century. Whereas in 1291 occupational names form almost exactly a quarter of the whole, in 1332 they have fallen to just over a seventh. Thus by the middle of the century when the vast majority of surnames have at last settled down, we find that in this buzzing hive of craftsmen occupational names are proportionately fewer than elsewhere. The answer to the problem of having so many tradesmen was to have fewer trade-names. However the balance was gradually readjusted by the flow of newcomers from the country, which has continued steadily ever since, bringing surnames formed in villages in ever-increasing numbers, while a much smaller proportion of Londoners retired to the country; so that in a few centuries the special character of London names was lost. It was not long before one could find a *Goldsmith* in a tiny village or a *Shepherd* in Cheapside.

No detailed Poll Tax returns survive for London, and the next taxation list after 1332 is that of 1411 in the reign of Henry IV, a long jump forward. The qualification for assessment is higher than in the earlier rolls, and therefore the names, being all of the wealthier class, do not make a fair comparison. They are very modern-looking on the whole, with a great preponderance of local names. The charm of this list lies in the fact that Richard Whittington himself, a leading citizen though not yet knighted, is one of the assessors, and one or two other of the names have a familiar look. There is, for instance, Lady Fastolf whose husband, Sir John, is away in France. It is often said that this name suggested the one so very like it to Shakespeare, but this real Sir John is the less substantial figure of the two. Next to Lady Fastolf on the list is Lady Bardolf, which intensifies the

Shakespearean atmosphere, and a little further down is Thomas Chaucer, son of the poet, paying a good fat tax from the comfortable inheritance he received from his father. In fact it is a list of prosperous citizens, and their surnames are all long established.

This concentration on London occupations is perhaps unjust to the other great medieval cities, but must serve here to represent them all. If a study of each of them could be undertaken, each would be found to have some special characteristics of its own, as well as much in common with the metropolis.

Chapter 11

THE CHURCH AND LEARNING

Although the canon law against the marriage of ordained priests, and the stricter vows of celibacy taken by the monastic orders, prevented the founding of families with ecclesiastic surnames on a large scale, yet by one means and another the whole hierarchy of the Church from the humble *Deacon* to the *Pope* himself is present in our directories.

It is generally said that all these names are nicknames, and so the majority probably are, but the statement is far too sweeping. In any case, even as nicknames they are a true reflection of the minds and speech of our forbears who readily called a pompous neighbour the *Bishop* or a shy young man the *Nunn*, using familiar figures from their limited experience of the world.

The celibacy which Norman archbishops tried to impress on the English clergy was very unwillingly received and never really enforced. There is no question that all through the Middle Ages many priests did marry, or at least had families who were accepted by society without much criticism. The twelfth-century *Life of Wulfric of Hazelbury* describes this holy man's close friend the parish priest who had a wife and son, and was beloved and admired by all who knew him; and Sir Anthony Wagner in his *English Genealogy* quotes many examples of reputable men of this period who were the sons of clergy. In Chaucer's *Reeve's Tale* the parson of Cambridge had a daughter whom he hoped to marry to one of high degree.

This is one side of the picture. On the other hand there was the official prohibition which did in fact keep the majority of priests celibate. The result is that instead of thousands of names derived from 'parson', the directory has only 430. Three of them are in the form of *Parsonson*, which make the position quite clear, and three refer to the *Parsonage*. Of the rest the great majority have a final 's' which is not usual for occupational names and strongly suggests that most of them were first used for servants, relations and other dependants who lived 'at the parson's'. We may also note here over a hundred examples of *Vickers*, including *Viccars* and *Vickery* (the Vicarage).

The Poll Tax returns, though they do not include the names of priests officially – the clergy being exempt from lay taxation – yet by listing their households show that in many villages the parsonage was a centre of hospitality, with more servants and dependants than any other house except the hall. The Yorkshire lists in which the names, being lately coined, are nearly related to current fact, include dozens of the type of Adam Parsonservant, Emma Parsonwoman, Henry Parsoncosyn, and Agnes Vicarcister. In due course most of such names would be shortened to *Parsons* and *Vickers*, and all one can say now with any certainty of such a name is that it referred to someone closely connected with the parish priest.

The word 'priest' is much older in English usage than the other two, and is often seen as a distinguishing name in Anglo-Saxon documents, such as 'Aelfsig Preost', a witness to a charter of King Edgar's. It began to be supplanted by 'parson' in village communities soon after the Conquest, but though there are fewer obvious examples of *Priest* among our surnames it is present more often than we might think in contracted forms. We see it in a number of local names: *Prescot* is the priest's cot or cottage; *Pressley* his field or clearing; *Pressland* his land, and these three names might easily be given to his man or servant, the *Priestman* or *Pressman* who cultivated his few acres and looked after his animals. We see now that *Press*, like *Prest*, is a contracted form of *Priest*; it certainly has nothing to do with printing. In thirteenth-century rolls one often sees a reference to 'the priest's son' (Thomas Prestson, Cumberland 1332). This is awkward to say as one word and, as Dr Reaney very reasonably suggests, it would be almost sure to lose the second 's' and become identical with the place name *Preston*. Something has been said of chaplains already (page 106); they were priests appointed to special duties, other than a parish.

England was full of them; some of them had families and they have left us the surname *Chaplin*.

So far these names are perfectly straightforward and may be accepted literally, but as we rise higher in the ranks of the clergy it becomes more likely at every step that the names are no longer related to real clerics but merely examples of popular humour. I do not mean to suggest that no *Bishop* ever had a son, but there is no recorded case of such a person using this surname. A twelfth-century Bishop of Ely had a son who became Bishop of London and Treasurer to Henry II, and was called Fitz Nigel from his father's Christian name. On the other hand when one sees, as one often does in the subsidy and manorial rolls, a mere peasant holding a few strips of land by villein status and set down as 'le Bishop', one knows that only a joke will explain it. I have seen the name occasionally also among the lesser members of the clergy, as for example 'Roger dictus Bisshop' appointed Rector of Stoke Wake in Wiltshire, in 1319, in which case the form of the name suggests a nickname, though well enough established to be put down in the Bishop's register. At this date the name was probably inherited, and it is not impossible that the man's father had been related to a bishop. It cannot be said positively that such a name was never factual, but it is certain that it was very often fictitious.

Another way in which this name must often have arisen was by the custom common in many towns of electing a 'boy Bishop' on the feast of St Nicholas, who was for several successive days paraded round the streets gorgeously dressed in cope and mitre. Such an honour would not be forgotten, and the boys in question might easily carry the name with them for life. We have over four hundred *Bishops*.

When we come to *Pope* we know it can only have been a nickname. From before the Conquest the word 'Pope' or 'Pape' had been known and used in England for the Bishops of Rome, and in this case there is no question that we might be dealing with sons, relations or servants. It sometimes occurs as an early surname of a village priest or chaplain, but as such it can only have been used jokingly, which seems to suggest an easy familiarity with the parson and a lack of veneration for the head of the Church. There is no question that it was often used ironically like other ecclesiastical nicknames for a pompous fellow or an unholy rogue. Matilda Pope from the Sussex Subsidy of 1296 could hardly have acquired it in her own right and must have inherited it from her father or late husband. She appears perfectly respectable, but when we read among the criminal cases in the Buckingham Assizes of 1227 that 'John Tabbe killed Jordan Pap in the prison of Alan Basset' we feel that we are in low company.

Turning to the monastic orders we see the same mixture of fact and irony. In the earlier part of our period most religious houses were conducted on austere principles, and monks led ascetic lives remote from worldly temptation. But by the thirteenth century, if we are to believe the violent contemporary criticisms, they were becoming rapidly more worldly, employing lay servants to wait on them, enjoying the good things of life, emerging more and more into the world, and provoking much adverse comment.

We may safely say that the names *Monkman*, *Monkhouse* and *Monks* imply lay workers at a monastery, but with the plain form *Monk* or *Munn* (from the French 'moine'), there is every likelihood that it was first applied to somebody as a joke, because he behaved like a monk or was particularly dissolute. Irony was always considered very witty. The name might also have been given to someone known or thought to be the son of a monk. Such things did occur, and there was no delicacy in the Middle Ages to prevent their being mentioned.

In this connection we cannot help thinking of the various clerical figures sketched for us so vividly by Chaucer: the fat, jolly **Monk** who loved hunting and good food, the wily Friar (*Frere* and *Fryer*) who was such a success with the ladies, the gentle, saintly poor parson and those hangers-on to the lower fringes of the **Church**, the Pardoner and the Summoner. The first has left few representatives, but the calling of the second – one of the most revolting figures in all our literature with his bloated face of which 'children were afeard' – is perpetuated in the sixty *Sumners* in the London Directory.

Once again, when we rise to the more splendid figures of the monastic orders, there is ample evidence of the use of their titles as nicknames. To take an early example, in the twelfth-century rental of Battle Abbey we find among the peasantry working the manorial land Aelfwin Abbat who held his strips in the common field by the payment of sevenpence a year and labour. We must take it that his friends called him 'Abbot' because of some fancied resemblance to the great man so high above them, or because he gave himself airs, or for one of a hundred small personal reasons that we cannot now guess. It seems a little lacking in respect, on the Abbot's very territory, but it was clearly accepted as his name by the monk who wrote the list of tenants. One begins to wonder, did the man perhaps sometimes hold the Abbot's horse or perform some other service that would entitle him to be called the Abbot's man more than the other villeins on the manor? But no. At such an early date, before 1200, the form of the name would betray the occupation. The absence of article or preposition or genitive case indicates a personal nickname.

In the same way it must have seemed very funny to call a humble man 'the *Pryor*', and especially so on estates belonging to a priory, where the Prior himself in all his dignity was a well-known figure, the actual employment on monastic land suggesting the type of nickname. Then again a plain statement of fact could soon be twisted into a joke. There are several early examples of surnames implying that their original bearers worked at nunneries. 'Robert othe Nonnes' was a draper in London in 1309; Adam Nunneman escaped from Newgate jail in 1326. Such names would easily shorten to *Nunn* (the form that is commonest now) slipping from what had once been truth to the kind of joke that people liked.

Of all the names vaguely connected with religion the most numerous is *Palmer*, of which we have seven hundred. The word implies a pilgrim who has been to the Holy Land and brought back a palm, or a piece of one, to prove it. He need not have any professional connection with the Church, though many itinerant friars claimed the distinction, and in fact the name appears from early times in all walks of life and all classes.

When we consider the large numbers of this surname (the same as for *Shepherd*) and the distance to the Holy Land, we are inclined to think that not all of them had been there. It was an age when a pious fraud could easily impose on the credulity of others, and, according to Chaucer, there was a ready sale for bogus relics. However when we remember that the period when surnames were formed coincides almost exactly with that of the Crusades we realize that large numbers of Englishmen at that time had actually made this adventurous journey.

Between 1096 and 1270 no less than eight of these great international ventures set forth from Western Europe and reached at least the shores of Asia Minor. The one best known to us is the third crusade when Richard I played such a prominent part, but in almost every one there was an official English contingent. In the fifth and seventh crusades this was led by the Earl of Salisbury, in the sixth by Richard, Earl of Cornwall, King Henry III's brother, and in the eighth by the prince who was soon to become Edward I. We are apt to think of a crusader as a mailed knight with a cross on his shield, a good picture to have in mind, but we should also remember that just as a king or earl could not set out on a quest without a great company of knights, so no knight could stir far without his retinue of men, and that all of them had to have grooms, cooks, chaplains, pages and camp followers. Consequently when these cumbersome armies at last got back to England, more reduced by sickness and mischance than by the arms of the infidel, there dispersed to their homes in many parts of England, not only knights, but also a great many lesser people who had actually seen the arid sands of Palestine and had in their baggage genuine palm leaves and other souvenirs from the Eastern Mediterranean. Such an army buzzing with tales of adventure returned to England in 1273 just at the peak period for surnames.

The word 'crusader' which we use with such confidence does not occur at all among our surnames. (*Cross* is always local – 'atte Cros', at the crossroads.) But some word must have served in common speech for those who had made this strange and adventurous journey, and the large numbers of *Palmer* suggest that it was often on men's lips at this time. No doubt many who had been no more than camp followers claimed pious motives for their journey impressively enough to earn the title. Others had really gone in a religious spirit, for the Crusades opened up the way, and organized parties frequently set out. Their zeal and their safe return is also recorded in the surname *Pilgrim* (including *Peagrim*, *Pegram*, and several other versions), but the far greater numbers of *Palmer* show which name was thought the more distinguished.

In spite of celibacy, the great medieval profession of the Church, with all its accretion of subsidiary attendants, has given us many modern surnames; but the other learned professions are almost totally missing from our directory.

The first colleges of Oxford and Cambridge were founded during the thirteenth century, and we look hopefully for any signs of academic distinction, but beyond the one all-embracing word 'clerk' there is practically nothing. The *Doctor* was a learned person qualified to teach others in divinity, philosophy, law, or even medicine, but there are only twenty of them. There is a little group of words that seem to be connected with schools (*Scholar, Scoular, Schoolman* and *Schooling*) totalling about thirty. But Professor Ekwall, whose word must be accepted as gospel on such a subject, derives the first syllable from the Old Norse 'skali', Middle English 'scale' or 'scole', meaning a temporary hut, which is found in many place names, so that our few 'scholars' are really only shepherds disguised by academic spelling.

The name *Reader* will not help us either, as it originally meant a man who cut reeds for thatching. The only name in any quantity that really implies some academic knowledge is *Latimer* or *Latner*, corrupted forms of 'Latiner' meaning a man able to speak Latin. There are fifty of these, but they have little to do with the universities. They occur frequently in legal documents from 1066 onwards and mean little more than a well-qualified clerk. Hugo Latinarius is described as an interpreter in Domesday Book.

Proctor suggests university discipline, but was first used, as it still is, for an official in an ecclesiastical law court. *Warden* could be the head of a college, or of other institutions, such as a trade guild, as could also the very general word *Master*. *Dean* is another word that could be academic or ecclesiastical, and cannot in any case be accurately distinguished at this distance from the local term 'dene', meaning a dell or hollow. As to literature, something has already been said; as an occupation it can hardly be said to have existed.

If the academic world is poorly represented, the law is little better. *Law* and *Lawson* come from shortened forms of the popular name Lawrence. However there was an Old English word 'law-man' (Brictric Lageman, Domesday Book) for one who knew and expounded the law, and the few examples of

Lawman might be assigned to that. In the surname period each manorial lord held his own court for minor offences and attended the Hundred Court or Shire Court to take his share of the work in more important cases. Law was no more a separate profession for the upper classes than fighting was. It was all part of a gentleman's life. Only the *Sherriff* (or 'shire reeve') was a real legal administrator in the modern sense, being responsible for the justice in a whole county. There are only twenty-four examples of this name in our list (in several spellings), but one would not expect many, unless as a nickname, and there is no sign of that. One does not see it among the names of the peasantry as one often sees *Bishop* and *King*.

Judge, on the other hand, and *Justice* must both be under strong suspicion of jocularity. It was only at the very end of the twelfth century that the system, instituted by Henry II, of sending royal judges round the country, began to be used to any great extent, and more than a century later that knights, scattered round the shires, began to be organized under the names of Justices. A word like 'sheriff', having been in use from Saxon times, could become a surname of literal meaning at an early date and continue in the same family, but in the late twelfth or thirteenth century a man important enough to be appointed a judge or justice would be sure to have a well established surname of his own before he reached that position of honour, though a name like *Justice* might sometimes be given to a servant or a lesser official of a court where justice was given. 'Judge' is a word that has always lent itself readily to metaphor. Courts and trials have a strong human interest, and a man inclined to lay down the law could easily earn the nickname 'judge'. That the surname is not a common one shows that the ordinary rank and file, accustomed to having their misdemeanours dealt with by their lord and his bailiff, knew little about these grand officials or their titles.

Constable is another word of Latin origin that came to us through the channels of Norman administration. Like *Marshall* its origin is connected with horses ('comes stabuli'), but it had left the stable far behind before it came into England. Again like *Marshall* it attained high honours in royal courts and castles – John of Gaunt held the title of Constable of England during the King's minority – but this kind of meaning never took root in England. Instead the word found itself a more humble position as a minor officer of the law, an attendant on the sheriff or bailiff in any of their courts. As early as the thirteenth century it was used in Manor Courts for men appointed to 'keep the peace' in individual villages; and a little later when manorial records become more plentiful we catch glimpses of these early village constables, untrained and unpaid, taking their turn in a difficult task, immortalized at one point as Dogberry, but continuing manfully into modern times. There are only sixty *Constables* on our list because the word is rather a late starter. That other manorial official, the *Hayward*, was already far ahead in the race, and even the *Pinder*, who impounded stray animals, is not far behind.

Before we leave the subject of law we must call to mind that surnames were largely formed before the days of trial by jury (the name *Jury* signifies residence at or near the jewery or Jews' quarter). If a case was difficult to settle it could be decided by ordeal or by combat, in the belief that God would give victory to the innocent. In spite of their fervent faith, prudent men of sufficient means, unless they were particularly young and vigorous, generally chose their strongest tenant or retainer to appear for them as their *Champion*. Indeed some Church dignitaries who often had legal cases about property to settle kept professional champions as part of their retinue, and no doubt God was often shown to be on their side. Opposed to the Champion was the *Challenger*, but the word *Champion* or *Campion* could be used for the combatant on either side and has made far more surnames.

In the realm of medicine we must not expect to find much. In the Subsidy Rolls from time to time one sees 'le Surgien', and surgeons must have been much in demand in the constant wars, but there are none recognizable in the modern directories. They have all been absorbed into the *Sargeants* who were armed attendants in the law courts (though they later rose to more distinction) and in any case are not very numerous. Then there was an Old French word 'mire' meaning a physician, which would account for some of our *Myers*, but there is also no question that others with this designation simply lived in the mire, not in a derogatory sense, just in a boggy place of which there must have been plenty.

As far as English speaking people were concerned, the general practitioner was the *Leach* or *Leech* of which there are 240 examples. In the villages many no doubt had recourse to the Wise Woman, who because of her sex has left no surname that I know of, but she is to be seen in the subsidies, and occasionally a son was called after her, as in the case of Ralph Wiswyf in Walsham-le-Willows in 1283. Perhaps the *Wiseman*, of whom there are 150, was a male version of the same kind of practitioner. These last examples of the art of healing, like the picturesque figures of champions ready to fight to prove a legal case, are perhaps hardly qualified to represent the learned professions, but they are none the less true representatives of the state of medicine and law at the time our surnames were formed.

Chapter 12

RANK AND STATUS

We must now consider those names which are hardly occupations at all but rather ranks and titles. They tell what a man is rather than what he does, and yet so often they tell both that they cannot be entirely separated from occupation.

Starting at the bottom of the social scale we can say at once that there is no surname derived from 'serf' or 'slave', although many of such people existed in England in the century after the Conquest. In fact no rank became a surname unless it was at least one step above the bottom. Historians writing about the social framework of this time have been influenced by the vocabulary of Domesday Book, with the result that we have been taught from our school days to speak of villeins, bordars, cottars and serfs, but the people in question did not know or use such terms, with the exception of *Cotter*, the only one of them that comes from an English word. A 'cot' or 'cote' was a simple shelter for man or beast, a primitive cottage in short, but as there was nothing distinctive about being a cottager there are barely forty *Cotters* in the directory, with about the same number of *Cotterells*. The latter, a French diminutive form meaning a small or insignificant cottager, sounds decidedly condescending.

The word 'villein' was used by the Normans in such a derogatory sense that it has only survived in our language meaning 'a bad man' and in theirs meaning 'ugly'. There is no sign in the directory that the English even knew the word.

A man without rank was just a 'man', as he still is in the army, and this unfailingly reliable word was often used in the sense of servant to distinguish the man from the master. This simple use, which is one of the origins of *Mann*, may be seen in many early examples such as Michael le Man in the Hundred Rolls. However there was never anything low or derogatory about this word; it always has a feeling more of loyalty than servility, and its breadth of meaning is too great to be pinned down to any rank.

A plain English word which remained always of low degree is *Hine*. Its first meaning was 'one of a household', again with a sense of clannish faithfulness. Later it acquired an excrescent final 'd' and as *Hind* long continued in use as a farm hand, especially in the North (having absolutely no connection with a female deer).

A rather similar word, this time of Scandinavian origin, meaning just a young man, retainer or follower, is *Swain*. It survives still in 'boatswain', but otherwise declined into a very rustic, love-lorn condition, having once been active and useful.

The first real upward step on the social ladder is made by the splendid name *Freeman* which stands at 660 in the directory. Here is a definite distinction that raised a man above his neighbours in a village so that they thought and spoke of him as *Freeman* or *Freeborn* or *Freebody*, or simply as 'the free' (which comes down to us as *Fry*). These all add up to 930, and the French form of the same word, *Franklin*, gives us another 360 without counting *Frank* which often meant 'free' but is complicated by other possibilities. Now we are right up in the high numbers.

The 'freeman' in Norman England was, roughly speaking, the descendant of the Saxon 'churl'. But at the Conquest these churls had for the most part sunk into some kind of bondage; the word was discredited and the expression 'freeman' took its place for those who managed to retain their independence, or to gain it later. In the thirteenth and fourteenth centuries personal freedom was much desired. Those who had it were envied, and many others were engaged in trying to obtain it by various means; therefore the word was often spoken. At a later date when most people were free it ceased to be a matter of interest, and both 'freemen' and 'franklin' faded out of general speech. They were words that had always been heard more in the country than in towns, for most of the inhabitants of towns were free, except for their apprentices who would soon become so. 'Freeman' in fact generally implied a man who cultivated his own land, with the right to sell it if he wished, owing the lord of the manor no more than the duty of attending his court and an occasional nominal payment.

'*Yeoman*' is derived simply from 'young man', and was at first applied to an armed retainer fit for active service. Its use as a single word was a little late for surnames, and so there are only a few – sixty – in our list, but it was in time to serve for the archers of Crecy and Agincourt 'who made all France afraid'. It is not to be wondered at that as these men returned from the wars and settled on the land, passing as it were from the fourth to the fifth age of man, the word 'yeoman' grew also a little older, solider and more prosperous, and gradually overtook the older 'freeman'.

No one could be blamed for thinking that the surname *Bond* represents the opposite of 'free', in fact the peasant bound to the soil. But our language is a complex thing, not always logical, and this is one of its pitfalls. *Bond*, in fact, is yet another word for a free farmer. It comes from the Old Norse 'buan', to dwell ('buande', dwelling), and referred originally to one who had settled down to cultivate the land, as compared to the invading warriors who still roamed at large. As Bondi, it was used as a Christian name before the Conquest (Bondi the Staller was one of the Confessor's household officials), but it also continued in general use as a common noun, and still provides the second syllable of *Husband* (a farmer with a house). 'Husbandman' retains the original sense better, and the Yorkshire surname *Younghusband* means 'young farmer'.

The similar word in 'bond-man' comes from the verb 'to bind', and the likeness between these two is coincidental. However they naturally became confused, and when after the Conquest the free English *Bond* (or *Band*) became by force of circumstances an unfree bondman, it is no wonder that the word went out of favour and, like 'churl', sank gradually into disuse.

Something has already been said of the word 'farmer' (page 98), which has been so firmly established for the last three or four centuries. It is the fifth in an honourable line; Churl, *Bond, Freeman, Yeoman,* and now *Farmer.* What will be the next? 'Agriculturist' perhaps. Or will 'farmer' hold its ground? Of the five it was *Freeman,* and its twin *Franklin,* that caught the full tide of surnames.

The social equal of a freeman in a town was a *Burgess* (380). We talk of the burghers of Calais or Carlisle, but there is no sign of this form in our surnames. A burgess was a resident of a borough with full rights and comprised the master craftsmen of all trades.

Beneath the craftsmen were their apprentices, now represented by sixty examples of *Prentice* and *Prentiss*. One might think such a name too temporary to keep for ever, and that when the boy grew up and became himself a master and a burgess he would acquire a more important name. But every surname that is still with us stuck fast at one time or another, and for many 'the sticking place' came early in life.

The surname *Master/s* seems almost too general to be of any particular rank, but it was probably used in cases where the word had a very exact meaning, the master of a ship, or of a trade guild, or the master mason in charge of a building, all important people with many men working under them. It would often happen that such a person would have a personal servant or assistant known as 'the Master's man', or '*Masterman*', and the fact that *Masters* (like *Parsons*) is far more common with a final 's' than without suggests that very often the name applied originally to his assistant rather than himself.

We now rise another step on the ladder and come to the *Knight*. We have met him before, but must think of him again in regard to rank. 'Knight' is one of those words whose meaning developed out of all recognition in the course of a thousand years or so. In Old English it meant simply a boy, and then a young servant, then a mounted attendant fully armed.

There was little distinction in our period between a servant and a soldier, and no real word for either. What every leader needed was a following of young men to serve him and fight for him. That is why so many words that later developed particular rank or status began by meaning only a youth. Of these *Knight* and *Yeoman* have run very parallel courses, but the knight started first, rose higher and stayed longer. The yeoman became a foot soldier and then a farmer; the knight, a mounted soldier and a country gentleman. The yeoman is now outdated, but the knight is more honourable than ever; only his average age is much advanced. He generally now receives the honour when his days of activity are drawing to an end, which would have much surprised the early medieval knight who had to fight for his living from an early age.

At the time of Domesday Book about five thousand small manors were held by the service of a knight's fee, which meant that their owners must follow their lord to battle when called on. These landed knights were generally known by the name of their manor or of some ancestor, and would be unlikely to acquire the surname *Knight*, but there were others of the same class who simply subsisted as the armed followers of some more powerful lord, living in his castle, accompanying him on journeys, ready always to spring to arms, or merely to add to his importance by swelling the numbers of his train. Such a man must often have been described simply as 'the knight', but if one of them were given a manor he would probably have thought it much more impressive to style himself Roger of Diddlington or whatever it was.

Again we cannot altogether rule out the possibility of some ploughboy, riding on one of his master's oxen with his long whip in his hand and his empty drinking bowl on his head, being laughingly dubbed 'the knight' by his companions. In the Battle Abbey rental where one of the 'villeins' was Aelfwin Abbat, another was 'Edwin Cniht'. This rustic humour cannot be ignored, but all the same I am inclined to take most of the *Knights* at their face value. But in doing so we must not magnify them too much into romantic figures of chivalry. Chaucer's 'parfait gentil knight' belongs to a century later than the fixing of surnames, and Malory, who has given us an idealized picture of the Knights of the Round Table, wrote late in the fifteenth century. The actual men from whom the modern families called *Knight* derive their names were horsemen in chain-mail whose highest duty was loyalty to their lords, and if we should meet one of them now we would probably think him anything but gentle.

The *Squire* was of the same rank as the knight by birth, but as yet unknighted. He served the latter as a page, as the apprentice served his master. But knighthood was an honour that involved one in arduous duties which could be troublesome, and many men were glad to pay money to exempt them from these liabilities. Sir Anthony Wagner tells us that under Edward I there were about three thousand men qualified to take up knighthood, but that less than half had actually done so. All such men were in a sense squires (or esquires) for life, which explains how this word, which once meant a youth learning the arts of war (and this is the meaning contained in the modern surname), came in time to signify vaguely a gentleman, and survives now in the curious abbreviation 'Esq' which has puzzled so many foreign postal authorities.

Batchelor, which once in the far past meant a cowherd (Latin baccalarius), had climbed to being yet another attendant on a knight, of much the same rank as a squire, by the time the Normans brought it to England, and even rose to being used for a newly made knight. But then it failed in the race up the social ladder and acquired instead a couple of very specialized meanings, one as a graduate of a university (BA), and the other as an unmarried man. In the latter position it fulfils such a useful function that it has never stirred from it since. But when it became a surname its principal meaning was that of a young knight.

It is interesting to observe the careers of the many words mentioned in this chapter that started out one after another as mere boys. Some, like the *Knight*, have risen to high honours, while others, like the *Swain*, are left far behind. The *Squire* has grown into an old-fashioned gentleman and is hardly likely to be with us much longer, but the *Mann* is more than a thousand years old and has never changed in all that time.

The next step takes us to the nobility and back into the realm of fun and mockery. The higher the degree the less likely that the surname spoke the truth. All the noble ranks are present in the directory, *Baron, Earl, Duke, Marquis, Prince, King* (much the most numerous), and even the Emperor in the form of *Kayser, Cayzer* and *Lempriere*, this last from the Channel Islands; but not one of them is to be trusted.

As with *Pope* it is obvious that the last three are not to be taken seriously, and the same verdict applies to them all. *Marquis* is a French title that was never used in England until the late fifteenth century. The first English *Dukes* were sons of Edward III, and before that, though the title was well known in England, its chief association was with Normandy. Neither of these French nicknames is common.

That the surnames *King* and *Prince* are not even remotely connected with royalty is certain. I have heard it argued that *King* might be a shortened form of 'king's man', but if this were so we should see contemporary evidence of it, and the evidence is decisive on the other side. A man employed in the king's service would have an official title, and anyone related to royalty, however irregularly, would be endowed with land or at least a place in a noble household and a name like Falconbridge. He could not possibly be a villein, and it is among villeins that one constantly sees this type of name. It is here that the Subsidy Rolls are so valuable, in that with every name they give the amount of tax due, thus revealing the owner's financial position. And there is hardly a village where one does not see at least one name like Adam le Kynge or Walter le Baron among the very poorest of the labourers. An example of an Earl in very low circumstances occurs in the Lancashire Assize Roll of 1246 when William the parson of Flixton claimed 'Adam the Erl' as his fugitive villein. It was stated that if Adam were not caught his chattels would be forfeit, but that he had no chattels.

The French word *Prince* superseded the Old English *Atheling*, but when we think a word is obsolete it probably still exists as a surname. *Ayling* and *Aylen* represent this fine old word, but whether it was used as a nickname or given as a Christian name by those who looked back to the old royal line we cannot say. It is found chiefly among the peasants.

Another interesting name which takes us back before the Conquest is *Child*. This was used in Old English just as we use it now, as an infant, and as such made a nickname for a childish person, but also at the same period it acquired a special sense of a royal or noble boy, apparently synonymous with 'atheling'. In the Anglo-Saxon Chronicle the last male descendant of the house of Wessex, the lineal heir to the Kingdom, is called Edgar Atheling or Edgar Child indifferently. It is true that at the death of Edward the Confessor he *was* only a child and therefore passed over in favour of Harold. This we might say was enough reason for him to be remembered always as 'the Child', a surname that stuck to him for life. But if this were the cause it was not the first time such a thing had happened. A number of Saxons had this nickname as grown men, among them Wulfnoth Child the father of Earl Godwin. Perhaps they had all inherited honours at an early age. Be that as it may, in the cen-

135

tury or two after the Conquest the word 'Child' was often used meaning a youth of noble birth, a heroic young man, almost a prince. That most romantic of all lines of poetry, 'Child Rowland to the dark tower came', illustrates both its use and heroic quality.

Child and *Childs*, the latter clearly being genitive, meaning the son or servant of the man known as Child, together make 240. They might logically be classed as nicknames, but their connotation is so close to that of *Prince, Noble, Knight* and *Squire* that they must be mentioned with them.

The title *Lord* differs from these others in that it did not refer to any special rank but was a form of address expressing loyalty to a superior of gentle birth. It might be used for anyone from the lord of a small manor to 'our sovereign lord the king'. But like the other titles of honour it became a surname as a joke.

We have now climbed the whole scale from the *Cotter* to the *Kayser*, finding as we reached the higher ranks that they were only a mockery leading us back to peasants. In doing so we have strayed from the subject of status into that of nicknames, which serves to show how hard it is to keep surnames in their proper categories. Indeed it is impossible to do so. Human invention will not fit into separate boxes; each one overflows and mingles with the next. Therefore while considering names of rank it seemed best to take them all together whether they were statements of fact or flights of fancy. Only the most numerous of them, *King*, has been reserved for the next section which must obviously be that of nicknames.

II. Nicknames

Chapter 13

APPEARANCE

Nicknames are as old as speech itself and are to be found in the earliest records of all races. They are unlike the other three classes of surname in that the latter all came into being for the practical purpose of identifying a man by an additional piece of information, but nicknames, although they do also serve this purpose, arise spontaneously from human inventiveness which bubbles up irrepressibly whether it is needed or not. The modern schoolboy is always sufficiently equipped with names, and if there is any chance of confusion with someone else he will be officially designated Major or Minor, or given a number, but that will not stop his companions from calling him by the most extraordinary names which sometimes remain with him for life.

This type of ingenuity flourishes particularly in a close community like a school where everyone knows everyone else, where jokes and opinions are passed round freely and the outside world impinges only slightly. Just such a community was the medieval village, where most of those who were born there would spend their entire lives, never going further from it than a long day's walk, perhaps to the nearest market town and back, sharing the same long hours of work, the same short times of play and relaxation, the same occasional festivals, the same worship in the church, the same hopes, fears, stories, scandals, superstitions and jokes. In such a community nicknames abounded.

Some people may prefer to think that their ancestors were the ones who lived in castles and were free to ride to London and France and even the Crusades. So no doubt many of them were, but there is no altering the fact that the majority of all our medieval forbears led lives that we should find incredibly monotonous, for when we try to imagine the confinement in one place we must remember also the total absence of books, papers, letters, radio and all the other cultural amenities on which we now rely. But the medieval villager did not miss what he had never known. It is sometimes suggested that these peasants were mere clods, but their capacity for thought and observation was as good as ours and perhaps better. When their chance came to rise in the world they often rose with extraordinary brilliance. In the meantime while still in semi-bondage they had enough to fill their minds. Instead of nuclear science they had the lore of saints and angels and magical happenings, which was just as exciting when just as ardently believed. Instead of news of the moon, the Antipodes and the Common Market they had tales of the Holy Land, France and London, or the shocking doings in the nearest monastery; then there was the question of justice in the Manor Court, the behaviour of the new reeve and the neighbours. Their range was smaller than ours but no less intriguing, and when it came to close observation of all around them, an exact knowledge of the woods and fields and fens and hills where they spent their lives, and of the wild creatures that shared them, in such matters they far excelled us.

These men, whose minds were not bombarded with other people's thoughts at second hand, were wonderfully creative. They had a strong turn for metaphor and could make a new name for anything out of words they already knew merely by an act of imagination, as is shown in the names they gave to all the wild plants: cranesbill, lady slipper, cuccopint, speedwell, day's eye, love-in-a-mist, toad flax, night shade, heart's ease, and many more; so that when a time came that everyone seemed to be needing an extra name, there was no difficulty about providing them. One man became a *Marvell*, another an *Angel*, another a *Nightingale*, another a *Wren*.

All nicknames are not of this imaginative order. Many are very plain statements of fact, like *Young* or *Short*, and might well be classed separately as 'descriptive' surnames. But it has already been demonstrated that when one tries to put names into tidy compartments they always overflow. Take a plain descriptive name like *White*. Very well, one may say, the man had white hair or a very white skin. But what about *Lillywhite*? Or *Lilly*? Before we know it we have slipped into the world of metaphor. Therefore, although I will start this review of nicknames with some of the simplest and plainest in order that the general pattern of thought may be seen, leaving most of the fanciful ones to a later chapter, I cannot be tied very strictly to this plan. We will group them according to meaning and see where they lead.

If today we are asked to differentiate between two men who have much in common, we look for the most obvious point of contrast and call them young or old, tall or short, fat or thin, dark or fair. Our surnames tell us how these same ideas were expressed in the thirteenth century. First we notice that there are far more *Youngs* (*Yonge* is the older spelling) than *Olds*. In the telephone directory there are over a thousand of the former to twelve of the latter (with another thirty of the northern form *Auld* or *Ault*). Such a striking contrast suggests that there was little tendency to call a man 'old' at all. The junior of two men was 'the Young' or the *Younger*, and that was sufficient to distinguish him, but the addition to his name given with such an obviously temporary intent might often stay with him for life. An early example comes from the Crown Pleas Roll of Wiltshire in 1249 in which a father, accused of sheltering his outlaw son, is sentenced to being outlawed also. Their names are Richard the Young and Robert the Young. The word once applied to the father as a youth has stayed to serve for the next generation. We will see this theme of youth reappearing in many common surnames. In the days when such tags were beginning to stick freely most people had one early in life and few reached old age without one.

However there are exceptions to everything, and some nicknames do indicate old age. *Whitehead* would seem to do so, though we will reserve judgement for the moment on *White*. *Gray* certainly seems to refer to hair, and the more picturesque *Snow* and *Frost* suggest a sprinkling of white on an ageing head. *Hoare* is an ancient word now hardly surviving except in 'hoar frost' and 'hoary'. It meant 'silvery grey' or 'very old'. The New English Dictionary cannot decide which sense came first, but this makes no matter; it was used in Old English to describe ancient stones, woods, and old men, frequently kings, always with a sense of veneration. So if a village grey beard was called 'the Hoar' it was with respect. Another word very similar to this in sound was applied to some women with no respect at all, and occasionally to their sons, such as John Horeson of Aldermanbury (1539), but there is so much early evidence of the use of 'hoar' as grey and venerable that I think it may be generally taken to have this highly respectable meaning.

As to size, *Tall* is too modern a word to appear as a surname, except very rarely. The proper English word to describe a tall man was *Long* (*Lang* or *Laing* in the North), or he could be called *Longman* or *Longfellow*. Edward I, who was very tall, was nicknamed 'Longshanks', but this does not seem to have survived in general use unless perhaps in the abbreviated *Shanks*. The opposite was naturally *Short* or *Shorter*, *Little* or *Littler*. These are rather less numerous than the 'long' names, but we shall find that there are several metaphorical names for small men, as for instance *Peppercorn*, which has been mentioned in connection with Spicers, but would do for any small round person.

When we come to the question of girth, the obvious word 'fat' does not appear in the directory at all. *Thick* and *Thynne* are nicely balanced with only seven and eight examples. The commonest adjective of width seems to be *Broad* (70), with its compounds *Bradman* and *Brodribb* (the real surname of Henry Irving). Then there is *Bigg* and *Mutch*, but none of these is common. Probably the word most often applied to a big man in Middle English was 'muchel' or 'michel', but these are now lost among the large numbers of our *Mitchells* which also represent the Christian name Michael. For 'thin' or 'slender' the usual word was *Small* (or *Smale*).

However it seems that when our ancestors were moved to comment on a neighbour's figure the result was likely to be something more picturesque. A thin man might be called *Bones* or *Smallbones*, or if he were a Northerner *Baines*, and a fat man was frequently called *Pudding*. This is a name that is seen regularly in the Subsidy Rolls but has, perhaps understandably, become extremely rare. On the other hand *Puddifat*, a strong visual metaphor from the pudding-vat, the big round vessel for boiling puddings in, has lasted remarkably well in a great variety of forms and spelling ranging from *Puddifoot* to *Puddiphat* which may be due largely to a certain Roger Podyfat, a prosperous citizen of London in the thirteenth century who made the name respected there. Pudding-boiling is as ancient an English custom as anything in our folklore, but the early pudding was more like a 'haggis' than a sweet pudding of modern times.

Nowadays we contrast people in respect of their colouring by calling them *Dark* or *Fair*, and both of these words have given us surnames though neither is at all plentiful. However it is from this very contrast that the nicknames with the highest numbers of all arise.

The Anglo-Saxons were predominantly fair-haired, though there must have been some variety among them even when they invaded Britain, and any intermarriage with the Celtic peoples whom they drove West would have increased the darker strain. Our names seem to confirm that a dark man was more unusual than a fair one, and therefore more noticed, but that extremes of both colouring caused interest and remark. Among the obviously dark types we have *Black* (with its variant *Blake*) and, the most familiar of all nicknames, *Brown*. Another common name for a dark colour is *Dunn* which in modern usage has come to mean an indefinite light brown applied chiefly to cows, but which was originally almost synonymous with 'dark'. Indeed both of these last two adjectives have grown lighter with the passage of time, as can be seen in Middle English writings in such lines as 'the sun that is so bright it shall become dun and black', and again, 'the world became brown, the sun was down'.

On the other side of the contrast we have *White, Bright, Gold* and *Fair*, in all of which the association of blond colouring and beauty are closely linked. The last of these is the least common. Its meaning in the surname period was nearer to 'beautiful' than blond, and it is found more often in compounds like *Fairfax* (fair hair), or *Fairbairn* (pretty child), than alone. *Bright* and *Gold* (or *Gould*) both refer generally to the shining golden hair that was much admired. *White*, which is far the commonest of them, must have been reserved for the true blond, the lily-white boy with the flaxen hair and fair skin ('not Angles but

Angels'), which is still quite common among English children, but rare in a natural state among adults.

Of course 'white' must sometimes have been used for old men with snow-white hair also, but in an age when life was inclined to be short and violent not very many men reached this stage, and there is abundant evidence of 'white' being used for young people. The Lady Wynflaed who died late in the tenth century left a bequest to one of her maidens, Aethelflaed the White, and in a ballad dated about 1330 the king had a daughter 'as white as whalebone'. These two examples, which in their dates span the whole surname period, show one of the ways in which the name was used in a complimentary sense. It was also used regularly for men, young and old, as far back as our records go, and at the time of the Conquest served as a surname for several leading Englishmen. In fact all these simple colour words, with the exception of *Fair* (which is not really a colour at all), were used regularly as personal names. It is certain that they all refer to hair and complexion and have nothing to do with such temporary adjuncts as clothes. They are all plentiful, with *Brown* and *White*, expressing the two sides of the contrast in the simplest terms, both running into four figures.

When we turn to the brighter, non-human colours the numbers fall very sharply, with the one exception of *Green* which is nearly as numerous as *White*. It has sometimes been said that it might indicate a forester in a suit of Lincoln green, and it may be so occasionally, but the great majority are local in origin referring to residence on the village green (page 269). A very poor second is *Scarlett* with a score of only thirty-five. This may arise from clothing; a scarlet cloak or hood would easily cause comment; or perhaps it is a nickname for one in the cloth trade concerned with dyeing this popular colour. Something similar may be said of *Blue*, *Bluitt* and *Blewett* which together make thirty. There are positively no Yellows, though the word is old enough.

Having found that the common colour names, with the exception of *Green*, are descriptive of human hair, we should expect many examples of 'red', for of all possible hair colours that is the one most likely to provoke comment. They are there in good numbers as *Read*, *Reed* and *Reid*, having retained the form and pronunciation of the adjective as it was in Middle English.

They must have been firmly settled as surnames and their significance forgotten before the word shortened in general use to the modern 'red'. Another offshoot from the same Old English root gives us *Rudd*.

Before we leave the subject of hair, which seems to have been much noticed by our forbears, we should glance at some compound forms such as *Blacklock*, *Whit(e)lock*, *Horlock* or *Horlick*, a corruption of the same name, and *Sherlock* which last means bright or shining locks. The last three of these names are all recorded as surnames in England before the Conquest. Then there is *Whitehead* and *Blackett* (originally Blackhead), *Dunnett* (dun or dark head), *Ballard*, meaning bald, and *Pollard*, cropped short. Another quality of hair is expressed in *Curl*, *Curley*, *Curling* and *Crisp*, the last, which is the most numerous, being sometimes twisted round (as a cockney will turn 'wasp' into 'waps') to make *Cripps*. A *Lovelock* was a fanciful curl, just as it is now. *Beard* with its northern counterpart *Baird* is also what it seems, and may occasionally have developed into *Barrett* (page 186).

In one way and another a man's head came in for more comment than any other part of him. Most of his physical features can be found in the directory, but in smaller numbers, and very often are not what they seem. *Bod(d)y* is generally short for *Baldwin*, but the word exists as the second part of several compounds such as *Freebody* and *Lightbody*, in the general sense of a person, as in 'anybody'. *Hands* comes from Hans, a familiar form of John, used by the many Flemings in England, but the compound *Whitehand* must have been a nickname for someone who appeared rather exquisite. It is close in thought to the nickname Beaumains given to the noble youth Gareth when he served in King Arthur's kitchen before he was made a knight. *Legge* is another form of *Leigh* (page 269), the general word for legs in our period being *Shanks*. Some unfortunates were known as *Cruikshank* or *Crookbain*; and a good many of our *Crooks* must have suffered from the same infirmity, though others may have lived by the crook of a stream. The word means a twist or bend. Another word meaning crooked is *Crump*.

Coming down to the feet we find *Whitefoot* to match *Whitehand*, but far more often *Foot* stands alone and unqualified. In

143

such a case we can only suppose that the original owner had some peculiarity that drew attention, a club foot perhaps. It can hardly have been an asset. This name is well documented as a nickname from before the Conquest when Godwin Foot was a landowner in Kent; it can be found in most succeeding centuries and is prominent today.

As with *Foot*, so it is with *Head*. It may occasionally be local for someone who lived on a headland, but the frequent early forms without any preposition of locality must be nicknames. In the Pipe Roll for 1130 we have 'Hubert cum Testa' who admits of no doubt. What was so peculiar about Hubert's head or Godwin's foot we shall never know, but there must have been something wrong with both of them.

The head has made more surnames than I have space to mention. *Greathead* and *Broadhead* are English versions of the name of the famous thirteenth-century Bishop Grosseteste, but in spite of that the significance was literally the same as the more modern 'fathead'.

When we look at the features of the face in detail we find that all have been noticed, particularly the eyes. *Blackie*, *Brownie* and *Goldney*, signifying black, brown and golden eyes, are straight description. *Brodie* (broad-eye), with its northern version *Brady* and its opposites *Smalley* and *Littley*, is the commonest of the group and may have had some metaphorical significance besides its literal sense of big eyes. *Hawkey* (hawk eye) is certainly complimentary; *Goosey* certainly not. There are a good many more possible names of this type, apparently comparing human eyes to those of various creatures, but as '-ey' is a very common place-name ending they should be regarded with caution. *Bulley* has local origins in England and France.

If there is no surname from the word 'nose' it is only because anyone making a personal remark about this feature would be inclined to use the more jocular expression 'beak', which as a surname retains the sound of the Old French 'bec' from which it came. The modern name *Beck* comes also from two other sources, both local. In early records they can be clearly distinguished as 'de Bec' (from one of several Becs in France and Normandy) and 'atte bec' meaning at the beck or stream. But it often appears also without any preposition, obviously as a nickname. In the last few centuries it has fixed itself on to magistrates and schoolmasters, and it is probable that the thought behind it was at first rude comment on a big nose and later the tendency of those in authority to poke their noses into other people's business.

Nicknames about men's mouths seem to have referred more to their speech habits than mere appearance. Two in particular may be noted, Black-in-the-mouth, which appears in the Subsidy Rolls of Cambridge and London, but has not survived unless there is a Blackmouth somewhere, and its opposite, Mildemouth, which may be traced through at least five centuries in the neighbourhood of Swanage, ending up as *Melmoth*.

Up to this point every name given in this chapter (with the exception of Beck) has been of English origin, and it is time now to consider their French counterparts. It should be borne in mind that all through our period, not only was French spoken among the upper classes, but also French people arrived and settled in England often complete with surnames formed in their native land. The development of fixed surnames took place simultaneously in both countries and on very similar lines, but on the whole the French were even more addicted to nicknames than we, and consequently most of our commonest ones have French versions, though often much modified by centuries of English pronunciation.

Thus to match *Long* and *Short* we have 'grand' and 'petit', both of which came in with the Conquest. The former soon changed in meaning from merely 'tall' to something more dignified and impressive, as befitted a Norman baron. As a surname it acquired a sharper ending making the familiar *Grant*, and as such became particularly common in Scotland. But it was established early in London too where Professor Ekwall has noted that William le Grant in the time of Stephen was the son of Wulfwin Graunt, an early case of a descriptive nickname becoming hereditary. 'Petit', which gives us *Pettit* and *Petty*, was often used in the sense of 'junior' as we use 'young', but might also mean 'small'. *Bassett* is another Norman nickname for a short man.

In the matter of colours, the French 'Brun' soon became indistinguishable from the native *Brown* which is an additional reason for its large numbers, but it was not so common a name in France as in England. The French, being a darker race than the English, were more inclined to remark on fair haired people than dark ones, and in a modern French directory it will be found that names meaning 'white', Le Blanc, Blanchard and the rest, far outnumber the Le Bruns and Lenoirs, whereas in England the opposite is the case. The word that the Normans brought into England in largest numbers for a fair man was 'blond' which, like *Grant*, had its final 'd' soon changed to a 't' to give us *Blunt* and *Blount*. We see it often in medieval documents from Domesday Book onwards generally Latinized as Blundus. Its diminutive forms, Blondel or Blondin in French, became *Blundell* and *Blunden* in English.

When the French wanted to indicate that a man was exceptionally dark, they frequently launched into metaphor and called him a 'Moor' in the form of le Maure or *Maurice*. This latter was the name of a saint and could be used as a Christian name or as an adjective. The English had had little direct contact with Moors before the Crusades, but the French, brought up on legends of Charlemagne's victories, knew all about them. Besides, the Vikings, from whom the Normans as well as the Scandinavian element in England were descended, had raided Mediterranean coasts in their long boats, and so a Moor, though a remote figure, was quite well enough known by hearsay to be used as a byword for a very dark man. One of the landowners in Domesday Book is 'Matheus de Mauretania', the Latin concealing the real name. It is possible that he had been to North Africa, but far more likely that he was very dark and his Norman friends called him 'Maurice'. In plain English his name would become Matthew Morris.

For red hair the Anglo-French 'rous' and its diminutive 'rousel' have given us *Rouse*, *Rowse* and *Russell*, our commonest nickname of French origin. A general term for a handsome Norman was 'le Bel'. This is one origin of *Bell* and the principal source of *Beale*. (We read in Mallory of 'la Beal Isoud'.) We cannot assess its numbers exactly, but it is far more common than the English equivalent, *Fair*.

Names like *Long* and *Short*, *Bigg* and *Little*, remind us inevitably of Robin Hood and his friend Little John. The thought of the latter is enough to remind us that a simple description may mean the very opposite of what it says. Everyone knows that Little John was a big man, and another of Robin's companions, the miller's son, was called 'Much' because he was so small. Does this undermine the whole theory of surnames bringing us true information about the past? Not at all, because only a very few names are suitable for this kind of badinage, and it is not hard to guess which they are, for although the subtleties of humour may have changed in seven centuries the simplest jokes seem to stay the same. In an unsophisticated group it still causes a laugh today to call a huge man Tiny, but this does not result in a wholesale use of opposites. The contrast must be very far-fetched and obvious, and the gambit not used too often, in order to cause even a smile. Our forefathers were not much different in this respect. They might call a bad character 'the Saint' (have we not done the same thing?) or a poor man a *Baron*, but most of the names they used were factual. After all, surnames were created for a practical purpose which would have been defeated if more than a small proportion were nonsensical.

However of all the ironic names the best attested is that of Little John. The story of his meeting with Robin, his christening in the forest and the adventures they had together were so widely known and loved that I think we may take it that many of the *Littles* and possibly the *Shorts* too were originally big men, named in a spirit of comradeship with those popular heroes whose jokes were passed round by word of mouth and echoed by Englishmen who longed to be like them. Whether the Robin Hood legends are old enough to have influenced surnames will be discussed elsewhere, but even if they are not, they reflect the kind of humour enjoyed in the Middle Ages.

So far we have paid little attention to clothes, and when we look for surnames inspired by this part of man's appearance we will find comparatively few. The garment with much the highest score is the one that provided Robin's own surname, but there is no reason to find any particular significance in that. If he was a real man, which can hardly be doubted, he probably inherited it from his father.

Dr Reaney shows that the surname *Hood* sometimes implied a maker of hoods, but I cannot believe that this special work, for which *Hodder* is the usual word, would account for more than a few of the examples in our directory, which total nearly a hundred. Hoods were made of the same materials as other garments, were often attached to them and required no special skill. It seems more likely that, just as a man's head and hair were the parts of him most noticed, so his headwear too would occasionally cause comment. Not that there was anything unusual in wearing a hood, which was the universal headgear for rich or poor during our period, but just as the words 'head' and 'foot' could stand alone meaning 'with an odd head' or 'a deformed foot', so 'hood' could imply that the man in question had a huge hood that nearly enveloped his face, or a new one that he talked of too much. There is evidence to show that *Greenhead* was often originally Greenhood – the unstressed second syllable easily losing its long vowel – and this may have implied a connection with the forest.

Other surnames from garments are few indeed. An interesting one is *Shorthouse* or *Shortiss* corrupted from Shorthose, a fashion brought in by Robert of Normandy who was himself known as Curthose; but this only numbers ten. It is plain that as far as appearance went it was the man himself that impressed his friends and inspired a nickname, rather than any passing fashion that he might adopt.

Chapter 14

HUMAN BEHAVIOUR

Having seen briefly in the previous chapter how men appeared to each other in our period, we turn to their behaviour, beginning with the way in which they moved.

In an age when only the upper classes rode on horseback and the majority of mankind progressed on its feet, the way in which they did so was much observed. They walked great distances and ran too when messages were to be carried for their lords and masters. It would be well known in every village who were the best runners, and such names as *Swift*, *Speed*, *Lightfoot* and *Golightly* would be well earned. Anyone called the *Hare* would be so named for his turn of speed, and I think the quality most envied in a *Bird* (or *Byrd*) must have been its ability to disappear so swiftly and easily into the distance. We say now of a car, 'It goes like a bird'; the phrase seems very modern, but many modern phrases are incredibly old. *Arrow* is another name that was probably used for a good runner.

Idiosyncrasies in walking were very quickly noted. *Proudfoot* is a particularly apt expression for one with a stately gait. Gilbert Prudefot was a sheriff of London in the eleventh century, and the name constantly reappears in the city records from that time to the present. *Steptoe* is also a real name; *Ambler* and *Tripp* had each his particular pace, and I think that *Trott*, *Trotter* and *Trotman*, which together score over a hundred, represent the style of a regular runner of long distances rather than a horseman.

In the rolls one sometimes sees Oxfoot, suggesting a very slow gait, but I know no modern example of the name, which probably merged with *Oxford*. *Sheepshanks*, which comes from the North, the home of plain speaking, suggests thin, wiry legs of the kind that would be more nimble than the *Cruikshanks* mentioned in the last chapter or the even unkinder French equivalent, *Foljambe*, sometimes seen as *Fulljames*, which means silly legs and can hardly have been liked by its first recipient. Other expressive Norman nicknames in this class that have stayed with us are *Bompas* or *Bumpas* from 'bon pas', a good pace, and its opposite *Malpass*, though the latter is also a place name. Then there is *Pettifer* (pied-de-fer or ironfoot), which may have referred to a mailed knight's protective footwear or to his heavy gait, and *Pettigrew* (pied-de-grue or crane foot). The crane was a long legged heron-like bird (now extinct in England) whom we shall meet again, and the way in which he lifted each large foot and placed it carefully before him was obviously well known. We do not seem to have the name in English, but *Crowfoot* shows the same exact observation of the typical movement of birds.

The English were not always on foot. There are about 150 *Riders* and *Ryders* and several *Rideouts* and *Gallops*, and when we come to think of it *Knight* is an English word.

If we now leave physical movement and come to the mind and character we will find that the attributes our ancestors valued and talked of most were courage, loyalty, strength, commonsense and cheerfulness.

The words used to describe personal bravery are mostly so old that they have changed their meaning since they were first used as commendation for fighting men. *Stark* meant hard and inflexible, and *Stern* much the same. *Snell* was brave in a quick, dashing style. *Sharp* and *Keen* both referred at first to the sharp weapon, but were soon applied also to the man who wielded it. *Smart* meant fierce in the sense of inflicting pain. As with the last two words the meaning was associated with the weapon ('an arrow keen and smarte') as well as the man responsible for it ('the Sarazin was keene and smarte'), but there was also a noun 'smart' referring to the pain so caused. As times became less savage the fierce quality of these three words was moderated to mean only courageous, or mentally keen, sharp and smart, and in the case of the last the modern American usage expresses this development much better than the modern English which has become mixed up, most unsuitably, with clothes and fashion. But when our forbears first acquired these same words as names they were still close in thought to the sharp edges and smarting wounds.

Moody or *Mudie* is another word that has changed its meaning entirely, its original sense being 'of a high and noble mood', in fact brave again so that *Muddiman* is a high commendation. *Bold*, *Doughty* and *Manly* have always kept much the same meaning, as have *True*, *Truman* and *Faithful*. Loyalty was esteemed as almost the highest virtue and closely akin to courage.

One of the Anglo-Saxons' favourite words for describing heroes and warriors was *Hard*, in the sense of unyielding and therefore again courageous. It has been a hard-worked word ever since, and in fact I can hardly form a sentence without it; but this 'hardly' which I have just used in such a weak sense was once worthy to qualify actions performed with intense courage and suffering. The Normans had a cognate word 'hardi', and between them they have left us many honourable surnames of which *Hardy* and *Harding* (the brave one) are the most numerous.

From the French also come *Stout* and *Sturdy* (though they both sound so English), the former having nothing to do with girth but meaning strong and reliable as in the sense of 'a stout heart' or 'stout fellow' (a fifteenth-century commendation), and the latter, according to the New English Dictionary, 'impetuously brave'. The French have also given us *Courage* and *Durand* (enduring), and *Savage* corresponding to the English *Wilde* which at first implied fierce like a wild beast. But the familiar adjective 'brave' which has gradually superseded so many of these fine old words came on the scene too late to make a surname at all. It was not needed. A profusion of names already expressed that sense.

As to mental ability, we have *Wise* and *Sage*, and *Pratt*, now obsolete, which meant astute. But the classic name for a man with good judgement is *Ready* or *Reddie*. 'Rede', that favourite old English word for good counsel and commonsense, lingered on in use until the sixteenth century. Why, I wonder, did it fade away, such a useful word which we sadly miss? Those who had it knew how to act in a crisis; they were 'ready'. Those who had it not, like poor Ethelred, could never put a foot right.

Then to describe the virtue of cheerfulness we have that pleasant group *Gay, Blythe* (with the variations *Bligh* and *Bly*), *Jolly* (which had a gay meaning in Old French before it acquired the 'pretty' meaning of the modern French word), *Merry, Merriman* and, best of all, *Merryweather*. With this last may be coupled *Fairweather*. Both these names occur in the Suffolk Poll Tax returns of coastal towns, their owners being described as seamen, good names for men whose lives and fortunes depended on the winds.

A descriptive surname of French origin that exists in several forms and is fairly numerous is *Curtis*, meaning courteous or polite. This, as far as I know, has no English equivalent. The cult of manners was apparently a purely French affair.

It must have been noticed that all the surnames given so far relating to character are complimentary, and when one looks for their opposites one finds nothing. Many are called *Strong* but none Weak. The surname *Weeks* is a variation of *Wicks* which comes from the common place name 'wick', meaning a small village or dairy farm. If a name has acquired a final 's' we may be sure it comes from a noun and not an adjective.

We have noted about twenty names relating to personal courage and endurance, but there is not one that I know of that indicates disloyalty, cowardice, or even timidity, unless we consider *Mouse* to have the last sense. But this rare name is such an extreme case that it may have originated like Little John as a name for a big, bold man.

The name *Coward* has of course no relation to this subject at all. It signified the cowherd and nothing else, and there can have been no confusion of meaning in the surname period or it would not have stuck and remained. The modern word 'coward' is not recorded before the fifteenth century. Its origin is uncertain, but appears to be French. The English seem to have found such a character so unspeakable that they had no word for it.

Of course there were derogatory surnames, a great many of them in medieval records, some so offensive that one wonders how they could remain in use for even one generation. When it is the case of a poor peasant being called Chickenhead or Slug (both from Dorset, 1327) one assumes that he could not help himself, but in the case of a rich man in full control of his affairs it is much more surprising. In Domesday Book, for instance, one of the Norman tenants-in-chief for Worcestershire is Hugo Asinus. There can be no mistake about it for his name appears also in French as Hugo Lasne (l'âne). One wonders how he liked it.

Rather similar is the case of an English thane who witnessed a royal charter in Norman London under the name of Robert Nagod (no good). He must have been a man of some standing to be called on for such an important duty. Did he enjoy the joke? Perhaps not. We know less about him than about Hugh the Ass who really was in a position to make his opinion felt. Professor Ekwall has collected a number of derogatory nicknames from early London records, even some expressing disloyalty, like Turncoat and Drawback, but such names did not last long.

The same tendency can be observed with names relating to appearance. Those that have survived, if not complimentary, are at least tolerable. We noticed that the name *Pudding* which was fairly widespread in the thirteenth century is very rare today. People have never liked being called fat, but there were medieval names of personal description far worse than that. I will mention only Broadarse and its fellow Wid(e)arse which still existed in the Parish of St Martin-in-the-Fields in the sixteenth century. But as the level of public taste rose so names of this kind vanished.

All this brings us to the conclusion that in the matter of such very personal names a certain amount of natural selection did take place. A man could never choose his own nickname any more than a schoolboy can persuade his companions to call him by a name of his own invention. The many names denoting courage could only be won in the hard way, and if an unflattering one was given there was little to be done about it so long as the victim remained in the same company, unless he could prove himself by physical violence to be worthy of a better description. A man of mild character might have to suffer all his life being called Milksop (a surname from thirteenth-century London), and his sons might inherit it, but sooner or later, unless they were also somewhat feeble, they would find a means of shaking it off. The best chance came if a boy left his native place and found work elsewhere, where nobody knew him. Then he would naturally avoid telling his new master his unwanted name, and thankfully answer to anything else that might occur to his master's mind.

Thus, over a period of many generations, the worst of the nicknames have been rejected. The process has gone on until the present day, but as centuries passed it became progressively a more awkward manœuvre. Apart from actual difficulties in the way, there is a kind of tenacity in most people, which makes them hold on to the name they were born with, and those who go to the length of changing it are a tiny minority.

But although our modern directories contain few surnames of which the original meaning is anything disgraceful, there are plenty which contain a note of disapproval or mockery. *Moneypenny* (many pennies), *Pennyfeather* (pennyfather), and *Turnpenny* are all names for misers. *Scattergood*, which sounds so like a public benefactor, was really a spendthrift, scattering his goods unwisely. *Dolittle* and *Drinkall* had their obvious faults.

A mild human weakness which has given rise to a good many lasting surnames in spite of their note of mockery is a tendency to being amorous. The Old English Leofman, meaning 'beloved', which had been used in all sincerity as a Christian name, before the Conquest, went gradually downhill in the following centuries until, as *Leaman*, it came to signify a lover of a disreputable sort. Its many forms, ranging from *Loveman* and *Luffman* to *Lemon*, total over a hundred, a far higher score than the French equivalent *Paramore*. There are many more names of this sort, *Truelove, Dearlove, Prett(i)love, Sweeting, Sweetman, Dear, Dearing, Dearman* and *Darling*, all expressions used by the Anglo-Saxons as terms of endearment and often too as personal names. The simple *Love, Sweet* and *Sweetlove* were generally women's Christian names; most of the others were masculine. All were originally terms of genuine affection, as many still are, but I suspect that when they were applied as nicknames in the surname period it was often with less kindness.

In the twelfth- and thirteenth-century rolls we see many made-up comical names on this theme. In the Lancashire Assize Rolls of 1283 there is a whole family, Emma, Richard and

Matilda, with their surname given in French as Pleindamurs. In the same decade the same name can be found in English, in counties as far apart as Cumberland and Cambridgeshire, as Fulloflove, and in the London Directory today it exists as *Fullalove, Fullilove* and *Fulleylove*. Another name of this type that is very widespread in the thirteenth century is *Spendlove* (in the sense of pouring it out extravagantly), sometimes contracted to *Spenlow* and *Spindlow*. These names have a pleasant sound, though sentimental, and have lasted well, whereas more disreputable ones like Wencher (from the Staffordshire Poll Tax) have long since gone.

The contrary principle also applied, that those who had names they were proud of – *Stark* and *Strong, Hardy* and *True* – would hold on to them and resist change, with the result that descriptive surnames of this type do represent the qualities our forbears most admired. In fact, side by side with unrestrained natural growth, the process of survival of the fittest operated from the start.

A glance at the table on page 329 will show that all the commonest nicknames are not only pleasant in character but short, simple English words, most of them extremely old, having been in use for describing human beings in this country for hundreds of years before they became surnames. However in the century after the Conquest the Normans brought in many new nicknames of the more complex type, and at the same time colloquial English, seeming to take on a new lease of life among the unlettered masses, produced a wave of new phrase-making which provided racy descriptions for every type of character. The usual form consisted of a verb followed by a noun, achieving its effect with the greatest economy, as with *Spendlove* and *Turnpenny* quoted above.

Only too many of these phrase-names were of the violent Spillblood, Crackbone variety which we cannot much care for now, and even in the Middle Ages they proved distasteful, only the more moderate of them having stayed the course. Of these *Shakespeare, Breakspear, Wagstaff* and *Waghorn* seem innocent enough though somewhat bellicose. *Brisbane* (break bone), is sufficiently disguised by its mixture of French and English to give no offence, while *Burnand* (burn hand), a name for the official who carried out the cruel sentence of branding criminals, is seldom recognized for what it is.

Some names of this type that have lasted to our time are even mild and gentle. *Makepeace* and *Playfair* are as pleasant names as anyone could wish to have. So is *Lovejoy*, though it may contain a note of criticism as being too pleasure-loving. *Hopgood* was a name for an optimist, related perhaps to that eleventh-century Suffolk peasant, Aedric Hopehevene (page 38).

The Normans were particularly given to this class of name, especially to the more violent ones, but few have survived. Perhaps the French phrase-name that has produced the largest modern numbers is Taillefer (cut-iron), with its *Telfers* and others (see page 34). Another that occurs in several subsidies is *Truslove*, in which the second part is from the Old French word for a wolf (see page 166), so that the whole name means 'bind wolf', a commendation for a brave hunter. A name that is now a byword for friendly enjoyment and bonhomie, is *Butlin*, which comes from 'boute-vilain', meaning literally 'push the peasant'. An archdeacon of Nottingham in the twelfth century had this nickname, and at that date may have earned it himself.

Some of these two-piece names are occupational. *Benbow* (bend-bow), is a nickname for an archer; *Rackstraw* for the farm hand who raked the stable yard. The *Catchpole* was the unpopular official who carried off the peasant's best hen (poule) as payment to his manorial lord. *Treadwell* and *Treadgold* were embroiderers (originally the first syllable was 'thread'). *Kellogg* comes apparently from 'kill hog', a nickname for a butcher, as also was *Knatchbull* ('knatch' meaning to knock on the head). *Hackwood* was for a woodcutter, who was also often called a *Hacker* or *Hackman*.

In some cases, even when the meaning of the words is perfectly clear, we cannot interpret the significance of the phrases with confidence. They are so very colloquial that without sharing the mood of the moment it is hard to catch their flavour. Was a man called *Drinkwater*, for instance, because he was really so eccentric as to prefer water to ale, the universal beverage for rich and poor, or was the very opposite the case? The two examples quoted by Dr Reaney of London tavern keepers of this name (about 1300) would seem to support the latter theory. (Incidentally the French *Boileau* is exactly the same thing.) *Planterose* was probably a name for a gardener, but what shall we say of *Pluckrose*? Is he just another gardener, or was something more important implied? It was not unusual for land to be held by the token fee of a red rose tendered at a particular time or place. Or again one's mind turns to the beginning of the Wars of the Roses. That particular occasion is much too late for coining new surnames, and not even historical, but it could be that the plucking of a rose and wearing it as a badge had been a significant action in times long past. Would the story have arisen if this were not the kind of gesture that men understood?

As for all the people who shook or wagged various objects, it is impossible now to say with certainty how or why they did so, but probably most were connected with a trade, office or traditional ceremony. Most of the phrases of this type that have remained as ordinary words in the language, like 'turncoat', 'cutthroat', 'killjoy' and 'spendthrift', are names of regular types, and therefore it seems likely that Shakespeare's name, if it was not just a picturesque term for a spearman, signified a trouble maker. E. K. Chambers, who collected early examples of this name with eighty-three different spellings from many parts of England, quotes the case of Hugh Shakespeare who, on entering Merton College Oxford in 1487, changed his name because it was held in low repute ('quia vile reputatum est'). If he could have waited just over a hundred years he might have thought better of it.

C. L. Ewen, whose large *History of British Surnames* is a monument of industry, packed with useful material, has unorthodox ideas about nicknames, which are not accepted by other scholars, and is at great pains to show that the name Shakespeare is not what it seems, even though he himself gives thirteenth-century examples of it in forms that are unmistakable. Shakespeare's genius is such a remarkable phenomenon that some people, unable to accept it on its face value, seem to think that it would be more comprehensible if it belonged to someone else, and in the same way even his name is subject to peculiar theories. It is a rare name but of a regular, well-authenticated pattern.

No name of this group is common. Most of those quoted in the preceding pages run to a dozen or twenty examples in the London Directory and are found in small numbers in other parts of the country. In thirteenth-century rolls they are more numerous, and those that have not survived far outnumber those that have. They failed for various reasons besides improvement in taste. Hold-by-the-head (perhaps a name for a wrestler) and Lye-by-the-fire, both from the Yorkshire Hundred Rolls, were too long; Catchfrensh, from the Hertfordshire 1307 Subsidy, was too awkward to say. Many died from natural causes. After all, the chances were against any one family surviving in the male line from the thirteenth to the twentieth century.

Of all the phrase-names the most numerous today is *Turnbull* (with a good hundred examples in the directory), a neatly expressed term for the strong man of the farmyard who could manage a dangerous animal. So we come back to the simple qualities of courage and strength which made a name that any family was glad to keep.

Chapter 15

THE WORLD OF NATURE

The familiar terms on which men and women used to live with wild creatures is illustrated by the give and take of bird names. The human names Robin and Martin were given so consistently to the redbreast and one of the swallow tribe that we now never call them anything else. The pye and the daw received the addition of Mag and Jack which stuck firmly on to their bird names, while several other names like Tom Tit were less firmly attached. In reverse, men often used a bird name for a person. It came just as easily to call a small man *Wren* as to call the little bird Jenny.

There was nothing new about this sort of thing in the surname period. As far as our records go back, men had used birds' names for nicknames. *Swan, Crow, Hawk, Kite, Sparrow* and *Sparrowhawk* can all be seen regularly as personal names before the Conquest. The general term for a male bird, *Cock*, which should not be narrowed down to the barnyard variety but embodies the lively, dominating spirit of all cock-birds, is one of those for which our evidence is oldest, for it comes from place names first spoken in the pioneering days of the Anglo-Saxons and existing only in speech long before it was written down. Cockington in Devon is the 'tun' of Cocca's people (O.E. 'cocca', a cock) and so on. Ekwall gives many clear examples.

By 1066 this name was already used as a surname – Alwin Coc is one of the dispossessed Saxons in Domesday Book – but it also continued as a popular first name of a familiar sort among the lower classes. Kok Forester and Kok de Mari (Cock of the Sea) are both from the Sussex Subsidy of 1296. As time went on it was used more and more for boys and servants and finally dropped out altogether, but not before it was firmly established as a surname, often taking a final 's' in the way of Christian names, which turned it into *Cocks* or *Cox* (see also page 193). We also have the diminutive form *Cockerell*.

Following the cock we must think of that other male bird, the *Drake*, but this is not always what it seems. No doubt some surnames are derived from the handsome bird, but more come from the even older word 'draca' meaning a dragon. Illiterate people have wonderful memories for legendary tales which they pass on verbally, such as that of Beowulf and his fight with the monster. Dragons loomed large in the folklore of the Anglo-Saxons and were sometimes depicted on their battle standards. Centuries later Francis Drake was known to the Spaniards by their very suitable version of his surname, El Draco, the dragon.

The bird name that has probably given us the greatest number of surnames is the *Hawk*. The fierce, wild courage of this bird which wheeled plentifully in our skies even a century ago and is now grown so pitifully rare, together with its magnificent powers of flight inspired our early ancestors with intense admiration, and its name appears frequently as a personal name in pre-Conquest records, not only as *Hawk*, in the Old English form 'hafoc', but also in the more exact *Sparrowhawk*. In the year 1050 the Abbot of Abington, whose name was *Sparhawk*, became Bishop of London. Both these forms can still be found in the directory and also the more contracted *Spark/s*. After the Conquest Havoc or Hawke continued long both as a first name and a nickname, often with the diminutive '-in' changing it to Havekin (found in the Hundred Rolls) and Hawkin. Either of these made a particularly suitable nickname for a falconer. The final step after they had passed into use as surnames was the addition of 's' to make *Hawkes* and *Hawkins*.

One complication should be noticed. The Norman name Henry, which came into England hundreds of years after men had been calling each other 'hawks', was soon abbreviated to Hal, and then became *Halkin* and coalesced with the popular Hawkin. Here we have an example of a new name being popularly assimilated to an old one and giving it a new lease of life.

The general love of falconry meant that all through the surname period a tremendous interest continued in the various species of hawks and falcons, and practically all have given us surnames, though none so numerous as the general term Hawk. We have in our directory a few each of *Falcon, Merlin, Goshawk, Muskett* and *Tassell*. The last two are the male birds of the sparrowhawk and goshawk, the female being the better one for bringing down the prey. Tassel is an early corruption from 'tiercel', and it may be remembered that Juliet calls Romeo her 'tassel-gentle'. A *Haggard* was a hawk who had been trained but reverted to the wild again.

Before we turn to the truly wild birds there are two more species that were partly domesticated by our forefathers, each giving a good number of surnames, firstly that of *Doves* and *Pigeons* kept in several varieties at every manor and castle, well known to everyone and especially suitable on account of their billing and cooing as names for lovesick young men or newly weds; secondly the *Peacock*, confined only to the establishments of the wealthy, but evidently known and talked of far and wide. This exotic bird was brought into Europe at an early date; the word occurs in Old English and turns up in several forms among our surnames, *Peacock, Pocock, Poe* and *Paw*. Descriptions of its magnificence must have reached the ears of many who never saw one, and it became proverbial for pride, that sin of which small communities have always been particularly critical. The name cannot have been given as a compliment, but the recipient may not have objected as it recognized him as a fine fellow. This is among the most numerous of bird names.

We come now to the more ordinary wild birds who filled the woods and fields and fens of that wilder, greener, more natural England of the Middle Ages. Those which have produced the most surnames are naturally the ones that have each some striking characteristic. The snow-white elegance of the *Swan* naturally made its name a compliment. A dark-haired person might well be called *Crow, Raven* or *Rook*, and the French version for this same family gives us *Corbett* and *Corbin* which are nearly as common. A tall thin man would readily be a *Crane* or *Heron*. The former, no longer seen in England in a wild state, was once extremely common, as many of our place names tell us. Cranford, Cranborne, Cranwell and many more were all places where they abounded. But they were esteemed a delicacy for the table and being even larger than the heron were well worth catching for that purpose; while added to the hazard of the fowler's net was the constant process of draining pools and marshes, which has continued all through our history depriving water birds of their habitat. The living crane has gone, but it is still with us in at least two metaphorical uses, first as a surname and secondly as the name of the great long-necked machines which now dominate our industrial landscapes, as once the original cranes dominated our ponds and rivers.

The French too made nicknames from this bird. But their word for it, 'grue' (*Grew*), is much less common than our *Crane*.

The people of the Middle Ages loved stories in which birds and beasts were the protagonists each endowed with a particular quality, and surviving examples of their literature include a large proportion of this sort of thing, such as various 'bestiaries' and poems like *The Owl and the Nightingale* and Chaucer's *Parliament of Foules*. Thus, apart from their own acute observation of nature, they had ideas of traditional characteristics for every bird. The owl stood for wisdom, but was also unlucky as an omen of death. Its numbers cannot be accurately computed because, though *Oules* and *Owles* belong to it, the more common form *Howlett* has become assimilated to a familiar form of *Hugh* (see page 215), and the Welsh *Howell* may have added to the confusion.

The *Eagle* (always a rare name) was majestic; the *Nightingale* was not only a fine singer, as also was the *Thrush* (*Throstle* or *Thrussell*), but was amorous as well. The *Lark* was cheerful and an early riser; the *Finch* was a byword for gaiety – 'Gai comme un pinson,' say the French, and a *Sparrow* for being quarrelsome in a noisy, merry fashion. The *Jay* was a gaudy overdressed fellow, in commoner style than the peacock; a *Starling* noisy and a blabber of secrets, according to Chaucer; the *Woodcock* was foolish and so was the *Quayle*; the *Bustard* was large; the corn-crake (*Craik* and *Crake*) had a grating voice; the *Partridge* was plump, and the *Coote* was bald.

So far all is fairly obvious, but when we come to some of the other birds we may wonder just what our forbears had in mind when they gave the names to their friends. Perhaps the name *Swallow* was given to one who was absent for long periods but returned periodically. It would have to be someone loved and admired, for few birds have inspired more poetic feeling; but more likely the bird's wonderful swiftness of flight made it a name for a fast runner. The tit used to be called the 'titmouse', a charming name for an amusing little bird, though which of its idiosyncrasies first inspired someone to call his friend by the name is hard to say. It has survived in at least two forms, *Titmuss* and *Titmas*. But what can be said of the *Bunting* and the *Pippitt* and the *Linnett*? And what of all the various water-fowl except that they are good to eat? Beside the *Coot* and *Heron* already mentioned, we have *Mallard*, *Teale*, *Sheldrake* (or *Sheldrick*), *Widgen*, *Bitte(r)n* (*Bittan* or *Bitton*), *Wildgoose*, *Duck*, *Diver* and *Dipper*, as well as *Goose* and *Gander*.

Looking at this list we cannot fail to remember that wild fowl formed a large part of the diet of our forefathers. Just as we observed that in thirteenth-century Billingsgate, where many fishmongers were crowded together, there was a tendency for them to have fish nicknames like *Herring* and *Pike*, so it might be that a fowler who was particularly adept at snaring one particular species might acquire its name. The bustard, now extinct, was particularly prized on account of its size; woodcock, quail and partridge were always appreciated, while the bunting, though small, was renowned for its delicate flavour. These birds were all netted in great quantities, and a young boy coming home with a basketful of buntings might well be hailed as Jack Bunting and keep the name for life.

So far our list of birds has consisted of words we still know and use, but there are also many archaic or dialect bird names to be found among our surnames. These include the *Ruddock*, or *Reddick* (robin); *Pinnock* (sparrow); *Puttock* (kite, a fierce, wild creature, and yet in 1023 the new Archbishop of York was Aelfric Puttoc); *Dunnock* (hedge sparrow, a gentle little bird, very different from the noisy house sparrow); and *Laverock* (the lark). The ending '-oc' was a regular Old English suffix with a diminutive effect that disappeared soon after the Conquest (dunnock, for instance, meant literally a little dark creature, ruddock a little red one). In modern surnames this suffix may be spelt '-ock', '-ack', or '-ick', but I have avoided too much repetition.

The old word most used for a woodpecker was *Speight* (sometimes also *Peck* or *Pecker*), a good nickname for a carpenter. The owl was sometimes called the *Povey*, the chaffinch *Pink* or

Spink, because that is exactly the sound of his favourite, often repeated chirp; a dove could be a *Culver* (and a dove house a *Culverhouse*); an avocet was a *Clinker*; a jackdaw was a *Kay* in the North and a *Coe* in the Midlands, presumably from his cry; while the curlew keeps the older form *Curlewis* in the surname.

Altogether I have collected fifty-seven different species of birds from the London Directory, some of them having two or three names, and no doubt more could be discovered. How many people in a highly educated modern group would be able to recognize and name correctly so many, let alone know them so intimately that the birds would remind them of their friends? I am afraid that some of them, if called a Bittern or a Bunting, would hardly know how to take it.

On page 330 a list will be found giving the bird surnames with a score of over fifty. One or two have been mentioned as being difficult to assess because of confusion with some other name, and another one in this doubtful state is *Daw*, which must often be a bird name – the mischievous daw would certainly have caused nicknames – but was also a regular familiar form of David. Below fifty the numbers trail away gradually down to the widgeon (*Widgen*), with only one. The only common bird which is hardly represented is the blackbird. Not so fine a singer as the nightingale, not so black as the crow, nor so plump as a partridge, nor so thin as a crane, it has just failed to hit any of the metaphorical headlines. The old names were. *Ousel* and *Mavis*, but though both exist there are none in the London Directory. The best it can offer is *Merle*, of French origin, and there are only three examples of that. There is no Cuckoo. It can be seen as a surname in medieval rolls, but was one that people managed to get rid of.

Another scarcity that I notice is among sea birds. The Old English word 'saefugol', literally 'sea fowl', was used as a Christian name and is to be met with in medieval records of many counties, particularly those with a sea coast. In the twelfth-century list of tenants of Battle Abbey three out of 110 men have this for their Christian name. It exists now as *Saffle, Seffle, Saffell, Seavill*, and perhaps other forms, and I suspect that it has sometimes been absorbed into the local name *Saville* which appears to be Norman though it has not been identified. But there is nothing from our coasts to compare with the detailed list of freshwater birds that we have just noted.

In the realm of animals by far the most numerous is the *Harte*. All Englishmen loved hunting, whether they were allowed to indulge in it or not, and to thousands of them no more beautiful sight could be imagined than a full-grown hart in all his pride of antlers, leaping swiftly through the thicket. Just as *Hawk* was a good name for a falconer, so *Hart* was especially suitable for a huntsman, and a quick, alert, skilful young huntsman at that. Such complimentary names were not easily bestowed.

Venery or hunting had a whole vocabulary of its own which can be confusing to the modern mind. Generally speaking, the *Hart* was the fully grown male of the red deer, the oldest and most honoured word for it. *Stag*, which came to mean the same thing, originally had a more general sense of a male animal of several sorts. *Buck* is the male of the fallow deer, slightly smaller than the red deer but also much admired. A *Roebuck* or *Roe* was smaller still. A *Brockett* was a young red deer with its first antlers. All these names are English, in spite of the Normans' attempt to monopolize hunting.

The most exciting animal to hunt in Norman England was the wild boar, which was deemed a noble adversary on account of its ferocity at bay. There are still in our directory a few examples of the surname it gave in full as *Wildbore*, though more often it has been contracted to *Wilber* or *Wilbur*. These are all rare. The better known name that survives from this animal is *Hogg* which meant, like *Buck* or *Hart*, the fully grown young male. The hog is a much maligned animal today. After wild boar ceased to roam our forests sometime in the sixteenth century, the word was used only for the farmyard animal and went rapidly downhill in the social scale. Now, instead of thinking of it as a noble quarry whose tusks were worthy to adorn the helmets of heroes, as described in Beowulf, we talk about 'road hogs' and 'going the whole hog' as if a tendency to greed were its only characteristic. To call a man a 'hog' now is nearly as bad as calling him a 'swine'. In the twelfth century it was quite a compliment.

The *Wolf* has already been mentioned as a favourite element in Anglo-Saxon names. In early times it seems to have had a supernatural quality which made it prominent in the mythology of all the European races. Consequently it was not only the English who made great use of the word in their name system. One of the most powerful of the Norman barons was 'Hugh the Wolf', or 'le Lou' in Old French. This word, of which the feminine was 'louve', merged into the totally different English word 'love', but the form used most frequently by the Normans was the diminutive *Lovell*, or 'little wolf'. Also from the Latin came the Italian Lupino and the Spanish Lopez showing the popularity of the same nickname in these countries. Even to this day in the restricted communities on Greek islands, where individual nicknames are often added to common surnames, Likos (the Wolf) is one of the favourites.

The German Wolff is so common, and so like our own word, that unless the double 'f' is preserved, they cannot be distinguished on a printed list; but *Wolfe* and *Woolf* are generally English. In this connection we should mention the *Lyon*, which though sometimes of genuine English origin is more often foreign. The hart, the wolf, the lion and the eagle are all symbolical creatures regularly adopted as surnames by the Jews, and some allowance for this fact must be made with each of these names. But whereas the last two are seldom seen in medieval English records and must be regarded largely as foreign imports, *Hart* and *Wolfe*, particularly the former, were common in England at a time when there were no Jews in the country, and owe the bulk of their numbers to English tradition and sporting instincts.

Almost equal to *Hart* in present-day numbers is *Fox*, with its other dialect name, *Todd*, also well represented. These high numbers are easy to understand, for the fox, besides being a plentiful animal to be chased and killed in any way at any time (organized fox hunting did not begin until the seventeenth century), had two very definite characteristics that would easily cause it to be used as a nickname, first its traditional cunning, the subject of endless popular tales, and secondly its colour. There must always have been a tendency among country people to call a red-haired man a 'fox'.

Other creatures with marked characters are the *Hare* with its turn of speed, the wild-cat or polecat, known formerly as the

Fitch or *Fitchett*, whose sharp teeth and claws and flashing eyes made it especially suitable for someone inclined to fly into a rage, and the *Brock* (or *Badger*), another very tough customer when brought to bay. Some of the characteristics that might cause a man to be called *Brock* are short legs, shaggy hair, and a strong smell.

The smaller wild animals have made few surnames, and probably many of these were given to the men who were expert in trapping them. In fact one gets the impression that, apart from hunting, our ancestors cared less for wild animals than for birds. There are forty *Moles*, fewer *Beavers*, which is only to be expected as they had disappeared from England by the Norman period, though they lasted longer in Wales and Scotland. (We should also remember that Belvoir in Leicestershire is pronounced in this way.) There are eighteen *Squirrels*, only eight *Otters* (unless *Hotter* is the same thing, which would add a few more), the same number of *Ferretts*, and of *Muzzells* or *Mussells* (an old word for 'weasel'), six *Coneys*, three *Stoats*, and just one *Mouse*.

Among domestic animals the *Bull* stands easily first, making an obvious nickname for the strongest man in the village, provided he has the right build and an obstinate character. It must sometimes have been given also to the man in charge of the bull, which might come to the same thing. *Bullock* was also quite a popular name, and *Stott* which has the same meaning. We have noticed already how surnames were often acquired young. In this case the boy who herded the bullocks, or perhaps the son of the man they called 'the Bull', might earn the name.

We must look, I think, for an even more youthful origin for *Lamb* which, although a mild creature, contrary to the general run of popular names, is yet numerous. Why, when people liked to be thought brave and strong, and hated any suggestion of timidity, has a gentle creature like a lamb made so many names? The answer must lie chiefly in the fact that there were so many sheep and shepherds that people's minds were bound to turn to that kind of creature for some of their metaphors, and the liveliness of the lamb is a much more attractive quality than anything the adult animal could offer. A shepherd's son would frequently have been called a lamb, especially if he had a thick crop of fair, curly hair. If he grew into a tough young man the name could continue as an ironic joke. At a much later period the soldiers who rounded up rebels after the Battle of Sedgemoor with ruthless cruelty were known as 'Kirke's lambs', meaning to say that they were like ravening wolves. This is long after the surname period, but proverbial sayings and metaphors of this kind seem to be dateless, and this is certainly one way in which this nickname could be used.

Another animal name which was probably used first for a lively boy is the *Kidd*. Perhaps it was a nickname for a good jumper. In any case it must have been acquired young. The adult goat (O.E. 'gat') is hardly represented at all, unless possibly by *Goad*.

The domestic cat was known in England well before the Conquest, but has inspired few nicknames, and those there were have been absorbed and swallowed up by the many abbreviations of the popular women's name Catherine, which often appears as Caterina or Catelina and is responsible for most of the *Catts, Cattells* and *Catlins*. *Kitcat* appears to be a diminutive for the animal. I do not know of any early example of this lively name, but Weekley gives one of Robert Pusekat who was killed in an affray in Corbridge, Northumberland, in 1256, whose name appears to be of the same ilk; but it seems to have gone no further. *Kitts* and *Kitson* are always familiar forms of Christopher or Catherine. Puss is a Dorset surname in 1317, but in the modern directory there is hardly a single name that can be ascribed with certainty to the cat.

We come now to the two remarkable omissions from our collection of animals, those two adulated friends of man, the dog and the horse.

The proper Old English word for a dog is 'hound', and though this is often found in place names it has made no surnames at all. The word 'dog', which is first recorded at about the time of the Conquest, seems to have been a low colloquial term to start with. Almost the only form in which it has survived as a surname is *Doggett* which comes from the curious nickname 'doghead' of which there are several early examples, such as Roger Doggisheved (the Old English 'head' was 'heafod') from Yorkshire, counterbalanced by Lucas Doggetayl from the Isle of Wight. But from the nobler word 'hound' there is nothing at all.

It is the same with the horse. There are, as we have seen,

a certain number of names for the men who looked after horses, but the animals themselves are simply not present. The only possible exception is *Steed/s* of which there are some forty ex-amples, but some of these are from the local word 'stead', often used for a farmyard, and some must be occupational in the same sense as *Steedman*, the steeds being the big, heavy horses used by armoured knights; but the two basic words, 'hengist' for the male animal and 'horse' for either sex, are strangely lacking from our list of animal nicknames. It is not that the words are not old enough. Everyone who knows any history at all knows that Hengist and Horsa are the first recorded personal names in our language. Because they are such a strange and striking pair it is often thought that they were ritual magic names for the leaders of tribes, or perhaps the symbolic figures depicted on their battle standards. In later centuries the White Horse was one of the emblems of the people of Wessex, cut on their chalk hillsides and carried as standards in battle. The word 'hengist' seems to have been so highly venerated that it ceased to be spoken at all. Its only survival in English is in 'henchman', the man who looked after the 'hengist', but this has given only a few examples of *Hensman* and cannot have been much used. 'Horse', on the other hand, has remained in general use ever since that fifth-century landing in Kent, but, though it appears in many place names, such as *Horsey* in Norfolk, it never seems to have been applied directly to a man.

What was it that caused the people of the Middle Ages to refrain from using the names of horse and hound as nicknames, when all the other familiar beasts of field and forest were pressed into service? Were these two animals too dear, too near, too much part of the human family to be seen objectively as typical of any particular qualities? Or is the reason for their omission due to some deep-rooted feeling of sanctity that belongs more to the ethnologist than the historian?

Our ancestors, with their inspired taste for metaphors, did not stop at birds and animals. The natural world was before them, and they used every aspect of it that they could see. Many fishes and other marine creatures from the *Whale* to the *Spratt* can be found in our directories, though none is numerous, and some like the *Pike* have other likely interpretations. It must however be admitted that little interest was shown in insects. One would not expect lasting names from the more objectionable ones, but I am surprised that so pleasant a creature as a butterfly, and one so susceptible of metaphor, was neglected. There is just one example in the directory of *Papillon* (French 'papillion'). The curious *Pamphilion*, which occurs in several spellings, has nothing to do with this subject, having its origin in a kind of fur trimming, fashionable in the thirteenth century. There are no examples of the English 'butterfly', and only nine *Moths*.

A good old English name that sounds deceptively like an insect is *Bugge*, which may often be seen in medieval rolls with its diminutive *Buggins* and probably originated as an abbreviation of an Anglo-Saxon Christian name beginning with Burgh. As a living creature 'bug' is not recorded before 1622, and it need not be supposed that Magot Bugge, from the Yorkshire Poll Tax of 1381, was thought to have an unattractive name, since both unfortunate associations developed since her day. Some later Buggs have found it a disadvantage, but the gentleman who in 1862 changed it to Norfolk Howard did not get over the difficulty, for the Oxford Dictionary now defines Norfolk Howard as a bug.

But though the *Buggs* are not really 'bugs', the *Grubbs* do seem to have originated as a nickname from the 'grub', but very long ago. The name is to be found in several counties in the twelfth and thirteenth centuries.

Turning to plants and flowers, we find, as we should expect, that the *Lilley* and the *Rose* have the highest scores, typifying white or pink complexions. *Flower* and *Blossom* would also make joking nicknames for exquisite fair-haired youths. All these sound more like names for girls than men, and were indeed so used, but they also appear from the twelfth and early thirteenth century as surnames for men. They could of course have been inherited from women, but even so they had to be borne by men at an early date, for it was only in the surname period that a man would be labelled with his mother's Christian name. A fanciful trio of names expressing flowery sweetness, with a note of mockery, are *Flowerdew*, *Honeydew*, and *Sweetdew*, but perhaps the most remarkable survival in this class is the poetical

Blanchflower which has lately risen to fame in the world of football. Floris and Blanchflower were idyllic lovers in a romantic tale made use of by Boccaccio. But there were *Blanchflowers* in Worcestershire in 1275 before Boccaccio was born. It must have needed generations of resilient men to carry this name intact for seven centuries.

Names of trees are nearly always local, telling that someone lived by an oak or an ash, but some words specifying parts of trees or bushes can only be taken metaphorically. *Sprott* means a sprout or young shoot. *Sprigg, Twigg* and *Spray* all exemplify the same idea of youth, while *Pinnell* (or *Pennell*) is a name for a tall young fellow as straight as a sapling pine.

An interesting name of this type is *Budd*. Like so many simple one-syllable nouns, it was used as a personal name before the Conquest as well as a common noun, and has survived for over a thousand years in both capacities. Its original meaning seems to have been connected with swelling. It was a small, round thing that would grow, and as such would make an apt nickname for a child, particularly a plump one. This root meaning of swelling shows how closely related the poetical idea of 'budding' is to the unromantic 'pudding'. Both words can be seen in several forms in the surname period, and are now represented by *Budd, Budden, Puddy* and *Pudden*.

These are just a few of the metaphors taken by our medieval forbears from familiar objects around them. But for the most part they looked to living creatures for words to describe each other, and especially to birds, which seem to have been their first love in nature.

Chapter 16

SPECIAL OCCASIONS

One of the most numerous of all surnames from nicknames is *King*, and we naturally ask why. That it is not a statement of fact connected with the King of England has already been established (see page 135). Any doubt one might have on this matter is dispelled when one looks through the Subsidy Rolls of any county and sees among the peasants paying their few pence, 'Adam le Kyng', 'Walter le King', and so on, occurring generally once or for one family only in each village. It can be found in much earlier records, even before the Conquest.

We see that this title of 'king' was a regular village name, as normal and widespread as those of the leading craftsmen. In numbers it is just behind *Baker* but ahead of *Wright*. To find its origin we must look for an activity as universal as building or baking, a custom which produced one leading performer or exponent. There can be little doubt that the May Day ceremonies are the best answer to this description.

The traditional festival of the spring, which lasted on into the nineteenth century in an attenuated form, sentimentalized by the poets, artificially boosted by lovers of antiquity, generally in decay but reviving a little here and there in strange new forms, this prehistoric festival was something real and important in our ancestors' lives. The coming of spring was more than a pleasure to the senses, though this was strongly felt as many fragments of medieval poetry bear witness, more than the prospect of plentiful food after a lean period; it was a deep stirring of religious excitement that was not basically Christian, though the Church did its best to contain it. To simple country people it was a fundamental part of their way of life, and the going into the

172

woods, the gathering of the may, the dancing and singing and crowning of a King and Queen of the May, was something to be talked of all the year.

We speak now principally of May Queens, because long ago, as people grew more sophisticated, the young men dropped out, leaving the leading roles to the girls, who enjoyed that kind of thing. (This taste is satisfied now by beauty contests, still complete with crown and robe and title.) But originally the King was as important as the Queen or more so, just as Robin Hood was more important in legend than Maid Marian, but she was necessary to complete the theme.

Whether the same young man continued as 'king' for several years, or whether a new one was always chosen, I do not know, but in either case it is clear that this rustic title often remained with a popular May King for life. He may have presided at other festivals throughout the year – hock time and harvest, Halloween and Christmas, as King of the Feast.

In some villages the leading figure in the spring ceremonies was dressed in green leaves and spoken of as 'the green man' or 'Jack in the Green', thereby personifying the figure of spring and linking the ceremony to ancient fertility cults. In this connection we should note again the great numbers of the surname *Green*, which in some cases I believe are linked with this ceremony. The name occurs very frequently in thirteenth-century rolls, nearly always as 'atte Grene' or 'de la Grene'. In the first case it was definitely local, but the second is vaguer and open to other possibilities. Whatever interpretation may be put on it, the name *Green* is exceedingly numerous, with nearly two thousand examples. There is also *Greenwood* to be considered which runs to 230 – local again on the face of it, but the number is higher than one would expect for this descriptive kind of name unless it had some particular importance. *Greenleaf* and *Greenman* are less common, but even more suggestive of these ancient spring rites.

Another name which we might well consider at this point is *Garland*. In the London Subsidy of 1319 we have William Garlander who, according to Ekwall, made circlets of gold and other precious metals often modelled in the forms of leaves for royalty and the nobility, as still worn by modern peers on rare occasions. But even in the thirteenth century so very few were entitled to wear these splendid forms of headdress, and their lasting qualities were so great, that as a craft it must have had few clients, and it can hardly have made a full-time occupation, only a name for a goldsmith who excelled in this speciality. It is much more likely that the name *Garland*, of which there are now seventy examples in the London list, arose more often, for someone who had been crowned as *King* of the *Greenwood* or of the *May* with a *Garland* of *green leaves*.

The surname *May* is not necessarily associated with this particular festival. It signified a general idea of Springtime, youth and blossom, and may have been given to any fair-skinned youth. 'He was as fresshe as is the month of May', says Chaucer of his squire. The word also meant, in early Middle English, a maiden, as in *Mildmay* which has the same idea of youth and purity, or it could be an abbreviation for Matthew (page 229) but in most cases the associations with spring must have been uppermost in the mind when the name was given.

It is not until the fifteenth and sixteenth centuries that we get any clear account of these May Day festivities, and by that time in many places the characters of Robin Hood and his companions had become identified or confused with the more ancient figures. But in the days when surnames were being formed and the May King was still supreme, Robin was alive, and tales of his adventures were spreading round England by word of mouth, not as legends from the past but as rumours of a contemporary hero who caught the imagination of ordinary folk because he expressed their own aspirations.

The wonderful thing about the Robin Hood cult is that, although it never produced anything of real literary merit, it is still so vigorous as folklore. All the popular art forms, films, television, musicals, cartoons, are incessantly using it on both sides of the Atlantic. His life – and who can doubt that he lived? – seems to epitomize the things most dearly prized by our race, now as well as then, freedom, fair-play, fresh air and fun. The historical Robin has never been definitely pinned down to any reliable fact. The earliest known versions of the ballads about him, which date only from the late fifteenth century, when they had already accumulated much unreliable embroidery, place him in the reign of Richard I, which may or may not be true. The earliest contemporary reference yet found that might relate

to him is a statement in the Pipe Roll for 1230 about the confis-
cation of the chattels of 'Robertus Hood, fugitivus'. The form
of the name as Robert need make no difficulty as Robin was
the common colloquial form of Robert and is always translated in this way into Latin. 'Fugitive' signifies an outlaw, so
this entry is in every way suitable as a reference to the true
Robin Hood. The difficulty is to prove that it is not just a
coincidence.

Another school of thought prefers to place Robin's life almost
a hundred years later, in the reign of Edward II. However the
Subsidy Rolls contain evidence which destroys this theory. In
the village of Walsham-le-Willows in Suffolk in 1283, one of the
villagers has the whole name of the legendary hero as his surname, being set down plainly as Robertus Robehood. His own
Christian name was probably spoken as Robin; and Robehod
('hood' generally has a single 'o' at this date) has been added as
a nickname. Perhaps he had impersonated Robin in the May
Day antics. That the name stuck to his family is shown in the
Subsidy of 1524 in which Thomas and John Robhood pay their
taxes in the same village. It also appears in the Sussex subsidies
of 1296 and 1332 as Gilbert Robyhod and Robert Robynhoud,
showing its early establishment as a regular nickname in widespread use. But this is not all. The London Subsidy of 1292
actually mentions an inn called the 'Robin Hood'. The reference
is to 'Adam le tailur ki maint devant lostel Robin hod' (who
lives opposite the Robin Hood Inn). This would seem conclusive.
It is generally stated that the earliest certain reference to
Robin Hood as a popular figure is in *Piers Plowman* which was
written between 1360 and 1390, but the first of those quoted
above is a hundred years earlier.

That the whole name *Littlejohn* was used as a surname we
know because it has lasted to our own time; there are twenty-
three of them in the London Directory. The earliest known
example, from the Hundred Rolls for Cambridge, is ten years
earlier than Robin Robinhood of Suffolk. Unfortunately it is in
Latin, 'Ricardus filius Parvi Johannis', but its significance can
hardly be in doubt. In the following century it may be found in
English also, but whereas it might have arisen in any case as a
nickname for a big man, compounds with John being comparatively common (cf *Prettijohn* and *Brownjohn*), Robinhood as a

175

surname is an unmistakable link with the outlaw. It must have died out from natural causes as many a rare name did.

If I have dwelt long on this piece of evidence, it is because it shows the close link between popular folklore and surnames, and how each can throw light on the other, and it proves that the Robin Hood legend is old enough to influence surnames, though it belongs to the latter part of our period. All his companions in the ballads, Tuck, A'Dale, Scarlett, Greenleaf and the rest of them, have surnames compatible with the early thirteenth century, and all, with the possible exception of Scathelock, are still with us. The name which above all seems connected with the famous outlaw band is *Merriman*, which according to the New English Dictionary was practically synonymous with *Outlaw* in the fourteenth century. Our directory had nineteen of the former and nine of the latter, and there should be no mistake about their ancestry.

It is sometimes said that the surname *King* arose from the acting of such a part in a miracle play. This is probably true up to a point, but could only account for a small fraction of its large numbers. Certainly surnames did arise from the presentation of the Bible stories in village churches, or in more ambitious style in pageants in the towns. That these dramatic performances are early enough for our purpose is certain, for they are referred to in William Fitz Stephen's life of Becket, written in about 1182 ('representationes miraculae vulgariter appellamus'), and Bishop Grosseteste, writing to his archdeacons in 1235, alludes with disapproval to 'plays which they call miracles and other plays which they call bringing in of May'. But when we consider these plays and the leading parts that were performed in them we find that the numbers of surnames arising from them are not at all large, except in the case of Biblical names like Adam or Joseph which cannot be assessed in this connection because they were in any case in use as Christian names.

The most numerous of the distinctive pageant names is *Angel* (160), which is not surprising as the part would involve the wearing of striking costume complete with wings, and would make just the sort of nickname to stick, whether taken in a complimentary or ironical sense. There are only five

Virgins, but twenty-one examples of *Virgo*, the Latin form showing the direct influence of the Church. Forty *Saints*, seven *Martyrs* and five *Postles* form a small but unmistakable group, and in some cases *Wiseman* might belong here too. But when we come to *Kings* and *Shepherds* the numbers are out of all proportion to these others, and we know that innumerable genuine shepherds were called by that name in a literal sense, so we can be confident that only a moderate number of each of these surnames can be assigned to the drama.

The names of the two central parts of the great play cycles, God and Jesus, were too sacred to be bandied about, particularly the latter which has always been scrupulously avoided for ordinary use. The only exceptions are the Oxford and Cambridge colleges of that name, which are quite out of line with general English custom and still cause embarrassment to some. The part played by the leading actor of the Passion Plays could only have been spoken of as 'our Lord', but I do not think it would ever become a surname in this sense, for this type of name would never stick without a touch of humour to keep it going, which would in this case have seemed too irreverent.

The early history of miracle plays is obscure, and we have few clear details of them before the end of the fourteenth century. But by that date they were already developing new themes in which personifications of virtues and vices and other abstract qualities pointed the moral or argued the problems of the main narrative. These allegorical figures are much easier to pick out from our surnames because they are not confused with real names and occupations. Their numbers are very small, as one would expect, because only a small number of people actually portrayed each part, and also this new turn of the drama is a little late. But all the same, a very respectable set of virtues can be taken from the directory, a pleasure for anyone to collect: *Virtue, Verity, Wisdom, Peace, Justice, Mercy* (generally *Marcy*), *Faith, Hope, Charity* and *Comfort*. The only one of these that is here largely under false pretences is *Hope* which is primarily a place name (see page 287). The rest, varying between five and thirty in number, are to the best of my belief genuine survivals of these moral entertainments. Whether *Chance* and *Bliss* should be in the same group is more doubtful.

Vices make a very much poorer showing. It is the same story

that we have had before. People simply did not like being called Avarice or Sloth and cast off the name when occasion offered, but we have five examples of *Greed*, just enough to show it existed, and fourteen of *Pride*. This theme had very long been established as an acceptable nickname. Well before the Conquest Tofi the Proud figures in the Anglo-Saxon Chronicle, and the large number of *Peacocks* show that this was the kind of vice of which some people were not ashamed.

The most dramatic figure in this kind of play was *Death*, and inevitably his name became a surname. But families who inherited it very naturally disliked the gloomy associations, and later generations often adopted the disguise of spelling it as *De Ath*, or *D'Eath*. There is some justification for this as there is a place in Belgium called Ath from which somebody could have come, but many early examples of the name as plain Dethe, at a period when place names were still normally written with a separate preposition, clearly sprang from the all too familiar English word. It would be surprising if it were not so. *Death* must always have been one of the best parts in a play of this kind, offering much more scope for a vigorous actor than a sickly part like *Charity*.

The name Devil, now found as *De Ville* or *Deville*, has an exactly parallel history. Again there is a possible local origin, from Déville in Normandy, which is indicated in some early examples; but besides them are quite as many cases of 'le devil' or, if the document is in Latin, 'diabolus'. As in the case of Death, the Devil would be an enjoyable part for a good actor, who would have no objection to retaining it as a nickname, for all his acquaintances would remember his performance. Even in the next generation it might still be spoken of, but to reach the twentieth century each name has had to last about twenty generations, and Death and Devil have only done so by assuming masks.

The men who acted in these early dramas seem from the first to have been called *Players*, but they were not professionals in the sense that Shakespeare knew the word. They were ordinary working people, playing parts for a short time only, and great occasions these must have been for them. Another kind of playing took place on the village green, or on the stretch of greensward outside a castle, when young men competed in running, leaping, wrestling and the use of weapons. It was here that the names *Playfair* and Playwell (now *Playle*), were probably earned. From skill with the quarterstaff such nicknames as *Hardstaff*, *Longstaff* and *Wagstaff* may come. The expert with the sword and buckler was called the skirmisher or skrimmager, giving us *Scrimgeour* and *Scrimshaw*, while the winner of the archery contest, in which the target was a gaily painted artificial bird known as the popingeay, stuck with bright feathers and fixed on a high pole, might win for himself the bird and its name which survives now as *Pobjoy*, *Pobgee*, *Popejoy*, and in other curious forms.

We have only half a dozen *Wrestlers* and *Rasslers*, but it was probably in this sport that the admiring term *Armstrong* won most of its numbers. (I cannot help feeling that the firm of West End jewellers *Longman* and *Strongitharm* would have been formidable opponents.) *Thrower* too might have been used in this connection, though it is also a technical term in the weaving trade, and *Holder*, though that is capable of several interpretations. The winner of the foot races won the *Game* or 'gamen', and from this latter older form the surname *Gammon* arises, having nothing whatever to do with bacon.

Champions who fought to settle legal disputes have already been mentioned. There must also have been 'champions' in these friendly contests, but this was a new-fangled French word, and on the village green the old-fashioned English *Kemp* or *Camp* would be the honoured title for the victors in the fights.

On these occasions there would be all sorts of entertainers to complete the pleasures of the day, *Hoppers*, *Leapers*, *Springers*, *Dancers*, *Pipers* and *Crowders* (or *Crowthers*). These last played a kind of rustic stringed instrument and easily outnumber the more modern sounding *Fiddlers*. Morris dancers inevitably come to mind when we think of this kind of assembly, but if it is true, as is generally stated, that they were first introduced into England from Spain by John of Gaunt, then they came after the close of the surname-forming period. But the name *Morris* was already there before them and meant, when used as an adjective, 'moorish', or in the vaguest possible way, dark-skinned, foreign-looking, or just *Strange*.

The days when work was relaxed and these festive gatherings took place were mostly associated with the feasts of the church. If a child was fortunate enough to be born on one of these holy days, the happy event might be commemorated in his name. If it were a Saint's Day it goes without saying that the name of the saint in question was a likely choice, and saints' names will fill a later chapter. But other more impersonal occasions were also used as names. We still often call a child born at Christmas Noel, and the French have also the regular name Pasquale, formed from their old word for Easter, Pasques. In medieval England it was quite usual to christen a child *Christmas, Nowell, Pask* (which survives also as *Pash, Paish* and the Cornish *Pascoe*) and *Pentecost*, all of which, beginning as first names, passed on naturally into the surname stage. Whether *Halliday* or *Holliday* was ever used as a font name or went straight into being a nickname for one born on a holy day, I am not sure, but it makes no difference to the final result. The pretty name *Loveday* was used as a girls' name before the Conquest and has continued in small numbers ever since. A 'love day' was a special day appointed for the settling of a quarrel or dispute.

Two names that show the importance attached to signs and portents at the time of a child's birth are *Storm* and *Tempest*, both recorded very early. In the Anglo-Saxon Chronicle abnormal weather conditions are often reported. Even in years which contain only the briefest mention of two or three events for the whole kingdom for a year, we see entries such as, 'This year happened the terrible wind'. A child born in the midst of such a frightening occurrence might always have it associated with him in the minds of neighbours. 'Young Thomas who was born in the great storm' becomes in time Tom Storm. In this connection we may reconsider *Snow* and *Frost*. They both occur early and often, without any article or preposition to guide us, simply as Alwin Frost, for instance, from Domesday Book. It is usual to say that they indicate white hair, but it is just as likely that in many cases they are referring to the natural conditions at the time of the boy's birth.

This brings us to that strange pair of names, *Winter* and *Summer*, both moderately common. *Winter* and *Wynter* score 315; *Summer*, which is generally *Summers* or *Somers* or *Sum-*

merson, 260. Before going any further it may be asked, why does Winter appear to be singular and Summer nearly always plural? In the first place this final 's', which has a tendency to attach itself to personal names, is possessive rather than plural, though its use is not perfectly clear; and secondly the reason why 'Winter' does not have it, is that in Old English it was declined in an irregular way, its plural being 'winter', the same as the singular, and its genitive 'wintra', whereas 'sumor' took the inflexions '-as' and '-es' in the normal way. After the Conquest the Old English syntax broke down; inflexions were lost or wrongly applied; 'Winter' as a common noun came in line with others; but as a personal name it resisted the addition of an incorrect '-s'.

This early form helps to prove its antiquity as a name, and there is clear evidence of its early use as a Christian name as well as a nickname. In a list of tenants of Burton Abbey, written soon after 1100, one man is put down simply as Winter, and as late as 1275 we see Winter Mariot in the Hundred Rolls. Therefore if we think of it only as a nickname for an old man we are quite wrong, for it was given to babies at the font. It is in fact yet another seasonal name, like Christmas or Pask, and if we turn back to early sources we will find that it can be narrowed down from the long period that the word generally implies to a particular and briefer period.

In the Anglo-Saxon Chronicle we are constantly told where the king was at Christmas, Easter and Pentecost because at those special dates he wore his crown in state and held great councils. As often as not, especially in earlier times, Christmas is called *Midwinter*. 'Then on midwinter day Archbishop Aldred hallowed him [William I] to king.' There are in our directory a dozen examples of this interesting surname which must have had precisely the same significance as *Christmas*. There are also at least fifty names derived from the old pagan word for this season, *Yule*, spelt in a variety of ways, *Yull, Youle/s, Youell* and probably others; and the name *Winter* must surely have implied that its owner was born – not in the winter generally, which would be far too vague – but during the special twelve days given over to this great winter festival, which, with its pagan traditions overlaid by Christian practices, was of tremendous importance in the lives of our ancestors.

Probably Summer was used as a personal name in the same way as Winter, though its early use is not so well documented. Dr Reaney explains it as being a contracted form of 'sumpter' which meant a pack horse or the man in charge of it, but though it may be that *Summers* has absorbed a number of sumpters and a few summoners too, it must also in many cases represent the summer season which meant so much to country people. The examples which he himself quotes from the Pipe Roll of King John's reign, of Geoffrey and Adam Sumer, appear to be personal, whether nicknames or patronymics. If they were occupational one would expect 'le sumer' at that date, and in surviving forms the almost universal presence of the final '-s', together with the form *Summerson*, strongly indicate a personal name. Our ancestors of that time, with their taste for allegorical figures, must often have personified Winter and Summer in dramatic form, or depicted them in tapestry or wall painting, not in churches, where the saints reigned supreme, but on castle walls from which they have long since vanished. Henry III, giving instructions for the painting of the chimney breast of the Queen's chamber at Westminster, ordered 'on it to be pourtrayed a figure of Winter'. He does not mention Summer, but obviously this too would have made a good picture with a rosy face and a garland of flowers. Anything so visual would readily make a nickname.

Spring, Summer and *Winter* are represented in our surnames, but none that I know of comes directly from 'autumn' or the older English word, 'fall', used in this sense. One might expect to find Harvest, which is a regular German name (Herbst), but there is nothing of the sort. I believe that the idea of crops and fruit and plenty is contained in the word 'summer'. To the medieval mind Summer and Winter were the two chief seasons. The spring festival was intensely important because it was 'bringing in the Summer'. 'Sumer is icumen in, Lhude sing cuccu,' sang the poet in the spring; but the fall was a sad time in comparison, when the year was beginning to die. The Christian feasts of this season, All Souls and All Saints, bring to mind the dead, coinciding with the pre-historic superstitions of ghosts and witches and goblins. Such ideas were not to be spoken of lightly, certainly not to be turned into nicknames.

Chapter 17

AN INFINITE VARIETY

In the foregoing chapters I have tried to arrange surnames derived from nicknames into some sort of logical order, but their variety and numbers are such that many remain which defy classification or interpretation.

A group that is hard to classify consists of names like *Cousin/s*, *Fellowe/s* and *Friend*. Nothing could be easier to understand, but exactly how did they become surnames? Looking through the early records one can see that they nearly always started as part of a longer expression, 'the miller's cousin', 'Robert's friend', and so on, generally referring to a stranger to the community, known only by his connection with a familiar person, and then abbreviated leaving only the relationship. Other names in this class are the obsolete *Neave* (nephew), *Eame* (uncle), and *Maw* or *Maufe* which comes from the Middle English 'maugh' which signified a relation by marriage. It forms the second part of several compounds with personal names such as *Hickmore*, *Watmore* or *Watmough*, signifying one of Hick's or Wat's in-laws. The North Country had a specially strong line in these family connections, as for instance *Bairnsfather*, in which the owner's chief importance seems to have lain in his paternity.

How, one wonders, did anyone remain in a house as a *Guest* long enough for the word to adhere to him and his forever, providing eighty examples in the directory? But the name did not then have quite the same significance as it does now. It meant a stranger and expressed the same idea as the obsolete Old English word 'unwine' (*Unwin*), which was literally 'un-friend' or 'not a friend', or simply an unknown person. It had, in fact, the same meaning as *Strange* or *Newcome* (more often

spelt misleadingly *Newcombe*). In old-fashioned country villages not so long ago a newcomer could be looked on as a
foreigner for years, and this mental attitude is expressed in
Newman which is one of the most numerous of nicknames.

A well defined group of names seems to speak with admiration
and affection of the very young; *Fairchild* (25), *Fairbairn* or
Fairburn, which is the same in origin (60), *Goodchild* (90),
Littlechild (13), *Littleboy* (6). I believe such names were mostly
spoken at first with all sincerity, and stuck through life partly
from habit and partly because later on the absurdity became
amusing. Modern cases of this kind of thing are plentiful; we
only have to think of Babe Ruth or Sonny Hale. The youngest
of all our nicknames is *Suckling*, and this must always have been
given jokingly to a very unsophisticated youth. Something has
already been said of *Child* which standing alone generally meant
a noble youth, but it could also be taken literally, as in the two
compound forms given above.

The familiar words 'baby' and 'boy' are both comparative
latecomers into English. The New English Dictionary has no
example of the former until the late fourteenth century when it
first appears as 'babe'. The latter is first noted about 1300. But
words were generally current for some time before they appeared in the kind of writing that would be preserved. 'Baby'
did just make a few surnames. I have seen examples of it in
early parish registers in Dorset, and there is one *Babey* in the
London Directory. 'Boy' must have been current much earlier,
and examples of it as a nickname can be found from 1066 onwards, though they are never common. Alwin Boi held land in
Surrey before the Conquest (Domesday Book), and Robert
Litelboie was a freeman of Leicester in 1202. The surnames
Boyes and *Boyce* come in many cases from the French 'bois',
corresponding to our *Wood*, but there is no question that they
also may represent the colloquial 'boy' which must have been
much used for a young servant. *Ladd*, with a score of thirty, is
more easily recognized.

Another group of names that strike a note of admiration, but
refer to the more mature, includes *Fairbrother*, *Fairman*,
Goodbody, *Goodfriend*, *Goodfellow*, *Goodsir*, and their French
equivalents *Bellamy* (bel ami), *Bonham* (bonhomme), *Bonser*
(bon sieur), and *Muncer* (monsieur). All these and the others

mentioned above are highly conversational in tone, and would hardly have made surnames unless they were frequently re-iterated. Someone must constantly have spoken of 'my cousin', 'my good friend', 'my little boy', for the label to stick. In many cases the words adhered, not to the person they described, but to the speaker. An overworked phrase can easily make a nick-name. A man who larded his speech with excessively polite phrases, 'good sir' or 'fair brother' and so on, too often repeated, would soon have one of these very tags fixed to himself, and an Englishman who aspired to add a sprinkling of French to his conversation in an affected way might easily find himself addressed as *Bellamy* or *Muncer*.

That a number of nicknames did arise from favourite forms of speech is certain. This brings us back to our old friends from Domesday Book, Roger Bigod and Roger God-save-the-ladies. Descendants of the former have been traced to the seventeenth century when the main line ended, but other branches are thought to have continued. The name still exists as *Bygott* in Yorkshire and in America, probably in true descent, and there are two in the directory.

Whether the other Roger has descendants still using some contracted form of his notable name is not known, but a small group with this sort of origin does exist. *Godsalve*, *Godsave*, *Godsiff*, *Godsall* and *Godsill* are all curtailed remains of pious wishes or imprecations. The last two of these probably represent the oath 'God's soul' which appears in the Hundred Rolls as the surname of a lady, Basilia Godsowele. *Mothersole* comes from 'by my mother's soul', the favourite oath of Ralph Modersoule of Lancashire (1313). *Godber* seems to be from 'God be here', a pleasant expression to use on entering a house. *Goatcher* is simply 'good cheer'.

From the French oath 'par Dieu' we have *Pardoe*, *Pardew* and *Pardy*, while from 'mort de Dieu' comes *Mordue*; but the most numerous of French interjections is the strong plea 'pour Dieu' (for God's sake), which has given us over seventy ex-amples of *Purdue*, *Purdie* and *Purdy*.

As names of this kind were extremely individual, few were ever common and many that we see in the rolls have failed to survive. Three that seem very typical of human speech at any period are Hugh Comment ('What'?), William Jurdemayn

(Tomorrow), both in the Hundred Rolls, and Henry Boiboi (from the Suffolk Poll Tax) whose voice calling his apprentice seems to be still audible.

The speech-names just quoted can be recognized as such by their nature, but there must be many others that belong to this class without our knowing it. After all we cannot expect to understand all the old jokes of so long ago, particularly the very individual ones that occurred perhaps in one single case, understood even then by only a few. For a modern comparison my mind reverts to the boys' school in which I have lived for many years. At the present time a highly respected master has a verbal nickname of this type. At one time he was called 'Bogus' because this was a word he was inclined to use in a caustic tone, being particularly genuine himself, but for many years now he has been simply 'Bogue'. How impossible for anyone of a future generation – let alone of centuries hence – to know the significance of such a name. Thus among the many thousands of English surnames we must expect some that no amount of study can explain, especially among the rarer names. 'Bogue', for instance, is probably unique. On the other hand any surname that is fairly common, and can be found in many parts of the country in the Middle Ages, and in large numbers today, must have a more reasonable origin which we ought to be able to discover.

A fairly common name that has puzzled many writers and is almost certainly a nickname is *Barratt* or *Barrett*. It has over five hundred examples in the London Directory and can be found frequently in medieval documents. The earliest example on record is that of Gamel Baret (or Bared), a Yorkshire landowner in Domesday Book. Gamel is a Norse word meaning 'old' which was often used as a personal name (surviving as *Gammell*, *Gamble* and *Gamlin*), and if this man's nickname was also Scandinavian it may have come from the Norse 'barthr' meaning a beard. However, there is little sign of this word recurring in this two-syllable form, either as a common noun or a name. Some other origin must be responsible for the crop of Barats (often spelt 'Barate') that appears in several Southern counties in the twelfth century. The only word that can account for them is the Old French 'barat' which signified cunning, trickery and fraud, and is now obsolete except in the legal term 'barratry'. This is a curious meaning for so common a name;

however, there are grounds for believing that its earlier significance was of a better nature, in fact something like business
efficiency, but that a deceitful note crept into it, causing it to
fall into disfavour and become obsolete, though not before it had
given rise to many nicknames.

In this way its history is almost parallel with the Old English *Pratt*. In the *Anglo-Norman Chronicle*, written in Latin
about 1200, we are told that Leofwine Prat was so called because he was 'astutus', but a century later the word 'prat'
according to the New English Dictionary meant 'trickery'.
Soon afterwards it became obsolete. This same tendency for
words originally having a meaning of capability to acquire a
disagreeable sense can be observed in several nouns and adjectives. 'Cunning' and 'crafty' originally meant clever and skilful,
and so did 'sly'. 'Knowing' is beginning to go the same way.
Have clever people always been inclined to become 'too clever
by half'? Or is it that the less clever have always distrusted
them? In any case the great majority of *Barratts* or *Barretts*
belong to this type of meaning. Some few may go back to the
bearded Viking from Yorkshire, some very few may be descended from the Norman Christian name Beraud (but there is
no real evidence for this), but most were examples of this colloquial word for a sharp dealer, which came into fashion just at
the right time to make surnames and disappeared again soon
after.

A surname that has caused much discussion without any
certain conclusion being reached is *Metcalfe* which totals just a
hundred in the directory. The early examples in the Yorkshire
Subsidy of 1301 are in almost exactly the same form as that
which exists today. It appears to be a nickname and the general
opinion of the experts is that it represents a 'meat-calf', that is
to say one being fattened for food, a 'fatted calf' in fact, which
in a medieval household would make a likely nickname of a
teasing sort for a plump young person.

Another curious nickname that is well known as a modern
surname without being common is *Quartermain*. Its early
examples, of which there are several of the twelfth and thirteenth centuries, all from Oxfordshire, make it perfectly clear
that the meaning is 'four hands'. But what did a man's friends
have in mind when they called him so? Does this perhaps belong

to the verbal class, springing from words that somebody spoke on a notable occasion? Dr Reaney interprets it as meaning 'a mailed fist', but I do not see it in this way. The French Poincaré, 'square-fist', might have this meaning and would at least signify a fighter, but 'four hands' seems more like a name for a very dexterous person. *Quatermass*, which has recently been given a sinister character by the influence of television, is a corruption of the same name. Incidentally the same idea of being quick with one's hands is expressed in *Hendy* and *Henty* which are variations of the word we know as 'handy'.

A name which appears to have a pleasanter interpretation than its real one is *Lovelace*. It sounds both romantic and well dressed, and seems particularly suitable for a Cavalier poet, but in fact it is just the same in origin as *Loveless*, which appears several times in the Hundred Rolls. There was no lace in medieval England. It seems an unkind name, but perhaps it was ironic and its owner had many loves. Another of this negative sort is *Carless*, meaning careless in the sense of carefree.

One might go on for ever picking out odd nicknames which require explanation, and there are many cases where none can be given with certainty. In *Stallabrass*, which exists in several spellings, the second part seems to be the French word for 'arms', but the first part remains a mystery. *Cramphorne* means 'crumpled-horn', but is this a metaphor for a cripple, or a description of the owner's cow? Is *Jellicoe* a corruption of the French 'Jolicorps' (literally 'merry-body'), or something quite different? Do *Peabody* and *Paybody*, which must be the same, signify someone who behaves like a peacock? Is *Lillicrap* a crop or flowering of lilies? In all such cases more evidence from an early date is needed to prove or disprove the conjectures.

When we look back over the whole field of nicknames what strikes us first is their enormous diversity. Individually their numbers are far lower than names of the occupational class, but their variety is even greater.

The list on page 329 shows clearly that the surnames in this class with the highest numbers are all plain Old English monosyllables, describing salient points of appearance and behaviour. But these simple terms are themes on which endless metaphorical variations were played. There were twenty different ways of saying a man was fair or dark or brave, and even more suggesting that he was a fine young fellow, a *Buck* or a *Cock* or a *Sprigg*, the theme of youth running strongly through the whole mixture.

The next salient point about nicknames is their antiquity, particularly that of the short, simple ones that have lasted so well. In the Norman period a wonderfully creative spirit among all classes of society produced a profusion of new nicknames, consisting largely of fanciful compounds and phrase-names; but none of these attained anything like the numbers of the short, Old English words that had been in use for centuries before the Conquest, both as common nouns and adjectives, and also as personal names.

In trying to study such names we are drawn farther and farther back into the past and can find no beginning. In an earlier chapter we considered nicknames from the animal and vegetable kingdoms, and noted that some of these, such as *Cock* and *Budd*, had been used in much the same way since pre-Christian times. We might have gone on to minerals, for they too were freely used as metaphors in the surname period, *Flint* and *Steel*, which typified the much admired qualities of hardness and endurance, being especially popular. But this admiration was no new thing, and once again this subject, if followed, would draw us back to that of early personal names. *Gold* and *Stone* (as 'stan') were regular Anglo-Saxon name-themes; *Cole*, meaning 'charcoal', was yet another of the many metaphors for a dark man, like the French *Maurice*, (like *Neal* and *Maurice*) that attained the status of a regular Christian name, while continuing in use as a nickname. It occurs frequently in Domesday Book either alone, as Cola, or in compounds such as *Coleman*. It was a name shared by the English, Celts, and Scandinavians, while the Normans used a similar idea in their diminutive *Carbonell* (a little lump of coal), a nickname for a small, dark man.

At this point classification breaks down altogether. *Carbonell* was always a nickname, but *Cole* and *Coleman* were more often Christian names. *Hawk, Cock, Swan, Winter* and many more were both, and no purpose is served in trying to distinguish the two uses, for the meaning is exactly the same in both cases. But it is of interest to understand them and how one merged into the other.

We have seen that most of the Anglo-Saxon names were formed by putting two words together, such as Dun-stan and God-wine. But of course in intimate daily use they were often shortened again to one of their elements, and it is from such colloquial use that our surnames sprang. We must also remember that as the upper classes were the first to adopt the new fashion in names, so it was the unlettered peasantry who continued longest with the old ones. Here in the vernacular the old names lived on in their simplest and shortest forms, so that it is certain that not only many nouns like *Cock* and *Hawk*, but also adjectives like *Bright* and *Good* and *Dunn* were in spoken use in the twelfth century as abbreviated personal names.

And when the Old English names dropped out of formal use altogether and even peasants christened their children William and Robert, all these old names and themes, which were still current in the language as ordinary words, made the easiest and most familiar nicknames.

Brown makes a good example of this double use. At the time of the Conquest it was still a regular Christian name (as Bruno still is in Italy), and occurs several times in Domesday Book simply as Brun. But within a few years it is to be found freely in the second position as a surname or a nickname, signifying, as it always had, that the man in question was dark. *White* took the same course. Many place names, such as Whittington which occurs in several counties and means the 'tun' of Hwita's (or White's) people, show it to have been a popular name for a leader of men in the pre-Christian pioneering days, and from then onwards it never ceased to be in use as a personal name of one kind or another. Brown, White and Black were all regular themes in the Old English name system, used in such compounds as Brunwine, Hwitheard and Blaecstan, and all three are recorded as surnames in the eleventh century and ever since.

In the list on page 329 I have classed most of these old favourites as nicknames because that was the way in which they were chiefly used during the surname period, but the fact that they had in earlier times been first names given at the font should not be lost sight of. Some of them will be met with again in the next section.

III. Names of Relationship

Chapter 18

FAMILIARITIES

Anyone who has given even a moment's thought to the subject of surnames knows that hundreds of them are formed from Christian names and imply that the bearers were the sons or other near relations of the persons named. Many years ago I formed the plan of counting separately all the surnames in the London Telephone Directory derived from popular Christian names in order to discover, by comparing their individual totals, which really were the favourite names in thirteenth-century England. The idea was basically sound; I had already tried it with trade-names and obtained interesting results; but I soon found that in the matter of Christian names it was a much more complicated undertaking, and could not be carried out with any approach to accuracy without considerable preliminary study. Whatever the value of the final list, the making of it taught me a great deal about medieval names.

The chief difficulty in the way of allotting modern surnames to the Christian names from which they sprang is the enormous number of abbreviations and familiar forms that arose in the Middle Ages, many of which have strayed so far from their original that they are quite hard to recognize. But it is in this very atmosphere of familiarity that the charm of the subject lies. It brings us close to the men and women who used these brief, easy-going names, Wat and Gib and Perkin, which in contemporary documents were nearly always set down formally as Walterus, Gilbertus and Petrus. If it were not for our surnames we should have little knowledge of what people called each other in those far off times. We should hardly know that David was Daw or Dawkin to his friends and that Richard became

Hick as well as Dick, but when we look in a modern directory and see the great numbers of *Dawsons* and *Hicksons* we begin to realize the popularity of such forms.

These familiar versions of Christian names are generally called 'pet-names' by writers on surnames, a term I do not much care for, but a useful one for distinguishing them from nicknames, which are formed from quite a different source. If, for instance, a certain Thomas is called the Fox or Lightfoot, it is a nickname; when he is simply Tom it is an abbreviation; but when the familiarity takes the form of adding a syllable to make it Tomkin we need a term for this new expression which is different from Thomas but derived from it. The common custom in making a name more intimate was first to shorten it and then to add to it. Thus Robert became first Rob and then Robin, which seems now to have a separate life of its own, but originated as a pet-form of Robert. In official medieval documents the name Robin is hardly ever seen, being usually written as Robertus. But hundreds of examples of *Robinson* and *Robbins* in our modern directories show how it was commonly spoken.

After the Conquest a great many diminutive and familiar suffixes of French origin began to be popular in England, chief among them '-in', or '-on', '-et' or '-ot', and '-el'. Often, after one of these had adhered to a name, another joined itself on too, giving such forms as *Hewlet* (Hugh -el -et), and *Tomlin* (Tom -el -in). They were used just as 'y' has been in modern times. We only add this to short forms; we never say 'Thomasy' but 'Tommy', and so it was in general with these medieval endings, a rare exception being William -ot (*Wilmot*). In later times some of them came into fashion again as feminine endings ('-ine' and '-et'), but in the Middle Ages they served equally for both sexes.

Another diminutive ending which became immensely popular was '-kin'. It is generally thought to have originated in Flanders (William I's wife was Flemish, and many of her countrymen came into England during his reign); but it gradually spread to all parts of the country, being readily joined to shortened forms of all the newly popular Norman and Biblical names, so that men hailed their friends as *Wilkin* and *Watkin* everywhere. This '-kin' had nothing to do with 'kindred' but was merely a diminutive suffix closely allied to the Old English '-ing', the French '-in', and probably the Welsh '-cyn', and its similarity with all these forms must have helped its rapid spread.

In the forms *Simpkin* and *Tompkin* it will be noticed that a
'p' has crept in to ease the transition from 'm' to 'k'. We must
accustom ourselves to these intrusive letters which often slipped
into a word to help it to glide more easily on the tongue, or to
give it a firmer ending, as in the case of the final 'd' which
nearly always attached itself to the end of Simon making the
surnames *Symmonds*.

Yet another familiar name-ending which sprang into popularity early in the surname period was '-cock', a word that had
been used as an independent nickname in England as far back
as our records go, and now took on a new lease of life as a mere
suffix. Added to a brief form of any Christian name it bestowed
on it at once a lively, cheerful character that was essentially
familiar and youthful. It seems to have been used chiefly for
serving boys who were inclined to be pert or 'cocky'; but boys
grow old; names bestowed on children come to be used by men,
and these '-cock' names have attained permanence in great
numbers. Thus we have *Wilcock, Simcock, Adcock* ('Ad' being
short for Adam), *Alcock* (for Alan), and a great many more. As
with most Christian names, when they passed into being surnames, a final 's' was frequently added, and quite often this was
combined with the 'ck' and spelt with an 'x', which is a very
practical short cut in spelling but tends to disguise the original
form. Until one has got one's eye in for this sort of thing, one
does not recognize *Wilcox* and *Simcox* as meaning Wilcock's or
Simcock's.

The way in which the new Norman names were truly taken to
heart and anglicized in pronunciation is shown by the fact that
it was always the first syllable that was retained and worked on.
The French in making similar pet-names have always been
more inclined to use the second syllable. Robert in France became Bertin; Richard led to Chardin; Thomas produced Masset
or Mass-in-et; Simon, Monet and so forth. Thus, though Robert
and Richard were originally Norman names, Robin and Dickon
are thoroughly English.

A particular trick that the English were much inclined to when
forming pet-names was rhyming. Robert became not only Rob
but Hob and Dob; Richard, Hick and Dick; Roger, Hodge

and Dodge. This Humpty-Dumpty, Georgie-Porgie kind of speech has continued with us into modern times, showing its vitality by dropping old forms and producing new ones. Robert no longer becomes Hob but is often Bob; William becomes Bill, which was never so in the Middle Ages; Edward, which in the nineteenth century was often Ned, is now more often Ted; but the total absence of Nedsons and Tedsons shows that these forms were not medieval. Cockney rhyming slang is yet another manifestation of this popular English tendency.

What is particularly noticeable in the surname period is that names beginning with an 'R' were rhymed far more than any other. In fact every popular 'R-' name has rhymed forms existing beside the original name. It appears that the English had a difficulty with this letter. To this day 'R' is the consonant which English children find hardest to master; nor is this weakness entirely confined to children, or anything to do with class distinction. Many of the highest in the land have a slight weakness in respect to this letter all their lives, and as a nation we tend to pronounce it less and less. We have lost it altogether at the ends of words and syllables, making no difference between 'farther' and 'father' and no 'r' sound at the end of either. The Americans and Scots have kept it in these positions, but we have let it go.

This ancient weakness must be at the root of our forefathers' tendency to turn an initial R into something else, preferably H or D. Three of the leading Norman names began with R, and though among the upper classes they retained their full forms, Robert, Richard and Roger, among the lower they were usually rhymed. That these rhyming forms represent the pronunciation of the English peasantry (who, it must be remembered, far outnumbered the gentry of both races), is undoubted. In Old English many common words began with an aspirated 'r'. 'Roof', for instance, was 'hrof', 'ring' was 'hring', and whereas the better class Saxons who adapted themselves to Norman rule learnt to speak some French and pronounce Norman names correctly, the peasant spoke the same names with a strongly aspirated English accent. He must have been laughed at for it by his betters. 'Hob', 'Hodge' and 'Hick' became in time recognized types for the simple countryman. One of the meanings given for 'hob' in the New English Dictionary is 'a rustic, or clown'. To 'hobble' was to walk with the heavy gait of a peasant, or 'hobbledehoy'. Hodge too is defined as 'an English rustic'. The food he ate was called 'hodge-podge' or 'hotch-potch', and the old country name for a snail, 'hoddy', again indicated his slow pace. 'Hick' has even crossed the Atlantic and started a new life there in this same old countrified sense, and perhaps Hob has kept him company as a possible origin of 'hobo'.

These developments are mostly later than the formation of our surnames, but they demonstrate the rustic character that this group of names came to typify.

These brief, familiar forms to which noble Norman names were reduced in the fields and farmyards, were mere starting points to which any of the diminutives and familiar suffixes could be added with local variations. Hob often became Hobkin, and the 'k' had the effect of sharpening the 'b' so that this form soon became *Hopkin*. The medial 'ch' in Richard was originally hard, and this early pronunciation survives in such names as *Ricketts*, *Hicks* and *Dickens*, while *Riggs*, *Higgins* and *Diggins* echo the sound of thicker speech. The later soft 'ch', which soon developed in Richard in the South and later spread over most of the country, can be heard in *Hitchins*, *Hitchcock* (sometimes softened further into *Hiscock*) and *Richings* which has acquired an excrescent 'g' simply because '-ing' was a familiar ending to the English.

I have picked out only a few of the many variations on the themes of Richard and Robert to illustrate the kind of thing that went on when the English nation adopted Norman names. It is strange to think that *Richings*, *Higgins* and *Dickens* are all exactly the same name, differing only in pronunciation; strange too that a Norman name like Richard with the addition of two French suffixes can produce such an essentially English name as *Hignett*.

Another point that is worth consideration at this stage is the old unwritten law of differentiation. In the Anglo-Saxon period the variety of Christian names was endless, and in one community it was rare indeed for two people to have the same name. But after the Conquest, when the new name system had swept the country, a small number of names became immensely popular. When one looks at the Subsidy Rolls where taxpayers are written down parish by parish, one is amazed to see the same Christian name, perhaps that of a former lord of the manor or a popular local saint, repeated over and over. In one village a third of the boys are called John, in another there is as high a proportion of Williams. How, one wonders, did they manage? Of course they had to differentiate them. One was plain Will, others were *Wilkin, Wilcock, Willett, Wilmot* and so forth. Even so they needed nicknames and other descriptive additions as well. But when the tax-collector set it down on the parchment roll that may still be seen in the Public Record Office, he wrote Willielmus for each one.

We see now that these many and diverse pet-forms were the English peasants' answer to the new fashion of Norman names. They accepted them and then knocked them into familiar shapes something like the names of their forefathers, just as the old lady who buys a smart new hat alters it to make it look like her old one. We have seen that the majority of recorded Anglo-Saxon names are of the formal two-theme type like Cuthbert and Godric, but besides these there existed a vast number of simple short forms such as Cutha, Goda, Cola and Wulfa, all of which would lose the final vowel and become monosyllables by the twelfth century. By the time the new Norman names were reduced to their simplest terms in the same way there was not much to choose between them and these old ones of native origin. Dodda or Dudda, for instance, appears in many pre-Conquest documents. Leofsi Dudde sunu (the son of Dud) owned land in Wormley, Hertfordshire, during the reign of the Confessor, and in Domesday Book Alwin Dodesone (surely of the same family) is recorded as a tenant in the same place. A century or so later if a Saxon was christened by the Norman name Roger, his friends would be liable to turn it into Dodge, and then Dod. The more things change the more they are the same. If your surname is *Dodd* or *Dodds* it is impossible to know if it comes from Norman Roger or Old English Dodda, but it is certain that it was among Englishmen that it became fixed in this form.

That these brief forms were mostly used by the lower ranks of society is undoubted, and is illustrated very plainly in a Latin poem written by Chaucer's contemporary John Gower on the subject of Tyler's rebellion. Describing the confusion and violence in the mob of peasants, he names individuals among them,

Watte, Thomme, Symme, Bette, Gibbe, Hykke, Colle, Geffe, Wille, Grigge, Dawe, Hobbe, Lorkyn, Hudde, Judde, Tebbe and Jakke, names that seem strangely incongruous interspersed with formal Latin, an effect which no doubt he intended to create. With a little modification in spelling all are modern surnames, and the only one of them not common enough to qualify for the list of favourites (page 332) is Tebbe, which comes from Theobald and is best known in such forms as *Tebbit*, *Tebbut*, *Tibbs*, *Tibble* and so on. Such names were not found in aristocratic circles. There they were Gilbert, Richard, Geoffrey, Lawrence and so on in full. But these Gibbs and Hicks and Geffs and Lawkins, though harshly put back in their places on the occasion described in this poem, were not to be kept down for long, and within a century or two many names of this type were beginning to appear in high positions.

So far all the variations of name forms mentioned in this chapter, the dropping of parts and adding on of others, were merely to make them more homely and friendly as Christian names. The additions that turned such names into surnames are quite another matter and may be briefly mentioned here. The most commonly used suffixes for the purpose are of course '-son' and '-s', which will be further discussed in the next chapter. They add still more to the great variety of different derivative forms for each simple Christian name.

Besides these two well-known patronymic endings, there are two more regular additions to personal names expressing relationship. The first is Fitz- which is simply the Old French 'fiz' or 'filz' meaning 'son'. (Its curious spelling appears to me to be simply a misreading of the Latin 'filius' which was often written in a contracted form 'filŝ', the line over the 's' which indicated the omission of letters making the 'l' look very like a 't'.) This was a short-lived development of the Normans in England, which never really took root. It was used freely by the top layer of society in the eleventh and twelfth centuries, and Henry II's expedition to Ireland resulted in several Norman families taking it there, notably the three sons of Gerald of Windsor who were known as William, Maurice and David Fitz-Gerald, each of whom had a great progeny of that name. But in England, though a few noble families have kept their early established

Fitz- names to the present day, the form soon dropped out of general use. However its use by Norman royal and baronial circles gave it a strongly aristocratic character, and ever since that period it has made a convenient method of creating new surnames for illegitimate sons of royalty, being used in that way right down to the nineteenth century when a number of *Fitz Georges* and *Fitz Clarences* were added to this exclusive category.

At the opposite end of the social scale from Fitz-, one more surname suffix which was frequently added to a Christian name is '-man', meaning a servant or attendant. It is very natural that such a person should often be referred to by his master's name, and that a distinction should be made between *Harrison* and *Harriman*. The possessive 's' which we might expect to find in such cases is always dropped. It was not the universal genitive inflexion in Middle English, as it is now, and at this time there was a strong tendency to drop unnecessary letters. We have many similar pairs, *Jackson* and *Jackman*, *Hickson* and *Hickman*, *Sanderson* and *Sandiman*, and so on. These forms belong chiefly to the North. In the South the relationship of one man to another, whether by blood or other ties, was more often expressed by the brief '-s' or by no addition of any kind, as with the name *Martin*.

Thus a Christian name could come all the way from the eleventh century to the twentieth with no change at all, or it could be shortened, lengthened and generally knocked about and still make the same long journey in large numbers.

Until all this business of pet-names and suffixes was thoroughly mastered I could not compile my list of the Christian names that had made the most surnames. Even so there remained some problems that could not be resolved, some abbreviated forms like Dod which could be derived from more than one name. All I could do in such a case was to divide the numbers between the alternatives. In spite of difficulties the count was eventually made with as much accuracy as possible, and the resulting list on page 324 gives a picture of medieval names for the whole country and all classes of society that is basically true. The figures must be regarded as an approximation, but a close one. Another student would arrive at slightly different results owing to different decisions on doubtful points, but these are generally concerned with comparatively small numbers, and the overall picture would remain largely the same.

The first thing that strikes one on glancing through these top-scoring names is their modernity. The very same set of names that were first favourites in Norman and early Plantagenet England are the first favourites of today, or nearly so. Some, well known now, are missing, and some little known were common then, but on the whole the change of fashion is remarkably slight for so long a time.

On the other hand, though the full names have stood the test of time well, the pet-forms revealed so clearly have mostly disappeared (except in surnames). A fond modern mother of a young Richard or Robert might call him Dick or Rob, but she would be hardly likely to call him Hitchcock or Hopkin.

Another striking point which emerges from this list is the enormous number of surnames it represents as compared with those of the two preceding classes. Not only does one Christian name produce a dozen or more quite different surnames, but many of these individual names exist in large numbers. If all the known ways of spelling each name were included, the list would be multiplied to an unmanageable extent. A straightforward name like Philip can be spelt in four ways merely by doubling or not doubling two of the consonants. As each version could have '-s' or '-son' added to it we have twelve possible forms before starting on other variations. A list of such a kind would be far too long, and inexpressibly tedious to look through, and therefore only the principal variations of each name are given. But the point must be made that if all the different spellings were included one Christian name could make fifty or more surnames.

In this list I have given only the Christian names which with all their derivatives give rise to surnames totalling over five hundred in the directory. There are forty-six which reach this number, and for purposes of comparison I have added the six native Welsh names which qualify by the same standard, bringing our list up to fifty-two. At least as many again could be found with numbers exceeding a hundred, of which only a few selected ones can be given. This may seem to belie the statement that after the Conquest a multitude of names gave place to fewer and more popular ones, but many of these names that have left us hundreds of surnames were already dropping rapidly out of use when the surnames were formed. In any case the population of England was something over two million in the thirteenth century, and about a hundred regular names is not very many among a million men.

Chapter 19

PATRONYMIC PROBLEMS

The completed list of surnames from men's Christian names, given on page 332, raises some general problems. Firstly the Welsh question looms rather large and must be considered here. It has already been pointed out that the native Welsh names are completely distinct, but those that are shared with the English, such as *Williams*, cause a complication. The fact that the Welsh have so few surnames makes their numbers highly concentrated, and therefore in putting names in order it is of interest to recognize their influence and assess it as nearly as possible.

A list of the principal surnames in Wales may be found on page 336 based on a Cardiff Directory. This city was chosen to match the other capitals of the British Isles given on the same page, but, doubting whether it was sufficiently typical of Wales as a whole, I also took statistics from five smaller towns in North and Mid-Wales, which verified that these leading names occur in much the same order all over the principality. The only difference that I found was that in North Wales *Roberts* and *Hughes* were higher while *James* and *Jenkins* were lower than in Cardiff; but these are minor points, *Jones*, *Davies* and *Williams* being easy winners everywhere. By combining all these statistics together I had a scale of numbers for popular Welsh surnames, and by comparing any one of them with a purely Welsh name (*Evans*) first in this Welsh scale and then in the London Directory, which I have used as a standard of measurement throughout, I was able to calculate approximately what proportion of its London numbers must be of Welsh origin. This experiment showed clearly that when the Welsh began using English Christian names they took to them in very much the same proportions as those in which they were used in England. As they also continued to use their own native names they did not adopt a wide range of English ones, only the dozen or so that were most popular, which multiplied fast. Consequently, when these became in due course surnames and overflowed into England they only swelled the numbers of what were already the leading names, and if we could subtract them from our list the general effect would be to telescope it, but not greatly to affect the order. The three leading names would lose some thousands, those following less in proportion to their numbers, most of those with low scores being unaffected.

The chief exception to this general similarity of order is David, which naturally enjoyed special favour in Wales on account of its patron saint and native princes. Its regular Welsh form as a surname is *Davies* and if we omitted this whole block of over sixteen hundred from our list the name would fall by many places. *Lewis* is so predominantly Welsh that I have classed it as such, though occasionally it must have originated from the French Louis, but it is far more often a shortened form of that most famous of all Welsh names, *Llewellyn*. It has also been used by Jews recently as an anglicization of Levi, so that altogether it is a difficult name to classify, though most individual families with this name know very well their country of origin, generally Wales.

At least 90% of the *Joneses* (and there are over three thousand of them) are of Welsh origin, which is not surprising, seeing that it is *Johns* with a Welsh accent. But no hard and fast line can be drawn between these two. They are so much alike that they must have overlapped and interchanged frequently, especially in counties on the Welsh border. By the end of the surname period John had easily passed William in popularity, the two of them remaining supreme favourites in England, a fact that is truly echoed by the Welsh surnames.

That *Williams* is nearly as Welsh in origin as *Jones*, seems at first puzzling. One would think that a name of such enormous popularity in England during the whole surname period would have left many English *Williamses*. But a renewed study of documents of the fourteenth century, when the bulk of English surnames were lately settled, showed that though William abounds as a first name it very seldom appears in full as a surname at this date. As with John its very popularity militated against its too frequent use in this way, unless in some variegated form like *Willett* or *Wilcock*. In earlier centuries noble families had often been proud to call themselves Fitz William, or simply William, remembering a distinguished forbear, but as the name became increasingly common they frequently acquired other more distinctive surnames, and in later times, when Tom, Dick and Harry were getting their second names in colloquial style, the usual form among them was Will, giving the regular English surnames *Wills* and *Wilson*.

But where the English had unconsciously held back from the most obvious forms of these names, the Welsh had no inhibitions. When the time was ripe for them they simply took their fathers' names in full, adding a possessive 's' to make up for the Ap (son of) which they used in their own language, with the result that *Jones* and *Williams*, the two most common names in Wales, are now among the first half dozen in England too. But though their numbers are almost entirely due to their Welsh popularity, we should remember that many families that adopted them on migrating to England did so several hundred years ago, and their descendants have long been completely English.

In the case of other leading names something similar happened but to a lesser extent. About three-quarters of the *Thomases* are Welsh, or were so once. With *Edwards*, *Richards*, *Roberts*, *James*, and *Hughes* the Welsh proportion is about half or a little under, but in each group on our list it is only the one form of the surname that is affected, the many totally English forms of the same names (such as *Thompson*, *Robinson*, and so on) serving to maintain a high total.

Even if the Welsh numbers could be taken out of our list, John and William would still head it; and though David would fall a long way, Thomas lose a few places, and Edward, having few popular variations to support it, slip down even further, yet on the whole changes of order would be few; those of interest will be mentioned when we look at the names in more detail.

The next question concerns the common patronymic suffixes '-son' and '-s' as applied to Christian names. Their use and

meaning may appear to be so simple and obvious as to require
no explanation at all, but the matter is more complicated than it
appears at first sight. The final 's', for instance, that came so
naturally to the Welsh as a possessive form, is a very late development in England, seldom met with before the late thirteenth century and not in any number until the fourteenth. At
the first thought, it seems that Robins must be a shortened form
of 'Robin's son', but this is not the way in which it happened.
The evidence shows that the surname was Robin first and developed a final 's' at a much later date, in fact the process was
the very reverse of what we should expect. Even the natural
Old English way of making a patronymic by adding '-son',
though we see it often at about the time of the Conquest, as in
the case of Alwin Dodesone quoted in the previous chapter,
disappears before 1200 and is hardly to be met with until the
Poll Tax of 1379 when it reappears in great strength, especially
in the North.

There is not a large amount of contemporary evidence on this
point because names are so often given in Latin, which conceals
their actual form, but there is enough to show what was going
on, and when we do find patronymic surnames written in their
natural form during this period, nine times out of ten they
consist of the father's name, quite plain, with no addition at all
whether formal or familiar, Robert Rolfe, John Roger, John
Hobbe.

But if contemporary evidence is in short supply, the evidence
of modern surnames is decisive on this point. Although all the
Christian names, that were still in high favour in the fourteenth
century, acquired these regular suffixes to some extent, the
names whose popularity had waned before that time do not
have them. This includes all the pre-Conquest survivals except
Edward and Edmund, which were revived at the latter end of
the surname period, and Cuthbert, which survived genuinely in
the North long enough to make a few examples of *Cuthbertson*.
But Godwinson (if it was ever used like that in one word, which
as far as I know is unrecorded) survives only as *Godwin* or
Goodwin. Nor do we ever meet a Mr Oswalds, Edgars or Ayl-
wards; such forms sound absurd. The same observation applies
to names of continental origin that were common in England in
the early surname period but not later. We have *Baldwin*,

Gerard, Randall, Austin, Osmond, Harvey and many more, all perfectly plain without suffixes of any kind.

The fact is that when we see a form like Godricson in an early record it is still making a statement of current truth, but as soon as it ceased to be true and became a hereditary surname the '-son' dropped off, as many other unnecessary inflections were doing at that same time. The mere fact of placing the name in a secondary position after the Christian name was enough to express paternity or descent.

This statement applies equally to French and English, and when we come to think of it the French have no patronymic affix as most countries do. Looking around we see 'Mac' in the Highlands, 'Ap' in Wales, 'O' ' in Ireland, '-sen' in Scandinavia, '-vitch' in Russia, but no equivalent in France. The son of Hugo is Victor Hugo, and that is the normal thing. 'De' refers only to places. 'Fitz-' developed only in England and did not last long there. But I am not suggesting that French influence had anything to do with the English practice, for it is the Anglo-Saxon Christian names that are most consistent in adding neither '-son' nor '-s'.

It is not until late in the thirteenth century, when the scribes are writing more and more names in a natural, unlatinized form, that a final '-s' begins to appear quite frequently. Oddly enough most of the earliest examples are of women, so much so that some writers have been led to suggest that the final '-s' was at first a regular feminine form. But it soon became far too general and numerous as a means of forming surnames for both sexes for that idea to be convincing. But the female element helps to emphasize the point that this '-s' represented dependence. Alis Dawkins could be the wife, widow, daughter or servant of Dawkin, the '-s' showing the possession or responsibility on his part. Equally the name might refer to Dawkin's son, or nephew, or man-servant or anyone in his household.

That this '-s' form began in a very colloquial way among the working people is made clear by the fact that we see it first far more on pet-forms than on formal names, and we can be certain that, before it appeared much in writing, people were talking about Tom Hobbs and Will Perkins, meaning 'Tom over at Hobb's place' and 'Will at Perkin's'. Written forms always lag far behind speech, but the spoken word will force its way to the front at last. We must remember that in the first century or so after the Conquest it was mostly the upper classes who were using surnames, and if a man was called Stephen Walter or John Philip it was perfectly understood that the second name belonged to his father or some remoter forbear of distinction. If he were Norman the prefix 'Fitz-' might be used; if he were English '-son' might be added, but neither was necessary and both had a strong tendency to drop off. It was a very different matter a century or two later when thousands of men of the peasant or servant class were needing second names, and their masters' names were frequently being used for the purpose. I believe it was this tendency that caused a strong revival of the suffix '-son' which now reappeared in force. It expressed a natural wish to distinguish Wat's son from his other miscellaneous dependants.

The earliest parish registers, which begin in 1538, show us the general state of surnames when the fixing period was over and everyone was provided with a family name, but the Welsh influence was still slight, especially in the Eastern counties. What we see is that by this time nearly all the surnames from familiar forms end in '-s' or '-son', but that most of the full-length names are still without any addition. This situation is exemplified in the modern surname *Gilbert* which is still generally without a suffix, though its pet-forms are generally found as *Gibbs*, *Gibson* and *Gibbons*.

The suffix '-son' needs little further explanation. Its late appearance as a permanent form is due to the final rush of surname-making in the late fourteenth century when every kind of ending was needed to give variety. It was much used in the northern counties at that time, and also in the Lowlands of Scotland. The Scots had their own distinctive Christian names, such as *Malcolm* and *Duncan* which like early English names became surnames without change, but Norman names spread into Scotland as they did into Wales, and when the Scots adopted surnames, which they did rather later than the English, hundreds of them became *Wilson, Johnson* and *Robertson* like their neighbours south of the border.

But whereas '-son' developed in a reasonable way from a genuine relationship, the final '-s', having once started as a popular form with a wider meaning, spread with little reason except as a catching fashion, with the result that families that had already for several generations been Robert or Wat turned willy-nilly into *Roberts* and *Watts*.

This new development can only be explained by the power of analogy. During the creative surname period the natural tendency had been to vary one name from another, but when that was all over and every family had a name which it took for granted, an opposite tendency towards uniformity began to work. If a number of names of one sort ended in '-s', a general feeling could easily arise that '-s' was the proper ending for this sort of name. We have seen that certain excrescent letters had a way of sticking on to names (like the 'd' on Symond) just to round them off and give them what seemed to the English tongue good endings. English speakers have always liked '-s' as a word ending, keeping all the Old English inflexions that ended in that way (plurals, possessives and third person singular of the verbs) at a time when they were dropping all the others. Anyone who doubts that the English find 's' a pleasant, friendly ending to a word should ask themselves why Barbara can sometimes be abbreviated to Babs, or why a cockney street-vendor will address a single customer not only as 'duck' but 'ducks'. Thus the '-s' ending attached itself particularly to the most familiar forms.

The full-length names resisted this addition longer than the short colloquial ones, and probably many more would have remained permanently without it if the Welsh influence had not affected them, but when during the Tudor period more and more Williamses and Robertses from Wales were to be found everywhere the force of analogy generally proved too strong. Anyone with a surname that differs slightly from a common one will know what a continual effort has to be made to preserve the small difference. Today, when the importance of spelling has been dinned into us since childhood we do make the effort; 'Two "t's",' we repeat incessantly over innumerable counters. But in earlier times when only a minority could write, spelling changed easily and with it small differences of sound, and a less common form could converge with a well-known one almost without those concerned being aware of it.

It is very noticeable that the surnames from Christian names that were most taken up by the Welsh were the most affected by this trend, and we have already seen that names that had gone out of fashion early, like *Austin* or *Allan*, were not affected at all; but in between these extremes the intermediate names were influenced only slowly or in part. This may easily be checked by looking through any early printed lists of surnames. In this way anyone may see that before 1600 *Philip, Walter* and *Adam*, for example, appear as surnames far more often without an '-s' than with one, whereas now the position is reversed. In the Catalogue of Wills of the Prerogative Court of Canterbury, which includes examples from all parts of the country, the section before 1558 contains twenty-seven examples of *Matthew* to only two of *Matthews*; from 1605 to 1620 the numbers are twenty to six; fifty years later they are twenty-five to twelve. So we see the '-s' steadily increasing until in the modern directory we have only thirty-one without it to 580 with; and this is not an unusual case.

Thus right into modern times this same tendency has continued. I was myself surprised when, indulging in a little personal genealogy, I traced the antecedents of my Cornish great grandparents of the name of *Johns*, only to find that as late as the mid-eighteenth century the whole family wrote it as *John*. Indeed at that date this latter form was almost universal in Cornwall, but when the family migrated to Plymouth in about 1790 they conformed with general usage and assumed an '-s'. *John* is still to be found. Again among family letters I find one of 1840 in which a great aunt, speaking of her husband, a prebendary of Salisbury Cathedral, advised her sister, 'Do warn your young friend not to address Dr Jacob as Dr *Jacobs* again. There is nothing better calculated to annoy him. But people *will* do it.' The last sentence seems to sum up the matter.

However it is to be observed that although surnames that were still in popular use as first names were liable to receive this addition right up to modern times, those that were forgotten were immune. This applies not only to early Christian names like Godwin, but also to pet-forms, and helps us to date the various fashions. For instance the once popular diminutive '-et', which we see in *Willett, Hewlett, Hignett* and others, must have gone out early, for it hardly ever has an '-s', but the '-kin' forms (*Perkins, Tompkins* and so on) are hardly ever without it, and therefore must have remained in vogue much later. In fact we have a useful means of dating names of this class.

We see now that the development of patronymics in this country is a long story. Many that were formed in the century after the Conquest have run the whole course unchanged; others of the same vintage received the addition of a final '-s' when they were already centuries old. In the thirteenth century a second great wave of surname-making may be distinguished when the masses were getting their names and every kind of variation and suffix was called into play. Then, later again, when English surnames as a whole had settled down, newcomers from Wales and Scotland brought more names of the same kind, each of their own special variety, to augment the mixture yet further.

Chapter 20

NORMAN FAVOURITES

Having taken some pains to discover which Christian names are most strongly represented as surnames in the modern directory, we go on to consider these winners in more detail and try to find out the causes of their popularity. In so doing we must come a little nearer to the minds and tastes of our medieval forbears.

Two distinct groups of names are clearly recognizable among them, on the one hand those of Teutonic and heathen origin, and on the other the literally Christian names taken from the Bible and the saints. Anglo-Saxon names belong linguistically to the former group, but they are notably lacking from this list of high scoring names. Edward, the one exception, owes its place to Plantagenet patronage and later Welsh popularity.

Let us take first the typically Norman names which belong to the first group, being Norse or Frankish in origin and similar in style to the Old English names, though seldom exactly the same. Of all the innovations the Normans brought with them, hardly anything has been so completely accepted and so long lasting as the names of those very men who leapt on to the shingle of Pevensey in the Autumn of 1066. Native institutions were largely to continue, the native language was to win through, but the personal names of the conquerors' race, particularly of the handful of leaders, once established on the top layer of society were to seep gradually down to all classes to the near extinction of those that were there before.

The name of the king led the way. William I was feared, and William II hated, yet nothing could stay the process of christening little Williams in the chapels of the new Norman castles and in the village churches. It took more than a century for the name to be truly accepted by the people, but by about 1200 it was supreme.

The other top-scoring Norman names, Robert, Richard, Henry, Walter, Hugh, Gilbert, Roger and Ralph, all totalling over a thousand on our list, are almost identical with those of the most powerful tenants-in-chief in Domesday Book. To this exalted group we should add Alan, a Breton name but one that was prominent in the Conqueror's exclusive circle, and high scoring like the others in the modern directory. Bearers of all these names were closely related by blood and feudal ties to William. His father had been Robert, and so was his half-brother, Robert of Mortain, and his eldest son, Robert of Normandy. Richard was the name of three former Dukes of Normandy, one of whom, William's great grandfather Richard the Fearless, had married the sister of Hugh Capet, founder of the French dynasty, thereby bringing the Frankish name Hugh into the family circle. Henry was the least prominent of them at the time of the Conquest, but as it was the name that William gave to his youngest son, born in England only two years later, it soon caught up the others. To his cousin, Walter Giffard, William gave land in ten counties; Gilbert of Ghent, his wife's nephew, received even greater endowments. Count Roger of Montgomerie (in Normandy) who styled himself on a charter as 'son of Roger the Great', distinguished himself at Hastings and became Earl of Arundel and Shrewsbury. Roger Bigod, who was given the earldom of Norfolk, was one of William's chief advisers. Ralf de Tankerville was his chamberlain, and several other Ralfs and Rogers closely connected with the new king received earldoms, bishoprics and other fat prizes.

Count Alan of Brittany (Alan the Red) brought a useful contingent to share in the English adventure and married one of the Conqueror's daughters. He was endowed with great estates, chiefly in the north-eastern counties, where the name of Alan quickly took root, and where his nephew Alan the Black succeeded him and became Earl of Richmond.

There is no question that it was the impact of this small, close-knit, conquering group that gave these names their tremendous popularity in the next two centuries. Later events were to give added favour to this one or that, or to bring other names to the fore, but, excluding saints' names for the present, no other names have ever surpassed those of the Conqueror's intimate circle. They were broadcast over England at exactly the right date to produce a full harvest of surnames, far greater than that caused by leading figures of equal importance but of later date.

This point is well illustrated when we look for comparison at the position of Edward on our list. Three successive Edwards occupied the throne for more than a century (1272–1377), two of them remarkably successful and popular, and yet their total of surnames is less than a quarter that of William. Hardly any pet-forms were coined from this name. Our directory has just five *Edsons*, three *Eddisons* and sixteen *Edkins* (and even these few must be shared with Edmund and several other Saxon names) to match against the thousands of *Wilson, Wilkins* and so on. If William could make so many surnames merely by being a king's name, why did not Edward – a native name – do the same? The answer lies in the dates of these kings. The three Edwards were too late. It is true that when Henry III, in pious admiration of two saintly Saxon kings, christened his infant sons Edward and Edmund, it was at the very height of the surname-fixing period. But the names in question were at that date so completely out of fashion that they had to make a new start. The king was so unpopular and babies so apt to die that it was not until Edward was grown up and beginning to show his mettle that his name began to come into fashion. By the time it had done so the tide of surname-making had passed and Edward had missed it or nearly so. But as a Christian name it returned slowly into favour and when the Welsh began to take fixed surnames later on, many of them were sons of Edward.

But to return to the leading Norman names, it is probably true to say that no name in all our history has been used with more affection than Robert, particularly in its familiar form Robin, or in its rhymed versions. The English gave it not only to their sons but to all sorts of living creatures that they looked on as companions. The friendliest of little birds became the 'robin'; the favourite hawk the 'hobby'; the faithful horse Dobbin, or else the 'hobby' horse, an expression which presently passed from a live horse to a toy one and in later days to a favourite pastime. To consort with one's friends was to 'hobnob', and the familiar spirit of the woods, anciently called the 'puck', became 'hob-goblin' or, if one wished to be really polite, Robin Goodfellow, surely the pleasantest name that could possibly be devised. It was very important to be on the right side of such a person.

When we consider all this, it seems only natural that that other Robin of the greenwood, who was probably the most popular man in England at the height of the surname period, should have this name. It has been shown elsewhere (page 175) that his name was a household word in various parts of England before the end of the thirteenth century. There is no reason to doubt that he flourished, as the legends tell us, in the reign of King John, and that the tremendous admiration which he inspired among the masses helped to give this name its special character. It was becoming a favourite, like Dickon and Will, before he was born, but his life must have given it an added impetus. We have seen that it took the name of William over a century to reach the masses, but with a popular figure like Robin Hood the soil was receptive and the harvest would spring up in less than half the time.

Richard and Henry, both stemming from early and popular kings, have very similar numbers. Henry I was liked because he spoke English and seemed to care for English interests, and set a seal on it by marrying into the old Saxon royal line. Henry II was an immensely capable and powerful ruler, and, as we have seen with William I, power seemed to produce a lot of namesakes. Richard I was really of little use to England as a king, more of a burden in fact, as he was always wanting money for his enterprises, but the Crusades that inspired him also stirred the hearts of his people, and they took an immense pride in the distinguished part he played in them. His personal popularity must have helped to account for a good many of all our *Ricketts*, *Dickens*, *Dixons* and *Hicksons* and all the rest of the tribe.

Perhaps the chief interest in the surnames derived from Henry is that they tell us so plainly how the name was pronounced in England in the Middle Ages. It was always Harry. The great block of over three thousand examples of *Harris*, *Harrison* and *Harriman* shows us the regular form, whereas a bare two hundred *Henrys* give the unusual and later form, which is largely Scottish. In Scotland the 'n' seems always to have been pronounced in the modern way, and an intrusive 'd' crept in after it, giving *Hendry* and *Henderson* which latter multiplied greatly as was the way with Scottish clans. The name was originally German, but the Normans got it by way of France, and their pronunciation of it was clearly much as it is in France now. 'Harri' indicates the Englishman's attempt at the French nasal 'n' and is much nearer to it than our modern pronunciation. In formal medieval documents the name is written as Henricus, a late Latin form invented by the clerks, but this has nothing to do with the spoken word. It was not until the sixteenth or seventeenth centuries when literacy was increasing rapidly that the spelling began to influence the pronunciation. Shakespeare uses the formal spelling in his titles, but in the text both spellings, the formal Henry and the phonetic Harry, seem to occur indifferently, and the latter probably represents the way in which he spoke the name in every case.

It has taken a long time for the old pronunciation to die out. In the last century it was still universally used as a pet-name for Henry, and is still so sometimes, but our surnames tell us that Harry was not originally a separate familiar form, but the standard English pronunciation of the name.

Another point of pronunciation that is made abundantly clear by the surnames derived from Henry is that in the Middle Ages the English had not the slightest tendency to drop their aitches. If they had done so it could not fail to be reflected in our surnames, just as the tendency to aspirate 'R' has been, and we should have hundreds of people called Arris. But there is not a sign of it. There are a few examples of the reverse process, of its being added to words that should begin with vowels. *Hoskins*, for instance, comes from familiar forms of names like Osmund and Osbern which were used by Normans and English; *Herrick* is a variation of the Scandinavian Eric. But such examples are few and probably arose from Norman confusion over the use of 'H'. The English made no such mistakes about their many names beginning with vowels, and in the case of names beginning with 'H' like Hugh and Henry, among all the hundreds of derivatives not one is without it. The custom of dropping aitches is a curious habit and comparatively modern, unlike the weakness with 'R' which, as surnames show, is much older.

A well-known surname that is partly attributable to Henry is *Hawkins*. Henry was sometimes abbreviated to Hal (another

sign of the English difficulty in ending with an 'r') and this became *Halkin* which could easily change further to *Hawkin*. On
page 160 it was shown that this latter form was also frequently
derived from the pre-Conquest personal name *Hawke* and that
the two merged together indissolubly. This is a parallel case to
that of Dod where a new Norman name was reduced to a popular form that coincided with one of the old ones.

Hugh was the name of several powerful Norman barons who
feature prominently in Domesday Book. Chief among them was
Hugh the Wolf whom William made Earl of Chester, with almost
sovereign powers on the Welsh marches. But the name was not
by any means confined to the West. A twelfth-century Bishop
of Lincoln was canonized as St Hugh, and a child in the same
city who was supposed to have been murdered by the Jews soon
afterwards was known as Little St Hugh, bringing more devotion to the name.

Derivatives of Hugh are innumerable in a literal sense because many of them are hard to identify with certainty. Coming
from the Old German 'hugo', meaning 'heart' or 'mind', it had
passed into French as Hugues or Hue, and in English ended
with the indeterminate 'gh' sound which was pronounced in
Middle English but has since disappeared, leaving so many
spelling difficulties behind it. The table on page 324 shows the
principal lines which the various familiar forms have taken, but
many of these are confused with other words, which makes them
impossible to compute accurately. There was an Old English
word 'hōh' for a hill which is very common in place names, as
for instance in the first syllable of Houghton and the last of
Ivinghoe, and this is hopelessly mixed with Hugh. In the
medieval rolls the distinction is clear as the place name always
has the preposition 'de' or 'atte' to show its nature; but now
Howe and *Howes* could be from either source. *Howitt* and
Howkins are both definitely personal. *Howlett* may be from the
man or a nickname from the owl.

Another problem is *Hudd*. This was a familiar name, often
found in the rolls, and used by Gower for one of his typical
peasants (page 197). That it was in regular use is attested by
370 *Hudds* and *Hudsons* in the directory, and it was certainly
used for Hugh, as an entry in the Curia Regis Rolls of 1212

makes clear when it refers to 'Hugh, the son of John . . . and John the father of the same Hud'. But where did the 'd' come from? Once again, as with Dob and Hawkin, the answer is to be found in the existence of an older native name. There were Huddas in England before the Conquest. Soon after it they had lost their final vowel and would have fallen into disuse. But the fashionable new name, Hugh, was near enough to the old-fashioned Hud to keep it going for another century or so.

Walter was generally pronounced without the 'l' sound, and probably in many cases the surname *Waters* belongs to the personal name, though in others it signified people who lived 'by the water'. But it is chiefly to the hundreds of *Watts*, *Watsons* and *Watkins* that the name owes its high score. It is rather the same with *Gilbert*; we have plenty of examples of the name in full, but far more of *Gibson*, *Gibbs* and *Gibbons*, showing its popularity with the masses. In the case of *Roger* it has been shown already that its pet-form, *Hodge*, became almost a synonym for a peasant, though Roger, in full, had been the name of some of the proudest and richest of earls and barons.

Perhaps it was excessive use by the lower ranks of society that caused some of these names,which had come into England with such éclat, to decline in the fifteenth century. Nothing could check the progress of the leading names. William, Robert, Richard and Henry went on like snowballs gathering momentum, but some of those in the second numerical rank, like Gilbert, Alan and Ralph, began to lose ground. Consequently they were not much used by the Welsh and received no large addition from that quarter.

Ralph is a name that is difficult to write of as one hardly knows what form to use. It is really derived from several different names that flourished among the Franks, Scandinavians and Anglo-Saxons and converged together in Norman England. To put a complicated story briefly, the principal Old English ingredients were 'rand wulf' (shield wolf), which became either Randal or Rannulf, and 'raed wulf' (counsel wulf), which produced Radulf; but either of these could be further contracted to Raulf, or Raul or Rawle. As the same names were favourites among the Normans, who had them from their Norse ancestors, they came into great prominence, as has already been noted, at the time of the Conquest. If we add together all the surnames in this group, the *Randalls* and *Rawlings*, and *Ralphs* and *Randolphs*, with their attendant pet forms, they produce a total of fourteen hundred. The detailed numbers show us that *Randal* and *Rawling* were the commonest forms in our period, much more so than *Ralph* which came into favour later on. (The 'ph' is due to the spelling of the Latinized version Randulphus.) We are told that the correct old pronunciation was Rafe. This may be true of the Tudor times, but in the surname period the 'Ran-' names and 'Raw-' names predominate.

It must also be mentioned here that like other Norman names beginning with 'R', all these names have their rhymed versions. *Rankin* and *Ranson* (sometimes changing unreasonably to *Ransome*) are matched by *Hankin* and *Hanson* (also occasionally *Hansom*, as in the case of the gentleman who invented the cab). Hawle would inevitably be lost in the multitude of Halls, of quite different origin, but *Hollis* and *Hollings* are still recognizable twins of *Rolles* and *Rollings*.

However we are in deep waters here. The name of the Viking who founded the Norman dynasty, Rolfe, is of partly different origin (hrod-wulf or red wolf). It was Latinized as Rollo, became Raoul in France, and as such is also responsible for some of the *Rolls* and *Rollings*. Then there is *Roland*, the heroic Frankish name with a score of at least four hundred, which also overlaps with some of them.

Added to all this there is the problem that some of the 'Han-' names are undoubtedly connected with John. It will now be understood why Ralph is a difficult name, but even if one omits all doubtful cases its score must be at least 1200.

Setting aside names of Biblical or classical origin for later consideration, we have now mentioned all the Christian names whose derivatives total more than a thousand in the directory. All have been Germanic or Teutonic in origin, with the exception of the Breton Alan which has been included because it came into England with the Normans. Linguistically the Breton names belong to a different group, but the few that became popular in England are conveniently considered here.

Between the numbers of a thousand and five hundred, still an impressive amount, comparable to that of such well-known occupational names as Fisher and Shepherd, we come to a group of names that were brought in by the Normans and flourished for a time (or they would not be so strongly represented now), but took only slight hold among the general populace and gradually expired as Christian names.

First among them is the unfamiliar Pagan. To modern ears it does not sound like a Christian name at all, especially as its meaning is the very opposite of Christian, but by the eleventh century meanings of first names were forgotten; personal associations were more important; and many parents must have given it to their sons at the font as it has left us over eight hundred *Paynes* and *Paines*. Its pet-form was *Pagnel* or *Pannell*, and altogether its score is higher than that of *Geoffrey*, for instance, which has held its ground much better as a first name.

The Norman *Howard* and the Breton *Harvey* have now come full circle. Both were regular Christian names in the Norman period, fell into disuse, but survived as surnames of noble families, and have now in modern times come back into fashion as first names again. Another Christian name that went right out is Hamo (from the Old German 'haimo' meaning simply 'home'). The five hundred examples of *Hammond* show how popular it once was. Its pet-forms include *Hamlyn*, *Hambling* (this name seems particularly liable to excrescent letters) and the much less common *Hamnet* which must have been already old-fashioned when Shakespeare gave it to his son.

Another in the same numerical group is Reynald, the Norman version of the Old Germanic Ragin-wald, or Ragnald in Scandinavia. This name was revived by nineteenth-century antiquarianism as Reginald, but the surnames *Reynolds* and *Rennell* give us the medieval pronunciation. Several other names of similar type began with this 'ragin' theme, which meant 'might' or 'power', names like *Rayner*, *Raymond* and the imitative *Rainbow* which is really a corruption of Reynbald. They exist also in shortened forms such as *Raine*, *Rains* and *Rainey*, none of which has anything to do with the weather. Reynald was still popular in the fifteenth century, late enough to acquire a final 's' as a regular thing, but the fact that *Howard*, *Harvey* and *Hammond* are without it indicates that as Christian names they had disappeared much earlier.

The last three names which definitely total over five hundred are all difficult to assess accurately. *Neel* or *Neal* was the Middle

English form of the name we know better as Nigel. It was originally a Celtic name belonging chiefly to Ireland where Niall of
the Nine Hostages ruled as a High King in the fourth century;
but at an early date it was picked up by Norsemen and spread
into all the lands they raided. The scribes of Domesday Book
wrote it down as Nigellus as if they thought it a diminutive of
the Latin 'niger', meaning black, and the modern name Nigel
is a back-formation from this. If we were to start counting
O'Neills and MacNeils the numbers would soon soar; many of
the Neills are abbreviations of these Irish and Gaelic forms; and
some of the *Nielsons* are of recent Scandinavian origin, but even
omitting all these semi-alien surnames we are still left with well
over five hundred English *Neal(e)s* and *Nelsons*.

A pair of names that cannot well be separated are Gerard and
Gerald. Their various forms show the early hard 'g' that was
retained longer in the North, as in *Garratt*, and the softer sound
that developed in the South, as in *Gerard* and *Jerrold*.

Humphrey just passes the five hundred mark, but would not
do so without additional numbers from Wales. The most distinguished man of this name was Henry V's brother, the Duke
of Gloucester, a great patron of the arts, who lived too late to
affect the name in time for English surnames, but its increased
popularity in the fifteenth century brought in a crop of Welsh
ones.

Apart from Edward only one Anglo-Saxon name reaches five
hundred. (In spite of royal favour Edmund scores just under
half that amount.) This is *Harding*, the brave one, and even this
has had some Norman help, for it has absorbed the name
Hardwin which, though typically English, was used by at least
one powerful Norman baron.

It will be seen that the numbers in this class are very high.
Even without the saints' names, which are just as abundant,
twenty-one Christian names with their derivatives score over
five hundred in the directory, and some ten times as many.

Below this number are many more Norman Christian names
in moderate numbers, of which we can pick out only a few,
names that are mostly forgotten, like Odo, Drogo, Milo, Falco
and Fulco, which have left behind them the surnames *Oades* or
Oates, *Drew*, *Miles*, *Fawkes* and *Foulkes*, the last sometimes
written with two little 'f's' which only represent the old style

of writing capital F. Guarin and Garnier are responsible for most of our *Warrens* and *Warners* (though the rabbit warren must claim some of them too). Almeric has produced *Amery*, *Emery*, *Emerson* and *Imrie*. Nor must we forget those two romantic paladins *Ro(w)land* and *Oliv(i)er*.

It is always of interest as we look at each sort of name and notice those with the most abundant numbers to turn our minds for a moment to the names which are very much fewer than we would expect. Among the Christian names of Germanic origin, like all these others that we have discussed in this chapter, the one which has the lowest score in relation to what might be expected is *Charles*. It is there, but with barely two hundred examples, less than a third of a name like *Pagan*, which most people have never heard of, and not a twentieth part of Richard or Henry, and without any pet-forms. And yet Charles the Great, or Charlemagne, had launched the name at the pinnacle of society on the Continent, making it one of the regular royal names of France ever after; and the Scandinavians had the same name in the form of Karl as one of their favourites. Thus one would expect it to have come into England in strength, but it did not. I believe the explanation of this can be found by considering the Old English word 'ceorl' or churl, which is cognate with Karl and Charles, and like them has the basic meaning of a freeman.

In England as in other northern regions this word was sometimes used as a personal name, just as Man was used in the sense of a manly young fellow. A sixth-century King of Mercia was named Cearl (of which the first two letters would develop normally into 'ch'), and there is one Carlo in Domesday Book. The word 'churl' was once an honourable name for those men who formed the middle rank of English society between the thane and the serf. However even before the Conquest many in this class were falling on evil days; after this event most of them were demoted to become peasants bound to the soil; and with them the good old word also suffered debasement. The English themselves stopped using it, and for those who had managed to preserve or gain their freedom the expression 'free man' was preferred. From the superior Norman attitude comes the unworthy adjective 'churlish', meaning ill-mannered like a peasant. I consider this misfortune to the English 'churl' quite sufficient to explain why the name which was so closely related to it linguistically never became popular in the Middle Ages. But it was much used in France at this time (as distinct from Normandy), and the small numbers we have may have come from there.

Every surname given in this chapter comes from the Christian name of a landowner in Domesday Book, and the proportions in which they occur there are extraordinarily similar to those in which they appear today in the London Telephone Directory.

Chapter 21

THE BIBLE

It is hard for us to realize how completely the English had avoided Biblical names until about the time of the Norman Conquest. This was partly due to their old custom of coining home-made names from their own language, and partly to a feeling of respect which made them shrink from presuming to take a holy name. This same feeling had to some extent influenced all the peoples of Western Europe and may be exemplified by the Popes, who for the first five centuries of Christianity took no names of persons connected with the life of Christ, preferring made-up abstractions like Pious and Innocent; and all through their history they have avoided the venerated name of Peter.

But by the tenth century ideas were changing, and the Normans, bursting into Europe like an explosive missile, had few inhibitions. Their Christian zeal, though new, was unbounded; crusades and pilgrimages suited them exactly, especially if difficult and dangerous, and their adventurous spirits led them into the Mediterranean as well as around northern coasts. For centuries English Christians had been making slow pilgrimages all across Europe to Rome, and sometimes even as far as Jerusalem; they had heard Greek and Roman and even Hebrew names, some connected with the Gospel stories, in ordinary use, and had come back home and christened their children Wulfric and Ethelwin as before. But the Normans, who only became Christian in the tenth century, were more receptive to new thought. When they invaded England they were almost all still called by the northern pagan names that we have been discussing in the last chapter. But within a few years many of them were off on the first crusade with the king's eldest son, Robert, and in the next generation the barriers were down and the saints' names from the near East pouring in.

In a way it is illogical to distinguish these 'Bible' names from the other Norman favourites, for, to begin with at any rate, they owed their popularity to Norman favour. Stephen and John, for instance, were kings as well as saints. They were singularly bad kings, it is true, but when we think of the immense impetus given to the name William by a king who was feared and hated by many, though admired by his immediate following, and by his son William II who was hardly liked by anyone, we see that we cannot altogether dismiss the prestige of royalty in the cases of John and Stephen. However the true religious feeling for such a name as John outweighed all other considerations, and once the Biblical names were admitted they increased on their own merits.

Let us look first at names from the Old Testament. Far the highest of them on our list is David, but if our subject is con-fined to English surnames David's score must be reduced by more than half. Nearly all examples of *Davies* are Welsh, and this is no mere echo of English popularity as in the case of *Williams*, but an expression of loyalty on the part of Welshmen to their own patron saint and native princes. We must also bear in mind that David is a favourite name among Jews, and that in modern times many of them have assumed the properly Eng-lish or Scottish forms of *Davis, Davison* or *Davidson*. According to my calculations on both these points, something over three thousand must be subtracted to leave David with a truly English total. But even so it will be seen that it was a popular name here in the Middle Ages. It is often to be found in medie-val rolls, both as David and in the abbreviated form Daue, giving us the well-known surname *Dawson*. It may seem a strange form for this name to take. There was in medieval script a great confusion between the letters 'v', 'u' and 'w', and how the short form was pronounced at first is not certain, but it has descended to us as *Daw* (a surname that can also be a nickname for the bird).

But the popularity of this name is due not only to the David of the Bible but also to the sixth-century Welsh saint who probably made the bigger appeal of the two, even to the English. It was Henry I who brought St David into prominence in England, and his motive was not entirely religious. The Norman kings had only a slight and partial hold on Wales which they always hoped to increase. The promontory of Pembrokeshire jutting out towards Ireland was of strategic importance, and Henry chose to settle there a colony of Normans and Flemings under his control. He also replaced the Welsh bishop with a Norman, and in order to placate outraged national feeling, rebuilt the Cathedral in the grand manner and used his influence in Rome to have David officially canonized and included in the international Christian calendar. From that time St David's became one of the principal places of pilgrimage in the British Isles. The long overland journey from England, through mountainous country full of danger from wild beasts and robbers, was enough to satisfy anyone's zest for adventure, while the sea journey was probably almost as hazardous. It was officially laid down by the English Church that two pilgrimages to St David's equalled in merit one to Rome, and its very dangers made it the more attractive.

We have immediately strayed from the subject of the Old Testament to a much more recent saint, but may take the occasion to note the pattern which will emerge as we look at these names of religious significance. Medieval people knew and enjoyed the principal Old Testament stories told by the priests, but when it came to naming a child they wanted a patron in Heaven. They were much more interested in the real people who had known Christ personally, such as the twelve Apostles, or in the saints and martyrs who had testified for Him since His death, and by signs and miracles been shown to be admitted to high honour in Heaven, than in heroes of ancient tales before Christ was born. Particularly they liked a patron not too remote from themselves. David, for instance, had lived in this island; if one made a pilgrimage to the very place and then named one's child after him, it should be of benefit.

After David the Old Testament name with the highest score, and that by a long way, is *Adam*. Just why the father of mankind had such a big appeal is not clear, perhaps it was because his was the best known of all the Bible stories, portrayed in stone and fresco and dramatic performances in churches everywhere. That it was a favourite with all classes is shown by the variety of its forms, some hardly recognizable. The familiar *Adkin* generally became *Atkin*, or *Aitkin* in the North, giving names like *Atkinson* which seem rather far removed from Adam, while *Adcock*, *Addison* and many other forms are plentiful.

The only other purely Old Testament figure with at all a high score is Elias, the Greek form of Elijah, which Norman crusaders brought back from the East in the form of Elis or *Ellis*. It became a great favourite in the twelfth and thirteenth centuries, particularly in its pet-form *Elliot*. Why, one wonders, did this particular name have such an appeal at that time, but so little staying power compared to other Biblical names? Can it perhaps be that the English took to it more readily than some because so many of the Anglo-Saxon names had begun with 'Al-' or 'El-' (contracted from 'Ethel-'), which gave it a familiar sound? You could christen your child with this exotic name to please the parish priest, and then call him something that sounded very like the name of your old grandfather.

David, Adam and Elias are the only names from the Old Testament to reach the thousand mark as sources of surnames. The next in numerical order is *Jacob*, but this would probably not be so high if it did not sometimes represent an early form of James, as will be explained more fully later. Its numbers have also been increased in the last century by Jews who have settled in England. However it should not be thought that this name, together with *Abraham* and *Isaac*, is entirely Jewish. They are all to be found quite frequently in English medieval documents, as for example Walter Isak in the Somerset Subsidy of 1327, and Agnes Jacobs and John Abraam both in Hertfordshire in the same year, a time when there were virtually no Jews in England, after their expulsion by Edward I.

All the Old Testament names that had good stories, like that of *Daniel*, attached to them made some English surnames, though not in great numbers. Several of them were pronounced somewhat differently at that time and exist as surnames in their old forms. *Joseph* was also *Jessop*. The fact that the name belongs to the New Testament as well as the Old and to a prominent character in the Christmas play, must account for its being found fairly often in early records and having a score of nearly five hundred. Moses was often *Moss*; Solomon nearly always Salaman which has come down to us as *Salmon*. Absalom is even more disguised as *Asplin*, having at a very early date turned itself into Aspelon in English. Noah, whose story has always been much enjoyed, was known in the form of Noe and has given us *Noyes* and *Noyce*. Abel survives as *Abell* and *Ablett*.

When we come to the New Testament, we see what real popularity can mean, particularly in the case of *John*. This name has long been a favourite in all Christian countries, but nowhere more so than in England. We need not search far for the cause, for the Gospels call John the disciple whom Jesus loved, and devout Christians seeking affinity with Christ could go no nearer. He and Peter were the two with the closest personal ties with Our Lord, and when once the barrier of respect was broken both names were seized on with avidity. There is also St John the Baptist, a figure of great inspiration to the crusaders who, after struggling across the burning sands of Palestine, could vividly imagine the ardours of his life in the wilderness, and feast their eyes in ecstasy on the waters of Jordan. They even brought back flasks of this same water to baptize their sons in England, sometimes naming them *Jordan* which became a fashionable first name for a brief period, leaving us over four hundred examples as surnames in the directory.

There are hardly any Johns in Domesday Book, and the two or three who are mentioned are probably priests. A hundred years later in the Index of the Pipe Roll, the name is still far behind William or Robert, less than a tenth of either. But in another century it is catching up fast, and once we are past 1300 it exceeds them, reaching its zenith in the fifteenth century. After this it spread through Wales, and still later the great crop of *Joneses* was raised there. In England the normal patronymic, which developed principally in the North (and also later in Scotland), was *Johnson*, often with an excrescent 't' creeping in like the 'p' in Thompson, making it *Johnston* which looks misleadingly like a place name. But the most completely English medieval form of this name is *Jackson*.

Many people have been much exercised in their minds as to how John could come to be Jack which seems so much more like the French Jacques, which in turn belongs to James. It seems very confusing, but is clearly set out in *The Oxford Dictionary of Christian Names* with a chain of evidence that is borne out by all the early records. Briefly, John came into England as Jehan or Johan, and was speedily reduced to one syllable, Jon, Jan or Jen in sound, varying in different dialects. The next step (chiefly in the South) was the addition of diminutive suffixes producing Jenin, Jenkin, Jankin and so forth, which account for the surnames *Jennings* and *Jenkins*. The form Jankin seems to have been short lived, almost immediately losing its first 'n' and being further shortened to the popular Jakke. I think myself that, though this name has no real relationship to the French Jacques, yet it may have been influenced by it to some extent. Englishmen in France must have heard this common name on every side among the peasantry, and this familiarity may have hastened the step from Jankin to Jack, which was in any case an easy one.

But such a popular name as John was bound to diverge into many forms. One group generally attributed to it is composed of those beginning with Han. In the Low Countries Johan became Han or Hans, and as the inhabitants of that region often overflowed into England, they may be responsible for this form of John, uncharacteristic of the English who seldom stressed a name's final syllable. These Han- names were used for Randal and Henry as well as for John, both *Hankin* and *Hancock* being found early and often in all parts of the country.

The next New Testament name in numerical order after John is *Thomas*, which again is no surprise. Having started with the advantage of apostolic rank, it was suddenly raised to further esteem by the wave of general emotion at the murder of Becket. After that it was St Thomas of Canterbury rather than the doubting Apostle who inspired the naming of so many little Thomases, who live still in our armies of *Thom(p)sons*, *Tomlins* and *Tompkins*. The variety of spelling is very great, and the divergence of familiar forms ranges from *Tonks* (by way of *Tonkin*) to *Tampling* (from Tom-el-in or *Tamlyn* in the North). As usual the majority of truly English names belong to these colloquial forms, and it was left to the Welsh to add their quota (about 1,100 in proportion to our standard list) to the plain, unaltered *Thomas*. The large Welsh contingent shows how the

227

popularity of this name, due to Becket, continued to swell after the settling of names in England.

Simon and Peter must be considered together, for they owe their numbers to the same great saint who, if his name were not thus divided in two would almost equal John. There was indeed another apostle called Simon, but so little is known of him that we can be certain it was veneration for Simon Peter that made the name rank so high.

In Middle English references to this Saint the name Simon (often written Symond) was generally preferred to Peter, as in Wycliffe's Bible, and the numbers of *Sim(p)son*, *Simmons* and other variants give an idea of its immense popularity. Probably one reason for the early preference for this form was that it coincided with the pre-Conquest name Sigmund which was Scandinavian as well as English and well known to the Normans. It appears in Domesday Book, and would inevitably be contracted to Simon, so that it must have seemed to eleventh-century Englishmen that the great Apostle who held the keys of Heaven had a very homely and familiar name. It is impossible now to sort out one origin from the other, but judging by other names of the two types we may say that much the larger contribution comes from the Saint.

But the name Peter was popular too, though not in the way we now say it. Our surnames reveal what may surprise many, that it came into England with a French pronunciation something like Pierre, at any rate in a single syllable without any 't'. It is true that there is quite a large contingent of *Peters*, showing that this modern pronunciation, influenced by the Latin form Petrus, came into fashion just in time for latecomers, including the Welsh, but by far the largest mass of surnames from this name are those with the sound of *Pears*, generally written *Pearce* or *Pearson*, with *Perkin* as the favourite pet-form. It must have been noticed how readily 'er' and 'ar' were interchangeable (as in Clerk and Clarke, Derby and Darby), and *Parkin* is just another form of *Perkin*, as *Parkes* is of *Perks*. However when we come to *Parke* we are on doubtful ground as some *Parkers* must have lived in the *Park*, which is an entirely different matter. This small uncertainty makes little difference to the large score of Peter.

The next Apostle on our list is *Philip* with a score of over two thousand. Like *Stephen*, which is also numerous, this is a Greek name which was current in Eastern Europe and in Rome in the Dark Ages where two Emperors were named Philip, giving it a general currency apart from its Christian significance. Philip was in fact less alien to the French and English than Hebrew names, and was the first Biblical name used by the French ruling family, as Stephen was the first in our own, Philip I being king in Paris at the time of the Conquest. Thus the name came early into England among the ruling classes. It was sometimes familiarized as Phillipot (*Philpots*) which produced the unexpected pet-form *Potts*, but this is the French way of doing it. *Phelps* and *Filkins* are more in the English style, but these are only moderately numerous. In fact the indications are that during the surname period it was used chiefly among the upper classes. There are over fifteen hundred examples of the full name, of which about a quarter are Welsh, and a much smaller number of pet-forms.

Andrew owes some of its numbers to Scotland where it was naturally popular as the name of the patron saint. But it was also much used in England, remaining, like Philip, chiefly among the upper class. *Andrews* is the English version, *Anderson* the Scottish, and they are nearly equal in numbers.

Bartholomew, on the other hand, was a great favourite with all classes, as is shown by its wide variety of popular forms, amongst which *Bartlett* and *Bates* are the most common, the former being the earlier. *Matthew* also came into England early and is one of the few names of this sort to be found in Domesday Book. Its popularity seems to have been mostly in the South where the French version, *Mayhew*, also flourished, sometimes abbreviated to *May* and *Makin*.

With *James* we complete the apostolic names, excepting only that of Jude or Judas, which was obviously not destined for popularity. It might be thought that surnames from James would come largely from the Scots owing to their many kings of that name, but though many of the *Jamesons* may be attributed to that rather later source, the name was well established in England before it reached the Scottish throne. One of the most important places of pilgrimage in Europe was Compostella in Spain, which claimed important relics of this Saint, including his head. It seems a long way to go from England, but medieval 'Cook's Tours' set off from time to time, generally by sea, and the pilgrims came back with the cockle shells they had found on the beach near the famous shrine. (The Wife of Bath had been there, of course.) This explains why the name came to England in the Spanish form 'Jaime' (from Jacomus), instead of the French form Jacques which comes from the first syllable of Jacobus. It can be seen that both these popular international names stem originally from the Hebrew Jacob. In England during the surname period both were in use, Jame or James as the popular version, while Jacobus, the Latin form, is seen in official documents. It was not until the Bible was translated at the Reformation that they were treated as two distinct names, Jacob being used for the Old Testament patriarch and James for the two Apostles.

Of other great names from the New Testament, the one that made by far the strongest impression on England was *Stephen*, a name highly honoured among Christians, especially in Eastern Europe and Asia Minor, as that of the first martyr. As a well-known Greek name it had continued in normal use in those regions, and was the first Biblical name to be used by a Pope. Later it was further familiarized in Western Europe by a general admiration for Stephen, King of Hungary, who embraced Christianity towards the end of the tenth century, bringing all his kingdom into the fold. This event may seem remote from Norman England, but it was significant even there. It must be remembered that before the capture of Jerusalem by the Turks, a persistent stream of pilgrims from the West had found their way to the Holy City, and one of the most dangerous parts of their incredibly difficult journey had been the passage through the wilds of heathen Hungary which separated the Christian empires of the East and West. Pirates in the Mediterranean made the sea journey even more hazardous. Consequently there was rejoicing throughout Western Europe when it became known that in Hungary pilgrims would no longer be harried and robbed, but helped on their way.

Among the admirers of the Hungarian Saint Stephen was the Count of Troyes who named a son after him and whose great grandson, Stephen of Blois, married William the Conqueror's daughter. Their own son, yet another Stephen, became King of

England. Once the name was introduced at this high level it was bound to create namesakes. Already in Domesday Book it occurs several times, probably among adherents of the Blois family who, like all William's relations, shared in English spoils. Like Philip and Andrew it never appealed greatly to the masses, and owes its large numbers far more to the full name (*Stevens* or *Stevenson*) than to popular forms. (*Stenson* and *Stimson* are the only indications of abbreviation, and neither of them is common.)

Other New Testament names which we might expect to rank high are Paul, Luke, Mark and Barnabas, but none of them is very numerous. Paul was probably the most used of the four, particularly in London where the great church made it familiar. The medieval spelling was very varied, Poule or Powle being often seen, and it has left a variety of surnames such as *Poulson* and *Polson* as well as the more obvious *Paul* and *Pawle*. But it cannot be counted because it overlaps with names of other origins, the local *Poole*, for instance, which is simply 'at the pool', and the Welsh *Powell*. *Pole* may also be sometimes from Paul, but the aristocratic De la Pole was plainly local.

Luke, which is much more straightforward, generally in the scholarly Greek form *Lucas*, with a less common pet-name *Luckett*, totals a little over four hundred. Mark was not common in our period, and the majority of modern *Marks*, also under five hundred, are Jewish. Nor is the name Barnabas much seen in medieval documents. One might think that the surname *Barnes* comes from this name, but it has quite different origins (page 71), and the only surnames that can be allotted to Barnabas with any certainty are *Barnaby* or *Burnaby* of which there are under ten.

Before leaving Biblical characters, we must remember one more name that is not strictly Old or New Testament, but quite in a class by itself, that of St Michael the Archangel. If we were to judge the popularity of Bible stories by the subjects of early medieval church carving, we should find Adam (and Eve) and the twelve Apostles easy winners, as we do in surnames, but very close to them would come the splendid, warlike figure of Michael killing the devil. The name was used regularly from the twelfth century onwards, spoken with a soft 'ch' which is still retained in the most usual form of the surname, *Mitchell*.

We must allow that some of the numbers of this surname belong to the common Middle English adjective 'muchel' or 'mychel', meaning 'great' and surviving in the modern word 'much', but as descriptive nicknames of this sort have on average very much lower numbers than patronymics, it is probable that the angelic name accounts for the majority of the twelve hundred *Mitchells*. *Gabriel* (with *Gabb* and *Gaby*) makes a poor second in the archangel class with only about sixty. But the real reason for this discrepancy lies in the fact that the Church celebrated the sanctity of all angelic beings on the one great festival of St Michael and All Angels.

Chapter 22

SAINTS AND HEROES

We come now to the saints who lived after the writing of the Bible, some of them historical figures, some hardly more than legendary. They are a vast company, giving a wide variety of names from many lands, and it is tempting to try to discover the special points that made a few of them highly popular in Norman England while others were totally neglected. Such seeking for motives is open to error, but the figures that show some names to have been used in thousands and others hardly at all are facts. The names in this class that pass the thousand mark in our list are *Nicholas* (easily ahead of the others), *Martin, Maurice, Lawrence* and *Benedict,* their numbers placing them among the chief favourites of our period.

Of St Nicholas, a Bishop of Myra in Asia Minor at about the end of the third century, hardly anything factual is known, but the legends told about his kindness and gentleness endeared him to the civilized world for ever. A saint who crept in at windows by night to leave dowries for poor little girls who needed them, and who put together children who had been chopped in pieces, restoring them to life, could not fail to be loved. The early Middle Ages was a period of great contrasts, when extreme gentleness and loving kindness, inspired by Christianity, flourished side by side with violence and brutality. At all times the influence of women must have been great in naming children, and it is no wonder that mothers longing for special protection for their newborn sons should choose St Nicholas, the patron Saint of children. Incidentally, the cult of St Nicholas which came into England early, as illustrated by scenes from the Saint's life on the Norman font of Winchester Cathedral, has shown extraordinary vitality in modern times, though the Santa Claus of the large department store is far removed from the saintly bishop.

The usual form of the name during our period was Nicol, as is shown by the plentiful examples of *Nicholls*, and *Nicholson* in over twenty different spellings. The Greek form, *Nicholas*, which was favoured by clerks in writing, was generally adopted rather later and is much less common as a surname. The obvious abbreviation, Nick, represented by *Nix* and *Nixon*, is less numerous than might be expected, the French Colle taken from the second syllable being generally preferred, particularly as Colin. The explanation of this is the same story as we have already had with Hud and Dod and Hawkin. In Domesday Book we constantly see the Old English name Cola which would soon become Colle or Cole. Thus the French style of abbreviating Nicol already sounded familiar to the English, and the union of the old and new names has resulted in the large numbers of *Cole* and *Collins*. In this connection it is impossible not to be reminded of Old King Cole who had a very old English name.

Martin is almost unique among high-scoring names in having hardly any variations. A few rare examples exist with the final '-s' or '-son', and a very few of the pet-forms *Martell*, *Martlet* and *Martinet* (some of which are probably latecomers from France); but the numbers of these versions are slight indeed compared with the great block of over sixteen hundred consisting of *Martin* only, or *Martyn*. This simplicity is due partly to the fact that the name already ends with the popular diminutive suffix '-in', the remains of the Latin 'inus', but far more to the very early date at which Martin reached its height of popularity as a Christian name. There were several popular medieval saints whose cults were brought in by the Normans, but devotion to St Martin was established in England many centuries before the Northmen even became Christian.

St Martin, who lived in the early fourth century, is said to have been a Roman soldier who became a Christian and played a great part in converting Gaul. Like St Nicholas he had engagingly simple stories told about him, as for instance the one in which he divided his cloak with a beggar, which proves him to have been much beloved. He has sometimes been called the patron saint of France, and really has a much better claim to the honour than the obscure St Denis who came into fashion later. Martin's life is largely historical, and his great work of monastic foundations, especially that at Tours, had a lasting and increasing influence on Christianity in Western Europe. It is no mere coincidence that the earliest recorded church in Scotland, that founded by St Ninian in the fifth century in Galloway, was dedicated to St Martin, while the earliest in England is St Martin's at Canterbury, founded by St Augustine.

St Martin's tomb at Tours was an honoured place of pilgrimage for Englishmen from the time they became Christians, and a closer link was forged in the eighth century when Charlemagne, in founding his school there for the education of Frankish nobles, appointed the English Alcuin of York as its head, and afterwards made him Abbot of Tours. When he died he was succeeded by another Englishman, and we can be certain that English monks, scholars and pilgrims constantly visited this centre of learning and venerated the name of Martin. It is no wonder that as soon as the new idea was established of using saints' names for ordinary people, Martin was almost the first choice of the English. But by the middle of the thirteenth century when the habit of making surnames out of colloquial forms was becoming general, and all sorts of suffixes were adhering to them, this old name was dropping out of fashion and was hardly affected.

The reason for the special popularity of *Lawrence* in England is less obvious. But he was held in great esteem in Rome where several churches were dedicated to him, one displaying the iron-grid on which he was roasted to death. His holy life as a deacon, devoted largely to the service of the poor, and his cruel martyrdom left a lasting memory, even in a city of so many saints and martyrs, and since many English pilgrims made their way to Rome and returned full of inspiration, so the fame of Lawrence spread to England, as can be seen today by the large number of *Lawsons*.

It is hard also to account for the great numbers of *Maurice* (consisting largely of *Morris* and *Morrison*), for he is a decidedly legendary figure. The story goes that he was an officer in charge of a Roman legion in Switzerland, who was put to death with all his men for refusing to sacrifice to the Gods, but one still wonders why he in particular, out of the great army of martyrs all over the Roman Empire, attracted so much attention. Like

235

St Martin, though to a lesser degree, he was well esteemed in Anglo-Saxon England, and when Hugh the Great, Duke of the Franks, exchanged presents with King Athelstan with a view to marriage with one of the king's sisters, the standard of St Maurice ranked very high among the gifts, which also included the sword of Constantine and the lance of Charlemagne, which was said to be the same one that had pierced our Lord's side at the crucifixion.

The Normans admired Maurice as a soldier-saint, and many examples of the name may be found among them, as for instance William I's chaplain, Maurice, whom he made Bishop of London. But an additional cause for the popularity of the name was its literal meaning 'moorish'. The Moors, or Saracens, were renowned as fierce warriors; the lands where they lived were remote and glamorous to Northern Europeans, and therefore the name had an exotic, romantic appeal as well as the significance of dark colouring (page 146).

The only other saint's name with a score of over a thousand is Benedict, the fifth-century hermit and monk of Monte Cassino, who founded the great Benedictine Order to which most of the monasteries in England belonged. The name *Bennett* of which there are a clear thousand shows the normal English pronunciation of this favourite Christian name of the early Middle Ages, which has been out of fashion now for many centuries, except in Cornwall where many old names have lingered longer than elsewhere. *Benson* is nearly always the son of Bennet and not of Benjamin, a name seldom seen in early records.

Between the scores of a thousand and five hundred we have *Patrick, Gregory* and *Augustine,* the last once popular as *Austin* or *Austen* but now, like Bennet, almost vanished as a Christian name.

The first of the three, represented chiefly by *Patterson,* was a popular name in the North of England where the influence of the Irish saints was strongest. In Ireland it is only moderately numerous as a surname, the commonest form, *Fitzpatrick,* showing Norman influence. The great majority of Irish surnames are of ancient Celtic origin.

Gregory the Great was the Pope who saw the English boys in the Roman slave market, and sent Augustine to convert their compatriots, but it is as a towering figure in the history of Europe in the Dark Ages and an inspiring leader of the Church that he was remembered, and not because of this special link with England. The many English *Griggs* and *Gregsons* show how popular the name was once. In Scotland it was even more so, but MacGregor is not included in our numbers, nor are any such clan names for reasons already given.

A name that totals about five hundred and seems to belong here is *Francis*, but in the medieval rolls it is nearly always written 'le franceys', meaning that the man so described was French. The lovable saint of Assisi, who made the word popular as a personal name in many countries, lived just too late for it to spread into England in time to make many surnames in that way. On the other hand the French Abbot *Bernard*, whose passionate eloquence inspired the second crusade, had one of those Teutonic names that was already well known in England and Normandy before he made it more so. It was generally written *Barnard* in England, and is the probable source of most of our *Barnetts*, though some of them come from the town near London. Even so its score is rather below five hundred.

So also is that of St Denis of France. With *Dennis, Denny, Dennison* and the sharper form *Tennyson* it adds up to 460, but some of the first two forms have other origins (pages 263 and 303), and the numbers attributable to the Saint are actually less than they seem.

But where, it may be asked, is our own patron Saint? Why among all these names from many lands chosen for English christenings is George so poorly represented? We do not find him until we descend in numerical order to the modest score of three hundred and fifty; and there, almost equal with St *Vincent* of Spain and St *Clement* of Rome we come at last to *George*. But whereas both these others show a variety of popular forms, such as *Vince, Vinson, Clemens, Clemmence, Clem* and *Climpson*, *George* remains perfectly plain. This is not on account of its having gone out of fashion early as in the case of Martin and Austin, as the evidence shows it to be late in coming into England; it indicates rather that George was used only by the upper classes, chiefly in the South, and failed to reach the proletariat, until all their surname-making was over.

The circumstances in which this Saint became attached to England are uncertain. That Edward III founded the Order of the Garter in his name in 1349 is known, but before that there is only a vague tradition of crusaders taking him for their patron. The red cross which they bore on their shields was later described as the cross of St George, but there is no real evidence to show when it was first so called. Of St George himself hardly anything definite is known. He is thought to have been a Roman soldier martyred in the persecution under Diocletian in Asia Minor, and it is certain that he showed outstanding courage in some way, for he was remembered with great honour all over the Near East, and the legends that grew about his name were all connected with heroic deeds. In the first crusade, of 1089, the Norman and English contingent were greatly encouraged at the height of their battle under the walls of Antioch by a vision of St George and St Maurice fighting beside them. But when they returned home, though some of them christened their sons Maurice, few if any did the same for George.

In the third crusade, a hundred years later, the name of St George was certainly used as a rallying cry for King Richard's army, and it is probable that he was already thought of as a patron. But the name still seems to have attracted little attention at home and is hardly ever found in documents before 1300. He must have still seemed strange and remote. One can understand that an English woman, choosing a saint's name for her child, would prefer one with a known burial place and shrine to which a pilgrimage might be made, or an exceptionally kind and sympathetic person like St Nicholas. If one wanted the inspiration of a glorious dragon-killing figure, there was always St Michael who could be seen depicted in many churches. Even the royal family, who had taken the lead in introducing George to England, made no personal use of the name for more than two centuries after Richard I's crusade. The first prince to bear it was Edward IV's brother, 'false, fleeting, perjured Clarence', who ended his inglorious career in a butt of Malmsey (if the story is true), an unfortunate augury for England's first attempt at a royal George. No name could seem more homely and English than George does now, but in the surname period it was exotic.

I find it even more surprising that St *Alban* should have such a negligible score. A soldier and a martyr, Britain's first, with a shrine conveniently situated on a great highway near London, where Offa had built a noble church, which was rebuilt by the Normans in great size and splendour, he seems to have all the requirements for a tremendous cult, but the surnames from his name, including *Albin, Albon, Allibone* and *Allbone,* amount to less than fifty. Fashion is indeed unpredictable. Perhaps his shrine was too easily accessible to be worth a pilgrimage. Perhaps it was a case of a prophet in his own country.

This thought brings us to the Anglo-Saxon saints, the very ones who should have been most loved and honoured in England. It is sad to see what low scores they have, compared to saints of France, Italy and even Asia Minor that were so popular in the surname period. But some genuine devotion to the English saints did remain, giving their names a little more staying power than the mass of purely secular Old English names which faded away so completely.

We must bear in mind that there were two St Edwards, but neither had done much to deserve the title. Edward the Martyr distinguished himself only as a promising boy king who was tragically murdered. Edward the Confessor was admired as a holy man, but his holiness consisted largely in a vague inefficiency in worldly affairs. Edward survived more as a royal name than a saint's name, but even so was nearing extinction when Henry III revived it.

But *Edmund* of East Anglia, king and martyr, shot to death with arrows (like St Sebastian) by the Danes, was truly loved and remembered, and his name survived in considerable numbers especially in the East Anglian counties and London, to which many young men from that part of England found their way. However, its score, even with somewhat late royal patronage, is only about 260, including several variants.

In the same way *Cuthbert,* the beloved monk of Lindisfarne, who, somewhat in the manner of St Francis, preached to the seals and the sea birds on his lonely island, was remembered and honoured in the North. His name survived there as strongly as Edmund in the South-East. It branched into various abbreviations and contractions including *Cudd, Cuddy, Cutts* and *Cutting,* and is probably the main source of *Cubit* and possibly of *Cobbett.* It may have more surnames than Edmund but cannot be accurately assessed.

Another great name in the North was that of St Oswald, Christian King of Northumbria, whose head was finally placed with great veneration in the same coffin as St Cuthbert's uncorrupted body, and both ultimately enshrined in Durham Cathedral. *Oswald* like *Cuthbert* survives in its full form, and also in several odd versions. I have seen it in the Parish Register of a Shropshire village, varying from Ostwald in the reign of Elizabeth I to Wostall in the next generation, and Woosall seventy years later, the same family being easily traceable throughout.

St *Dunstan* is represented by nearly fifty examples, and St Alphege, another Archbishop of Canterbury, by rather more, which is not surprising, seeing that he was stoned to death by the Danes only a generation before the Conquest. His name survives both in the French pronunciation *Elvidge* and the English *Elphick*. St Swithin, on the other hand, the Bishop of Winchester, whose name has been oddly connected with the weather, has no example in the directory; but there is probably one somewhere.

The names of other Anglo-Saxon saints will be found on page 335 in a list of Old English personal names.

The question of who received the title of Saint and who did not was a chancy affair in early times. If anyone in England deserved canonization it was Alfred, the champion of Christendom who brought a whole heathen nation of invaders into the Christian Church. But he was not martyred, nor did he live as a recluse. It was hard for a family man who died in his bed to become a saint, however great his virtue. Alfred's name was remembered and honoured, but not quite in the same way as it would have been if his place in the hierarchy of Heaven had been officially ratified.

We will leave the mass of ordinary secular Anglo-Saxon names for the next chapter, and for the moment look further back into the Dark Ages at that other heroic leader who fought against the heathen in this island, Arthur. He too might well have been given the name of Saint. Although his life is hardly more than legendary, he is just as historical as George or Maurice, more so than many Celtic saints like *Ives*. The Celtic peoples who cherished his fame and the stories of his exploits and death were particularly lavish with the title, but it was never awarded to this heroic figure. Nor indeed was his name much used in Wales or Cornwall; only in Brittany was there a continuous tradition that kept the name of Arthur in use.

There are about a hundred examples of *Arthur* in our directory, but according to G. F. Black, the authority on Scottish surnames, the Highland MacArthur, of which it is a simplified form, is derived from a Gaelic name meaning a bear, and has only a coincidental likeness to that of the legendary king. But a few, genuinely linked with him in memory, did come into England with the Breton contingent in the Conqueror's army. We see them occasionally in documents of the period, generally Latinized as Arturius. One of them, for instance, was a Canon of St Paul's in 1104, and from them are descended the few *Arters* (less than twenty), which are the only surnames that can definitely be derived from this great, half legendary hero of our own. The even rarer *Harter* has probably the same origin.

As to his knights, the name of *Tristram*, a prince of Cornwall, was just kept alive in this remote corner of England where memories seem to be longer than elsewhere. *Kay* also continued in the West, though now confused with other surnames (page 71), and Gawain, whose story exists in an early metrical romance, survived in the North and West as *Gavin*. But there is no sign of Launcelot or Galahad, and though the Arthurian legends gradually found their way into the repertoires of minstrels and courtiers, until by the fifteenth century they were among the favourites of the upper classes, they did not produce Christian names in England. If the Breton Prince Arthur, heir to the English throne, had not been murdered, it would have been very different. But he was, and after that the name was probably thought unlucky, as it seemed to be when tried again in Tudor times. So if we are looking among modern surnames for British saints and heroes, Arthur is just a notable omission.

In this review of surnames from Christian names, we have descended all the way from John with its thousands, in our chosen scale of measurement, right down to Arthur with only about twenty. Among those with a high score there is only one that I have failed to mention in detail, and that because it belongs neither to the Teutonic names of the Northmen nor to the Bible, nor the later Christian saints and heroes. *Alexander* is the only secular name with more than the merest handful of

241

examples that comes from the ancient history of the classical world. It was a name whose great prestige in Europe had never faded. It remained current all through the Dark Ages, especially in Eastern Europe, and was used for Popes and Emperors in the West. The name of a conqueror (though not a Christian), it was just the sort to appeal to the Normans.

Even so the numbers of this name would not be so high were it not for Scotland where three Alexanders were kings in the twelfth and thirteenth centuries, establishing the name there as strongly as William in England. If we ask how it came to Scotland in the first place, it was introduced by Queen Margaret who, as a child, had been brought up in exile in the Christian court of King Stephen of Hungary, where she had received influences from Eastern Europe which she would not have had in England. Alexander I was one of her sons. So the name came into England from the North, the twelfth century being a time of much friendly intercourse between the two countries. But meanwhile the Normans had brought it into the South as well, in the French form Alisaundre, which became common as Saunder. On the whole *Saunders* is the southern surname, *Sanderson* the northern.

When we look for a pattern in the popularity of these saintly and heroic names, we find it intricate and complicated. Sometimes local saints seem to have an appeal, but on the whole the stronger preference is for those of foreign origin. Alexander of ancient Greece was thought much more of than Arthur of ancient Britain, a hundred times as much according to the figures; the Roman soldier Maurice, martyred in Switzerland, was as greatly preferred to the Roman Alban martyred in similar circumstances close to London; Lawrence, the deacon, tortured to death in Rome made thirty times as many names in England as Alphege, the Archbishop of Canterbury stoned to death at Greenwich.

We see that affection for a name was a slow growth. George fails principally on account of the late date at which he was brought to the attention of the English, rather than his geographical remoteness. Arthur was not part of legends of the English; on the contrary he belonged to their enemies whom they had driven into the West, and his return to England as a hero of romance was late in the surname period.

Many children no doubt were given the name of a Saint because they were born on his special day. This one might suppose would, by the law of chance, hardly favour one more than another. But it happens that some saints, like both the St Johns, have two festivals each, and certain Saints' Days fall at particularly important times of year, which give them an added interest. St Michael's Day, for instance, at the end of September, is associated with the harvest and became an important landmark and dividing point of the year, and St Martin's Day, 11th November, follows close upon All Saints and All Souls, which themselves coincide with the great autumnal festival harking back to pagan times. This was a time of ancient rites and superstitions, also of feasting; and St Martin, because of this association, became the patron saint of feasts. These two great occasions marking the end of summer and coming of winter, Michaelmas and Martinmas, must have added much to the special character of the two names.

Likewise both Nicholas and Stephen have their days close to the Christmas festival, which must have given their names cheerful associations. It is this chance that must be largely responsible for turning St Nicholas into Santa Claus.

Although many saints' names have been mentioned, there are still others with sufficient numbers to show them to have been well known in medieval England, though they do not compare with the soaring numbers of the leading names. St *Lambert*, a seventh-century bishop martyred in Germany, scores over three hundred, but the originals of some of these may have been homely lamb-herds. St Gervaise and St Eustace, both Roman martyrs, give us the surnames *Jervis* and *Jarvis* (250), and *Stacy* (150). St *Leonard*, patron of prisoners (200), and St *Giles*, of cripples (180), each had a natural appeal. St *Anthony* (120) was said to be the patron of swineherds, but was probably chiefly admired as a famous hermit. *Jerome, Valentine, Sylvester* and *Hillary*, all under a hundred, are some of the other saints' names occasionally used in the surname period.

To say that medieval people thought much of the saints would be inadequate. Heaven was a reality to them towards which their lives were hopefully bent, and these names, taken from its glorious company to be given to their children, represent some of their deepest feelings and beliefs.

Chapter 23

PRE-CONQUEST SURVIVALS

When we were looking at nicknames we were constantly drawn back into the past and found that those that had made the most surnames were the ones used by the Anglo-Saxons. With Christian names the opposite is the case; the post-Conquest names being the most numerous, and yet, though the earlier names are not obvious, they are present with us in far greater numbers than might be supposed.

The new favourites brought in by the Normans stand out like the leading characters of a drama, but anyone who studies the scene will be aware of a great company of supporting cast filling up the crowd in the background. Among them are no individual names which survive in large numbers, few even whose totals reach three figures in our directory, but there are literally hundreds of different surnames from this source. The Anglo-Saxons liked to create variety in their names, and that variety is still with us, though largely unrecognized.

There are two main reasons why we are so unaware of the presence of these names. One is that, being so old and long disused, they have suffered more battering by time than names that came in later and remained well known. As they grew less familiar, so they became more liable to erosion and, like ancient stone carvings worn away by wind and rain and covered in moss, they can remain in full view unrecognized for what they are. When we meet a Mr *Alston* we do not instantly think of Athelstan, nor does Miss *Kemble* remind her friends of the Saxon Cynebeald.

The other reason is that few modern people are familiar with more than a score of Anglo-Saxon names, so that even when they have survived in excellent condition they are still unknown. *Darwin*, for instance, is hardly changed at all from Deorwine (dear friend), nor are *Gladwin* or *Goldwyn* (glad friend and golden friend) much altered. They are pleasant Christian names straight from pre-Conquest England, but most people now would think of them only as surnames.

This is not the place to elaborate on sound changes, but a mention of one or two that took place regularly will help with a recognition of such names. The Old English hard 'c' nearly always changed into a modern 'ch' sound, except in the North. ('Church' is the same word as the Scottish 'kirk'.) We have met this change already in the case of Richard, which remained Rickard long enough in the North to make many surnames with the hard sound. This common name-theme 'ric' was much used by the Anglo-Saxons, but generally in the second position, and nearly all their names, ending in this way, now end with 'rich' or 'ridge'. Thus Eadric became *Edrich*; Leofric, *Loveridge* or *Leveridge*; Godric, *Goodrich* or *Goodridge*, but the northern *Goodrick* survives also.

The letter 'r', always an uncertain affair in English, had a tendency to change its position We see this in many common words, as for instance 'bird' which was 'bridd' in Old English, while 'beorht', which formed the second part of many Anglo-Saxon names, has developed into 'bright'. But it could also become 'bert' as in Cuthbert, or 'birt' or 'burt'. In early West Country parish registers the surname *Burt* appears even within one family, spelt indiscriminately Byrt and Bryt, as if the pronunciation consisted of nothing but the three consonants and the vowel hardly mattered. The result is that we often have double forms like *Seabert* and *Seabright*, *Fulbert* and *Fulbright*. In history books the old royal name Aethelbeorht is generally given in a simplified form as Ethelbert; in Domesday Book it is written Ailbert or Albert, but the surname *Albright* is the true representative of the normal English development. In *Albutt* the 'r' has been lost altogether. Some of the *Alberts* in the modern directory must be of genuine Old English descent, but others have come in recent times from the Continent where a cognate form of the same name existed.

There was a general tendency towards shortening which was

much needed. Many of the Old English names seem impossible mouthfuls, but when whittled down they are manageable and pleasant. It was a great improvement when many of their cumbersome diphthongs became single vowels. How much better Edward is than the original Eadweard, with all its vowels fully sounded. It reminds one of the slow drawling speech of West Country dialects which probably do echo these early sounds. Many other vowel changes also took place, of which I will mention only two that affect several names. The first is the change of ō, which made Godwine become *Goodwin*, the second the change of ā, which caused 'stan' to become 'stone'.

Final letters often dropped off from name-themes; the 'f' sometimes did so from 'wulf' and 'leof', the 'g' always from 'wig' and 'sig'. Thus Cenwig and Wigmund became *Kenway* and *Wyman*; Wulfsig and Leofsig became *Wolsey* and *Livesey*; and Leofwine contracted to *Lewin*. Many more such examples may be found on page 335, but they will be better appreciated if the general principles underlying these changes are understood. Wulfric developed naturally into *Woolrich*, and then an intrusive 'd' slipped in to ease the passage from 'l' to 'r', giving *Wooldridge*. Wulf was a much used name-theme from the earliest recorded times, and exists in many surnames, sometimes easily recognizable, as in the case of *Wolfit* which comes from Wulfgeat – the Geats being a race of legendary heroes of whom Beowulf was one – sometimes whittled away almost to nothing. Cuthwulf, for instance, a name that needed some whittling, survives as *Cuttle*, *Culf* and *Cuff*. Saewulf (sea wolf) has become *Self*.

Aethel, the theme made famous by the kings of Wessex, occasionally survives with the 'th' still intact, as in *Etheridge* which occurs as Etheric in the Anglo-Saxon Chronicle. But far more often it lost the 'th' and kept the 'l', arriving at 'Ail', 'Al' or 'El'. The last two of these are frequently indistinguishable from that other royal theme, Aelf, which was inclined to lose its 'f'. Thus Aethelric and Aelfric both became Alridge, and then, as in the case of Wooldridge, acquired a 'd' in the middle, and so we have the names *Aldridge* and *Eldridge*, either of which may come from either name, or from Ealdric which had the 'd' in it already and also became *Oldridge*. Together this group produces 350 examples, a small score compared with Norman names, but quite high among Old English survivals. If your name is one of these three you cannot tell whether the original thought behind it was of a noble-, fairy-, or old-ruler, but you can be sure that the ancestor from whom it descends to you was English and lived not long after the Conquest.

It must be remembered that hundreds of Scandinavian names were mixed with the English ones before the Normans came, their general style and origins being so similar that little distinction need be made between them. However they had some special name-themes of their own, such as Thor-, which provides the first element of many surnames such as *Thirkell* and *Thurstan*, and a great many short forms that have given us well-known names like *Gunn*, and *Finn* and *Orme*, the last signifying the legendary serpent against which heroes fought. The famous Danish Cnut survives as *Knott*. The two races were so closely welded together before the Conquest that when we speak of the English after that date the Scandinavian element is included.

Some of these Old Norse names were almost identical with English ones, and some were also used by the Normans who came of the same Viking race. Rannulf, or *Ralph*, has already been mentioned (page 216) as coming from several sources and owing its popularity in England chiefly to its use by prominent Normans; while the typically Northumbrian Osbeorn and Osmund (now *Osborne* and *Osmond*) were also shared by Scandinavians and Normans, and borne by notabilities at the court of William I. One of his nephews, who became the first Bishop of Old Sarum, was later canonized as St Osmund.

While thinking of these names of double provenance, we should also notice that several of the continental names of Germanic origin that the Normans had adopted had cognate Old English forms. For instance *Herbert*, which comes from the Old German 'hari-bert' (army bright), coincided exactly in meaning and nearly in form with the Old English 'Herebeorht'. The two coalesced, but it was the Norman favour that made the name popular in the surname period. Other names in this class that were famous among the Franks but have counterparts in England are *Godfrey*, *Goddard*, Theodoric and *Theobald*. The last two have given the pet-forms *Terry*, *Terriss*, *Tebbitt*, *Tibble* and many more, all showing that the French pronunciation was the one in vogue in the surname period, and yet such names existed in pre-Conquest England.

One more name that is typically English in form and character, but which was reinforced from the Continent at the Conquest, is *Baldwin*. The Conqueror's father-in-law was Baldwin V of Flanders, which shows that the name was strongly entrenched there and must have been much used by the Flemings who came into England at that time. Its ramifications have given the surnames *Boddy*, *Bodkin* and *Bawcock*.

All these names must be classed as Anglo-Norman. Their use by the newcomers gave them a different line of development from the purely Old English names, which retained their own character, resisting foreign influences and new fashions to the last.

Much has already been said about the two-theme Anglo-Saxon names like Leofric, and the point made that they could be reduced to one of their parts for colloquial use. That this happened in all classes is shown by occasional scraps of evidence, such as the name Wuffa for an early king of Essex, which must surely have been a pet-form of one of the Wulf- names; and Cutha for the West Saxon King, Cuthwulf. But as time goes on these short names appear less and less among the ruling classes.

It would be convenient to call them monosyllables, but though they reach this state in the surname period, nearly all these short names had a final vowel that was sounded in Old English. The most regular masculine ending was 'a', which early chroniclers, trained in Latin, found so hard to stomach that they altered Beda to Bede (which it would have become in time), though they inconsistently left Penda and Offa in their original state. While some of these one-theme names are identical with common words like Good and Bright, others are so old that their meaning was lost long ago, names like Wada and Cada, Botta, Hudda and Tukka that were growing old-fashioned soon after the year 1000, though they continued in colloquial use for another two centuries. They seem infinitely remote from the present day, and yet they are with us still as *Wade*, *Cade*, *Bott*, *Hudd*, *Tuck* and many more. It is always a possibility with a one-syllable surname that seems to have no meaning, that it comes from one of these simple, ancient names.

It has been said that Old English Christian names became sur-names without any additional suffixes. This is true of the two-theme names, which normally remain perfectly plain, as *Aylwin*, *Seward* and so on; nor do any of the short names take the fami-liar endings which adhered so freely to the new Norman ones. But one suffix that was entirely English was used very frequently on all the short names. This is the ancient '-ing' which from the earliest recorded times signified a dependant, a child, a son, or just someone small and familiar. In the Anglo-Saxon Chronicle we read that Aethelred was 'Eadgaring', meaning 'the son of Edgar', but the sense was generally far wider and vaguer than that. An Aetheling, for instance, was either the son of a noble person, or a young noble person. (We have the same double meaning in 'prince' which suggests youth but also a royal de-scendant of any age.) The only certain sense of '-ing' is that of belonging. *Wilding*, for instance, means a person who belongs to the Wilds, or 'the wild one', or the son of a man called 'the wild'. It was a most useful suffix that made an adjective into a noun, linked a son to his father, and generally expressed attachment and familiarity.

I quoted 'Edgaring', but that was used in an official chronicle. In ordinary speech, '-ing' was never applied in this way to full-length names. But it was used constantly to round off the short ones, and therefore we have *Gooding, Harding, Bolding, Golding, Manning, Whitting* and many more, their form showing them all to be personal names. The most numerous of them is *Harding*; the Old English 'heard', which was much used in name-making, had a cognate form in French which came in as a nickname later as 'le hardi' or *Hardy*. But Harding is a typical Old Eng-lish form often seen in eleventh-century records. Robert Fitz-Harding, who was given Berkeley Castle in the reign of Stephen, was the son of a Harding, son of Eadnoth, a prominent English-man in 1066, and the fact that the name was used in this way with the Norman prefix shows how completely it was accepted as a regular Christian name.

On page 335 will be found a list of Anglo-Saxon personal names with the modern surnames descended from them. They are not arranged in numerical order like the list of later favourites, partly because their structure is much better seen when they are grouped by their themes, but chiefly because it is impossible to count them with any approach to accuracy. One difficulty in the way is their frequent similarity to place names. For instance, 'stan', the early form of 'stone', was a favourite name-theme, but also a regular place-name ending. Surnames like *Winston* and *Alston* can come equally from the name of a man or a village. And again the tendency for 'r' to change its position means that Alfred and Wilfred have sometimes become *Alford* and *Wilford*, coinciding again with village names.

Then there is the problem of some old names being swallowed up in new ones. *Alwin* must sometimes have been absorbed into *Allen*, and Aethelgeat into *Elliot*; the popular Cola or *Cole* has become mixed with *Collins*, and Hudd used as a pet-form for Hugh. Altogether there are too many doubtful cases, and the numbers that could be listed with certainty are unrealistic compared with those that are really attributable to this source.

And yet this list, which is only a selection, shows that what the Old English names lack in individual scores they make up for in variety. I have aimed at including the best known surnames from the best known Anglo-Saxon names, but far more exist. It is like collecting all the pebbles of a certain colour on a large beach; one cannot ever begin to think one has gathered them all, or even half. The English scholar, Searle, and the more recent Swedish scholars, Redin and von Feilitzen have recorded literally thousands of these names from contemporary sources, but for every one that was written down on a piece of parchment that survived, there must be others that were never recorded.

Can we say which of these many names were most popular at the time of the Conquest, and which survived it longest as Christian names? It is really impossible to pick out favourites, only favourite themes with which endless different permutations were made. The one that occurs most often in the eleventh century is Wine, meaning 'friend'. (Why did this word become obsolete?) It exists as a surname in good number as *Winn* and *Wynne*, and might be more common if it had not been generally the second part of the name which was not so often used in abbreviations.

The God- (or Good) names were perhaps the most popular. *Godwin* alone has 340 examples without counting any of the

Goodes or *Goodings* some of which must rightfully belong to this source and would perhaps bring it to five hundred. It might seem that the Earl Godwin was remembered more than his unlucky son *Harold*, whose name including the contracted form *Harrod* scores barely a hundred, but probably the overbearing earl had much less influence than the general liking for the two themes, 'God' and 'Wine'.

The Aethel- and Aelf- names were much used, merging together in one syllable as has been noted, but there were so many forms of both that their numbers are much divided. Their popularity was a last expression of loyalty to the old royal line. Sae- and Sig- are also indistinguishable, so that *Sewell* can be from Saeweald or Sigweald.

Another favourite theme was Leof (*Love*), which could be used alone as a Christian name for either sex. Both Leofwine and Leofric have left a good many surnames, but in the case of the former the matter has been complicated by the fact that its natural derivatives, *Levin* and *Lewin*, have sometimes been adopted in modern times by Jews (page 76), but individual families do not need much knowledge of their genealogy to rule out or admit this possibility. If their surname is not Jewish, it is not only English but Old English.

The same complication affects the popular Old English name-theme Wulf (*Wolfe*). A number of Germans, whether Jews or not, have this surname, generally recognizable as foreign by a double 'f'. But the large numbers of compound Anglo-Saxon Wulf-names listed on page 336 prove that the short form must also be English to a large extent.

Another Saxon name with a comparatively high score, is the plainest name of all, *Mann*, with its diminutive *Manning*. We have met this before in the occupational section as a mere description of rank, distinguishing a man from his master, but there is no question that it had long been a popular personal name with the English from the early days when places like Mansfield got their names, to Domesday Book and later. It may be compared to Carl among the Franks and Norsemen, and Svein or Sweyn with the Danes, which both have the same, simple meaning.

Many compound names were formed with '-man' as the second part. The surnames *Blackman*, *Whit(e)man*, *Coleman*,

Seaman and *Goodman,* all of obvious meaning, were originally Christian names, though they were probably used as nicknames at a later date. The last of these won itself a very special place in English speech. Because it was typical of the Old English style of name, and its meaning suggested virtue and reliability, the name *Goodman* lingered in use as a type-word for an old-fashioned countryman of respectable standing. As late as the eighteenth century many a yeoman farmer was referred to by his neighbours, not as Master or Mister Brown, but as Goodman Brown.

Of course *Brown* was popular, but although it was used as a Christian name, either alone (as it occurs several times in Domesday Book), or in compound form, such as Brunstan, and had a regular diminutive form, *Browning,* it made such a natural description for a swarthy fellow that it must owe its numbers largely to its later use as a nickname. It would slide very easily from one use to the other. Let us imagine a young couple with a baby son to christen. Father, a diehard of the old school, wants to call him Brunwine. Mother wants to be in the fashion and call him after the new young lord of the manor. She gets her way, and he is christened Richard, but he turns out dark haired, and Father, who never liked Richard, calls him Brown. Mother, forgetting her grand ideas, calls him her little Browning, and so do his friends. When he grows up and attends the Manor Court to claim the few strips of land that had been his father's, his name is written down formally as Richard, and Browning is added as his second name.

This kind of thing must often have happened, giving these old names a prolongation of life as nicknames after they had ceased to be thought suitable for the font. But in dwelling on these many familiar forms we must not forget the hundreds of full-length two-theme Old English names that have descended to us a trifle battered but not familiarized in any way.

Just as the surnames formed from the new-style names brought in by the Normans represented at first the ruling classes and then, at a later stage and in more popular forms, the general mass of the people, so it was with the Old English names. The shortened ones and the '-ing' forms were those likely to remain longest as popular nicknames, while the formal two-theme names are regular patronymics from an earlier date. They represent those thousands of Englishmen in the century or two (at most) after the Conquest who did not quickly adapt themselves to Norman ways. And though the majority of them under Norman rule were only peasants, there were many who retained some of their former lands, and some authority. People whose surnames became permanent at such an early date were on the whole of the upper class, and therefore a family with one of these full-length pre-Conquest names as a surname has every reason to think of the ancestor from whom it derives as an Englishman of good standing born before 1200 and possibly within living memory of Hastings.

We now return to the question as to which of these names were most common just after the Conquest, and which of them lasted longest as Christian names. It has been hard to answer because of the Old English tendency to make an infinite variety of names, but by the eleventh century the new idea of naming after great men was beginning to make an impression, and certainly Alfred, Edgar, Edmund, Edward, Cuthbert and Godwin are all quite well represented (according to the moderate standards of this class) both in contemporary records and the modern directory, while a number of others such as Sewald, Aelfric, Ailward, Leofwine and several of the '-ing' names have similar numbers. These are all names that a priest would think proper to give at the font, but if the question is not, 'What official names lasted best?' but, 'What did Englishmen call each other as they worked together in the fields?' then the answer would be something like, Wolf, Man, Brown, Good, Gold, White, Ed, Al, Bert and Stan, and to any one of them they might add the familiar '-ing'.

It has been said earlier that the pre-Conquest Christian names had disappeared within two centuries of the Conquest. This is a sweeping statement, but (if we exclude the short, common themes like Brown and White that continued as nicknames) it is not too strong. From the accession of Edward I in 1272 we have the evidence of the Subsidy Rolls, giving a comprehensive view of all classes. To test this point I took a thousand consecutive names each, from lists for London, Suffolk, Sussex, Cumberland, Yorkshire and Dorset, and found an average of just under 2% of pre-Conquest men's names as Christian names, the proportion

253

varying only a little from one county to another. They were present as surnames in quantity, in fact in rather higher proportion than we have them now, but they were no longer given at the font.

These old names may still be found quite plentifully in records of the time of King John and the early years of Henry III. But about that time the last generation who bore them was dying out, and in a few decades they had all gone. It must have seemed sad for the old men that the names of their forefathers were being forgotten, and they can have had no notion of the extraordinary degree of immortality these same names were gaining by being transferred to a secondary position. We can imagine old Snelgar and Cuthbold mumbling together by the smoky fireside about the tiresome habits of the young people, and deploring, among other matters, the new-fangled names which were ousting the old favourites. But as their grandsons, Tom, Dick and Harry, rode off as part of the escort of the local Lord, who was himself following a greater man – shall we say to Runnymede – the old men would hardly notice that these boys were hailed by their companions as Tom *Snell* and Dick *Cobbold*, and could have no conception of the new careers on which these names were being launched.

The pre-Conquest names that became permanent surnames at such an early date have lasted so long and well because they had that desirable quality in surnames, variety. Ceasing to be first names soon after 1200, they made excellent second names, and came through the rest of the period, when such matters were still fluid, in large numbers, without any change other than the natural modifications of time, because they served the purpose so well. The more unusual they were, the more likely to last, for people like a surname that does not sound like a common word but only like a proper name.

Chapter 24

METRONYMICS

Throughout this section we have been considering surnames derived from men's Christian names, but at the height of the surname period when casual designations of a colloquial sort were sticking fast, a great many of them came from names of women.

No one need think there was anything derogatory about this. It is true that an illegitimate boy might be called by his mother's name, but it was equally natural and usual to refer to the son of a highly respected widow in the same way, or even, when the father was alive but away for years on some distant expedition or married to a dominant wife, the lad might be spoken of among the neighbours as belonging to Moll or Alison or Margery.

We see a great many such surnames in the thirteenth-century rolls, a higher proportion than we have today. Presumably some young men did not like a feminine name tagged on to their own and managed to acquire more manly ones while such things were still fluid, but a great many have stuck, more than is generally recognized, amounting to at least 10% of all names of relationship.

These maternal names seem to occur very often in the records of legal courts, possibly because boys brought up by their mothers more often got into trouble than those who had fathers. For instance in the Court Rolls of the Earl of Lancaster in the reign of Edward II, we find William the son of Moll and William the son of Magg fined together for trespass, ninepence and threepence respectively. They had probably been out poaching, and Will *Mollison* seems to have been the worst offender. Or, a more serious affair from the Wiltshire Crown Pleas Roll for 1249,

'Adam the son of Agnes struck Adam the son of Edith with a knife so that he died on the third day. Adam, son of Agnes fled. The jurors say he is guilty. So let him be exacted and outlawed.'

These two entries are translated from Latin, but of course the Latin was itself a translation of the words spoken in court. The young men, whose Christian names by chance are the same, were called something like Adkin *Annison* and Adcock *Eady* by their friends, but the clerk would know better than to write that down. He would make it as formal and correct as possible; and yet the words of the witnesses have endured in spite of him, and are in our directory though not in his record.

These women's names surviving in modern surnames exhibit in their smaller compass the same characteristics as those of men. Some are survivals of pre-Conquest names that we hardly know; others of royal names that spread from the few great ones to the masses; others show the popularity of certain saints. All combine to reflect the tastes and feelings of their times.

Anglo-Saxon women's names are even more formidable than the men's and require much natural erosion to make them tolerable. They were formed in the same way of two parts, of which the first was the same as the men's, but the second consisted of feminine words, though to our way of thinking there is nothing gentle or feminine about many of them. 'Gifu' (gift) and 'flaed' (beauty) are pleasant enough, but other very popular endings include 'gyth' and 'hild' which both mean 'war', and 'thryth' (strength), hardly the themes we would choose now for girls.

'Burg', meaning a stronghold or fortified place, seems a particularly forbidding theme for including in a girl's name, but was much used. It is exactly the same word as the one that ends numerous place names in a variety of spellings and pronunciations (bury, burgh, borough and so on), which makes it often impossible to recognize as a woman's name. Wigburg, for instance, which must have been quite popular even after the Conquest, judging by the number of different surnames that have derived from it (page 337), seems about as unfeminine a name as one can imagine. Ethelburga, as the Queen who brought Christianity to the court of Northumbria is generally called, was actually Aethelburg which would normally become Elbury or

Aylbury or some such name, sounding much more like a village than a lady.

These formal names belong to classic pre-Conquest types, but in the later Anglo-Saxon period, as with the men, we find softer and gentler names developing, such as *Sweetlove* and *Loveday*, to give them in their modern form, often shortened simply to *Sweet* and *Love*.

With these Saxon names one is constantly facing the difficulty of deciding how to present them. In their original spelling they look outlandish to those not used to them. Some have a modified later form, such as Edith, that is much more acceptable; others are better known by a Latin form made up by chroniclers, which does not represent reality. Take Aethelthryth, for instance. It looks so alarming that one could feel no surprise at its going out of fashion, but actually it lasted better than most. It had the advantage of belonging to a saint who founded the Abbey of Ely, and was remembered with great devotion. 'Th' often turned into 'd', owing to French influence, and the clerks, writing in Latin, added the inevitable final 'a' (regardless of the fact that in Old English 'a' was a masculine ending) so that the lady has come down to us in history as St Etheldreda. In the nineteenth century that great admirer of the Anglo-Saxons, Charlotte Yonge, gave the name to the heroine of her highly successful novel *The Daisy Chain*, rightly omitting the spurious 'a'. Of course Etheldred's brothers and sisters called her Ethel for short, and this new name swept the country for a generation or two. But this was an artificial growth. The real development of Aethelthryth was to Aildrid and Audrey, which was still alive among old-fashioned country people in Shakespeare's day, and the fillip he gave it sent it the rest of the way. But before his time it had made the surname *Awdrey*.

One of the few Anglo-Saxon women's names that is well known (in its Latin form) is Godiva. The name of the celebrated Lady of Coventry was really Godgifu (good gift), but by the end of the eleventh century it had been whittled down to *Goodeve*, a pleasant sounding name with a dozen examples in the direc-tory. A similar name that has also survived quite well was God-gyth which became Goodeth, and then simply *Good(e)y* of which there are over fifty. But this last form could equally belong to Goodeve and must be shared between the two. Just as the men's

Good- names came to be used as types of old-fashioned country men, so their feminine counterparts, often shortened to 'Goodie', lingered on in peasant speech. It seems a far cry from Lady Godiva to 'Little Goodie Two Shoes', but there is a link.

But of all Anglo-Saxon names the one that probably lasted best was Eadgyth, or Edith. At the time of the Conquest it was unrivalled as a royal name; Edward the Confessor's queen (Harold's sister), Harold's own queen, and his mistress, Edith of the Swan Neck, all had the same name. There is some little confusion about the last two ladies, uncertainty as to which of them was Edith the Fair who appears well endowed with land in Domesday Book, but the ex-queen is the likelier candidate. The name can be seen in medieval records as a Christian name after almost all the other Saxon ones, male and female, have gone. It is still there in the early parish registers, especially in the South-West, though very countrified and out-moded, and in fact stayed the whole course to the Victorian revival. It is responsible for *Eade*, *Eady* and *Edis*, and probably *Eddison* too, for at the height of the surname period it was far more numerous than any of the men's 'Ed–' names.

The name Edith has brought us to the subject of queens, and, as with men's names, we see that once the eleventh century is reached with its new style of name-giving, the prestige of royalty outweighs all other influences. The first Queen of England whose name has made many surnames is even earlier than Edith, Emma of Normandy, the only woman to be twice Queen Consort, first of Ethelred the Unready and then of his conqueror, Cnut. She was a selfish, time-serving creature who infuriated even her saintly son Edward the Confessor, but as wife of two kings, mother of two more, and sister of the Duke of Normandy (William's grandfather), she was immensely influential. It is not likely that her name was much copied in England in her lifetime, for at that date the English so much preferred their own names that they designated her Aelfgifu. It was in Normandy that her name must have spread at first, and so it came to England again among the wives and daughters of the Conqueror's knights and barons, giving us *Emms*, *Emmett* and others. Some of Emma's many relations are shown in the family tree in the endpapers.

Before we follow any further in the train of Norman queens, we must remember a queen of English lineage whose name, Margaret, was destined to take deep root in this island. Her romantic history is well known, but worth repeating, for it makes a vital link between old and new royal lines, and between Eastern and Western European culture.

In 1016 when Edmund Ironside died and the Danish Cnut had become the ruler of England, Edmund's infant son Edward was taken from the country to a safe refuge in the hospitable court of Hungary, lately made Christian by its King Stephen. There the exile grew up and married a lady related to the Emperor of the West and had three children, a son whom he named Edgar, hoping that one day he might be King of England, and two daughters, who received the Greek names Margaret and Christina.

When the Saxon line was restored in the person of Edward the Confessor, younger brother of Edmund Ironside, and it became clear that he would have no children, having, some said, taken a vow of chastity, he should have recalled his nephew from Hungary at once to be his heir. Eventually he did so, late in his reign, but when Edward 'the Exile' did at last reach England with his wife and children, he almost immediately died, before he had even seen the king. 'Alas, that was a rueful time', comments the Anglo-Saxon Chronicle sadly, and the event does seem not only rueful but highly suspicious. A few years later, when the Confessor died, the child Edgar was passed over in favour of Harold, because of the need of a grown man as king at such a time; but when Harold was killed and William victorious the hopes of the nation clung forlornly to the 'Child', as they called Edgar, and to his sisters. With some faithful attendants this young family set out to escape from William's power by sea and, driven by storms, landed at last on the coast of Scotland where the young King Malcolm received them kindly, fell in love with Margaret and made her his queen.

The Chronicle makes much of this story and dwells proudly on Margaret's virtues and holiness and her achievement in spreading Christianity and enlightenment in Scotland, and the thoughts of many Englishmen must have dwelt sadly at this time on their twice exiled royal family. As William's iron grip on England strengthened, hopes centred on Edgar Atheling faded to despair, but when a generation later Henry I married Margaret's daughter it was an act of immense popularity. Meanwhile Margaret's name, exotic though it was, spread quickly in England as well as Scotland, even before her canonization in 1250, its popularity being shown by the many forms into which it branched, Meg, Mag, Mog, Margery, Madge and others, often rhymed with an initial P. And all these forms made surnames, as can be seen on page 339.

The name of Margaret's sister, Christina, who became the first Abbess of Romsey, was also soon absorbed. Indeed the surname *Christie* is far more often from this source than from the masculine Christopher which is seldom seen in England before the fifteenth century.

Before we leave Margaret it should be mentioned that there was another saint of this name who had a considerable cult on the Continent, but I cannot think she was responsible for more than a small fraction of the surnames derived from the name in England. She has much in common with Saint George, being an obscure character from Asia Minor with no real historical basis for her legend, which is also concerned with a dragon. She may have had some romantic appeal among Norman ladies, but this must have been slight compared to the deep emotions of pride and nostalgia felt by the English for their own princess, who had proved worthy of highest heavenly honour, as well as love and loyalty on earth.

Turning now to the names of Norman queens we find that Matilda reigns supreme. To us the name sounds faintly comical, but this was far from the case in the eleventh century. In the hundred years following 1066 four queens bore this name; Matilda of Flanders, wife of the Conqueror; Matilda of Scotland (daughter of Margaret and Malcolm, whose real name was Edith but who assumed the name of Matilda on her marriage with Henry I); their daughter Matilda, who struggled against Stephen for the crown after her brother had been drowned in the White Ship; and, lastly, the wife of Stephen, who was again, inevitably, Matilda. In fact one could say that during that century of Norman rule all the royal ladies distinguished enough to be remembered in our history were called Matilda. After this it seems that everyone was sated with the name, and when it had run its natural downward course through all classes it disappeared more completely than any other royal name of either sex has ever done, an attempt to revive it in the nineteenth century having little success. But its regular descent from royal palace to rustic hut and oblivion took at least two centuries during which time surnames were formed freely from all its versions.

We all know how the history books vacillate between Matilda and Maud, and surnames do exactly the same thing. The name was Germanic in origin, composed of the two themes 'maht' and 'hild', might and battle, just the sort of things the Normans liked. In French it was contracted to Mahild, Mauld, Molde, Mawt and so to Maud, and the general use of such forms in England is reflected in such surnames as *Maude, Mould, Moult, Mowatt, Maw* and *Mawson*, though the last two have at least one other possible source (page 183). The Latin form was Matilda, and there must have been some popular version close to this in sound, for we also have a distinct group even more numerous than the other, from the abbreviation *Till*, giving us *Tilly, Tillett, Tillotson* and others. Altogether there are well over three hundred derivatives of this name in the directory, and among women's names it probably ranks highest in number, with Margaret close behind it.

Two other names much used in Norman court circles and destined for wide popularity were Alice and Isabel (to use their modern forms). The Germanic Adelhaidis came to England in various contracted forms. William I's sister (mother of King Stephen) was known as Adela; Henry I's second wife as Adelicia, but the English people, taking the name to themselves, soon reduced it to the simple Alis, often adding the familiar '-on' to make *Allison*. Isabel, an early version of Elizabeth, seems to have come from the south of France. It was used in England even before King John married Isabella of Angoulême in 1200, but no doubt that event increased its numbers. Its popularity in the following century is proved by the variety of pet-forms seen in the surnames it formed: *Ibbs, Ibbott, Nibbs, Niblett, Libby, Bibby* and of course *Bell*, though this last has obvious other sources.

The only other English queen's name early enough to influence surnames, excluding Berengaria who never set foot in

England, is Eleanor. The dynamic and influential wife of Henry II, Eleanor of Aquitaine, cannot have failed to leave many namesakes, and the gay, extravagant Eleanor of Provence, wife of Henry III, unpopular though she was, must have kept the fashion going. Yet a third Eleanor, the adored wife of Edward I, followed her, and we can be sure that by this time the name of these three queens must have been widespread. But its colloquial forms are too easily confused with others for us to be able to pick them out with any certainty. *Ellen, Ellett, Ellis, Else, Elkins, Elson* and *Nelson* could all be easily from this feminine source, but there are other sources too, mostly masculine, for all of them, Ellis, for instance, and the Saxon El- names (derived from Aethel), and, in the case of Nelson, the Celtic-Scandinavian Neill. Eleanor is certainly represented among all these forms, but we cannot pin her down in any of them.

Bible names for women were slow to come in, and the old taboo on using the names of sacred persons still held for the especially holy name of Mary after those of later saints were admitted. It is seldom to be found before 1200, but spread rapidly in the following century, generally in the pet-form Mariot which accounts for the majority of our *Marriotts*. *Marris* and *Marrison* are less numerous, as also is *Marion* which came into favour late in our period. Maid Marian is probably a fifteenth-century embellishment to the Robin Hood legend. The 'r' being, as usual, a difficulty for some, Mary often turned into Mally and Molly, giving us *Malleson* and *Mollison*. (The change from 'a' to 'o' is exactly parallel to that in *Maggs* and *Moggs*.) It is highly probable too that some of the many *Morrisons*, which really seem too plentiful for Maurice, may be attributable to this source. Also it is certain that not all the *Malletts* are descended from the Norman baron who fought at Hastings, some being the English sons of little Mary.

Very few other women's names from the Bible were used in England in the surname period. Magdalen, pronounced Maudlin, is sometimes seen and must be responsible for *Maudling*, though some of its forms may easily be confused with those of Maud. For men the names of the Apostles had enormous appeal, and parents wishing to place their daughters under the patronage of these important saints did not hesitate to give them their names with or without feminine modification. Thus we see many examples in the rolls of Johanna as well as Johannes, but in actual speech the girls' names, which were to develop into Joan and Jane, differed so little from the boys' John and Jan that it is quite impossible now to say which of the numerous Johnses, Joneses and so on derive from female names.

It is the same with several other names from masculine saints. Philip was certainly used sometimes for girls, and though clerks wrote it in Latin form as Philippa, and it is now known in that form, it seems from the evidence that this and other men's names of foreign origin were sometimes given to girls without any alteration. There is a distinctive feminine form of Peter in Petronel, which survives as *Parnell* and *Purnell*; but with many masculine names, as with John, though we know they were sometimes given to girls, we cannot pick out the feminine forms. There is no sign among surnames that the Latin final 'a', so often added to girls' names in writing, was ever pronounced in common speech, but rather that it was omitted, or turned into 'y', a traditional feminine ending as the list on page 339 makes clear. This takes us back to the Old English names in which some of the most frequent endings of women's names, such as 'thryth' and 'gyth' and 'gifu', end up as little but this single vowel.

A masculine saint's name that was much used for girls is that of the patron of France, St Denis. Its Latin form is Dionysius, and though this is not very often seen in the rolls as a man's name, it appears quite frequently as Dionysia. In this case we have reason to be grateful to the clarity of Latin, for if it were written in English we should often see no difference of sex in its form, which would be something like Denys in either case. But it is likely that the original of *Denny* was often a woman.

Elizabeth and Ann, such invariable favourites of later days, were hardly used. The former occurs very occasionally, shortened to Beth which gives the rare *Bethell*. Bette is quite often seen but is nearly always masculine, as in Gower's *Peasants' Revolt*, and seems to be one of the pet-names formed from Bartholomew. *Anson*, *Annett* and *Annison*, which sound as if they came from Anne, almost all belong to Agnes, a favourite from an early date, which was regularly pronounced without the 'g'.

A fair number of *Eves* can be found to match the numerous Adams, but otherwise Old Testament names had little appeal for the ladies. They much preferred saints and martyrs of later times, particularly if there was a pathetic or romantic story attached. Catherine, Cecilia, Lucy, Agatha and Agnes were all virgin martyrs whose cults have made English surnames. Of these the favourite was Agnes. A young girl, martyred in Rome in her early teens rather than submit to an unchristian marriage, and seen afterwards in visions clad in robes of purest white, she became a symbol of chastity and patron of unmarried girls. But placing girls under her protection did not imply that they should remain virgins. On the contrary, St Agnes' Eve became a great occasion for rites and ceremonies connected with the hoped for object of happy marriage.

Another saint's name that became extremely popular for girls in our period was Juliana. This saint is not in the English calendar, but was a favourite with the Flemings for whom she had a local interest, and Miss Withycombe in *The Oxford Dictionary of English Christian Names* attributes the introduction of the name to them. In any case it became so common in England at one time, shortened to Jill, *Gill, Gillet* and so on, that it sank to being a term for the lowest type of girl, a 'jilt' in fact, after which it went right out, leaving behind it probably more surnames than any woman's name except those of queens and the Virgin Mary. But their numbers cannot be calculated as they are confused with abbreviations of masculine names such as Giles and Gilbert and the French form of William, Guillaume; the name *Julian* could belong to either sex.

In the twelfth and thirteenth centuries close contact with Europe brought a flock of new names into England from the tales and romances told first in the courts and castles of the great. Queens from foreign countries were influential in bringing in new culture from abroad, and what was said and done at the court was sure to spread. Eleanor of Aquitaine, for instance, was a woman of wide experience who had herself travelled to the East and loved to encourage poets and scholars. In her son Richard I's reign many Englishmen widened their horizons in the Crusades, and then, during the next two reigns, Isabella of Angoulême and Eleanor of Provence both came from the pleasure-loving South of France with minstrels and courtiers in their train, bringing new touches of romance and imagination to our grim Norman castles.

It was as if a new wind was blowing, and with it came an outburst of romantic names. Some were classical – Cassandra, Ismenia, Sybilla, Constantia. One sees them in this formal Latin in official lists, but the surnames from them (page 339) show the sort of thing the girls were really called.

Some came from the Arthurian legends. Guinevere, sometimes written Gwenore or Gaynore in medieval romances, has left the surname *Gaynor*. Iseult, a favourite not only in Cornwall, but all over the country, has left many versions.

Some are purely fanciful, made up out of pleasant attributes like Jocosa (or *Joyce*), or Amabella, which was soon reduced to Mabel, Mab or Mob, the 'b' often becoming sharpened to 'p' (as Hobkin becomes Hopkin) giving surnames like *Mappin* and *Moppet* as well as providing a name for the Fairy Queen.

Many fanciful, high-flown names came briefly into fashion at that time. Dry legal documents are brightened with references to Melodia, Scientia, Theophania, Celestria and dozens more, making us realize what pleasure women found, as they always have, in novelty and romance. They vanished away in a few decades giving place to plainer and more enduring names, but their brief flowering season coincided with the peak point of the fixing of surnames, so that many of these rare, short-lived girls' names have left rare but long-lived surnames.

Some of the better known names of this Norman and early Plantagenet period were revived by the late Victorians in their zest for all things old, and to our ears seem to belong more to that period than to any other. Alice, Isabel, Mabel and Maud sound like a Victorian tea party in the Rectory garden; we can almost hear the ping of tennis balls and the rustle of muslin blouses, but the real background of these names is castle walls and timber cottages in the time of the Crusades.

We have said that surnames from women's names are like those from men's on a smaller scale. Certainly we see similar pre-Conquest survivals, none individually numerous; we see also the influence of royalty and the Bible, with Matilda and Mary balancing William and John; and we see the great popularity of later saints and the special appeal of one or two with local interest. But there are points of contrast too. The men are more conservative in their tastes than the women. Having passed from the Old English names to those of Norman rulers and Christian saints, they showed little disposition to venture further. Alexander is almost the only man's name from the ancient world of Greece and Rome to attain much popularity, and this is largely due to the three kings of Scotland of that name. The Arthurian legends produced little effect on the naming of sons, but it is typical that, whereas the numbers of Matilda and Mary are only small, fractions of those of William and John, the score of Iseult is at least four times that of Tristram.

In another respect these metronymics have a distinctive character. They are all colloquial and belong to the true surname period, and the height of it at that. Surnames from men's names are complicated by the latecomers, the Welsh and to a lesser extent the Scots, deliberately adopting names of English type. But such people always took the names of their fathers. Mothers' names were never taken deliberately. They only developed naturally out of daily speech, generally in their most familiar form. At the very same time that Hob and Perkin and Wat and other men's names of this sort were sticking to their sons in thousands, *Maudling* and *Bibby* and *Mogg* were adhering in smaller numbers to fatherless boys in the same spontaneous way, without any thought of posterity.

IV. Local Names

Chapter 25

THE ENGLISH LANDSCAPE

Of the four categories of surnames we have left the largest to the last. Though names of relationship seem to exist in endless numbers, those derived from place names are even more plentiful. And yet few of them are individually numerous. In any large group of English people it would be found that nearly a third had names of relationship, and only a slightly higher proportion of locality, but if one were to count, not the people in each group but the different surnames, it would be found that the latter group contained by far the most.

However there is one class of local names which exist in good numbers. This, as we might expect, consists of general terms like *Brook* and *Lane* and *Hill* which tell us the exact spot where our ancestor was living when he acquired the name. They are not aristocratic in origin, though they may be of intermediate class, representing a freeman. A landowner of any importance would take his name from the whole village where he lived, which would be known twenty or even a hundred miles away. But such designations as *Ford* were given to people whose lives were spent in one village where there was only one ford, and one cottage by it, and where no one could doubt the identity of Adam at the Ford. The same sites were often occupied for many generations by one family, and such names may sometimes be as old as those of the gentry at the hall, though there was less occasion in early times to write them down.

The study of local history fits in very happily with observation of this kind of name. My own most concentrated work in this field has been in Hertfordshire, particularly in Great Amwell and its adjoining parishes, where the Subsidy Rolls of Edward I and II, supported by Manorial Court Rolls of the same date, give a detailed picture of the rural population there in the years around 1300. A good many of the villagers owning strips in the common fields had at that time fixed names of the type that gave their address, and a detailed knowledge of the locality enabled me to place them exactly. In most cases the spot is still inhabited, often by a substantial Tudor or Georgian house, showing how the descendants of these villeins grew into prosperous yeomen. John atte Hethe lived on the edge of a stretch of wasteland still known as the Heath, Laurence atte Welle by the ancient well that gave the village its name, Aliza atte Lane in a turning off the main road, still spoken of locally as Hailey Lane or just 'the Lane'. These families continued in these places for generations after the names first appear, and at any time after 1300, when sons went off to London or elsewhere to try their luck, they probably took these local names with them.

As with occupational names, so also in this class the commonest are those that refer to the most important features of village life. Every village must have its water supply, and therefore *Brooks* and *Wells* are plentiful. Let us also note in passing that surnames tell us unerringly which words were most freely used in the early Middle Ages. *Stream*, which formerly referred to a big river, is a rare name, nor is *Rivers*, whicu came late from France, very numerous, but the land was watered by innumerable *Brooks* and *Bournes* in the South, and *Becks* and *Burns* in the North. Some people lived on their *Banks*, and others by the *Ford*. Then there were *Pooles* and *Lakes* and *Meres* (or *Mears*) and of course *Waters*. It was a wet country with a good deal of *Marsh* and *Myer* and *Mudge*.

The other natural feature which appears in endless forms, expressing truly its omnipresence in medieval life was the *Wood*. Woods were everywhere, playing a vital part in village economy, supplying many of the needs of man and beast, and yet at the same time in many places a traditional enemy to be driven back to yield to cultivation. Round many villages there was so much woodland that detailed names sprang up to specify its different regions, as the *Greatwood*, *Broadwood* or *Littlewood*, the *Harwood* (hoarwood), or the *Blackwood*, meaning the one with dark evergreen foliage as compared to the more usual *Greenwood*, the

Birdwood, and the *Grisewood* where the pigs were driven daily ('grice' being an obsolete word for 'swine'). Close beside each of these somebody lived, perhaps at the *Woodgate*, or in the *Woodhouse*, which, like the *Moorhouse*, referred to its position rather than its construction.

There were other common words for woods that are less familiar to us; *Grove*, for instance, sounds vaguely poetical but was a very ordinary word for a small wood or distinctive group of trees. An early form of the same word was *Grave*, or even *Greave*, which becomes confused with *Grieve* (see page 91). In the thirteenth century England was still full of groves, many of which even then were falling victims to the axe.

The most numerous of all these local names from common nouns is *Green*, and no name could be more typically English. We have seen (page 173) that in some cases it may be a nickname associated with the spring festival, but the plentiful examples in medieval rolls of 'atte grene' show that it is generally local, referring to the village green round which the huts of the villagers were grouped and on which their geese fed and social life centred.

Close after Green comes *Lee* with its variant spellings *Lea* and *Leigh*. This word originally meant a clearing or open glade among woods, and is a common ending of place names (as '-ley') because such a place made a suitable site for a settlement. But by the surname period the woods had receded further and the word 'lea', still in very common use, had come to mean different things in different places. Generally it was a stretch of grassland suitable for pasture, often meaning much the same as the green, whereas the *Meads* or *Meadows* were for hay, and the *Fields* for cultivation. But in any one village each of these terms was applied exactly to a definite place about which there could be no mistake. We think now of a village as having many fields, but in Norman times many villages had just the one area under cultivation where everyone from the lord of the manor to his humblest tenant had his strips. Even though it was divided into two or three fields for agricultural purposes, these generally lay close together on the best land available, so that to live 'by the field' could be a definite description.

Acres too, which seems now a vague expression unless relating to exact measurement, meant originally 'arable land', its significance in fact being much the same as 'fields', and not vague at all. A *Croft* was a small enclosure, a very different matter from the meaning of a small farm, later developed in the Highlands, and a *Close*, as the word implies, was well fenced in or 'closed'.

Some names of this type specify very exact spots indeed, related to detailed features of the village. A family could live by the *Church*, or by the *Pound* where stray animals were kept, or at the *Corner* or the *Cross*, which generally meant the crossroads, or by the *Wall*, or the *Style*, or the *Stubbs*, or *Stocks* of cutdown trees (which we would call 'stumps' today), or even under one particular *Tree*. It must have been a very noble and historic tree to need no further description, perhaps marking some ancient meeting place of the Hundred. The name of a particular species is much more usual.

In an earlier chapter I amused myself with a list of birds but I leave it to my readers to compile one of trees. There are at least twenty, some partly disguised. For instance the words 'at the', which were generally used in Middle English in the contracted form 'atte', became 'atten' when the noun that followed began with a vowel, so that a man lived not 'at the Oak' but 'atten oke'. When the preposition was dropped, the 'n' often remained sticking to the noun, leaving us the three tree names *Nokes*, *Nash* and *Nelmes*.

Rountree refers to the mountain-ash or *Rowan* (*Gowan* in the North), whose scarlet berries were the striking feature of some early dwelling. *Sweetapple* is a charming name in contrast to the sour *Crabbe*. These two may refer to the owner's disposition rather than his proximity to the trees, and *Cherry* may be an allusion to his nose, but any one of them might stand beside a cottage and give its owner a name. *Plumtree* clearly did so, and on the whole tree names are almost always local.

Thorne is easily the most numerous tree name in our directory, but if we were to start thinking of compound surnames at this point we should see visions of a land full of trees, often growing by the grassy lea, *Oakley*, *Ashley*, *Thornley* and scores of others, some like *Ashcroft* and *Thorndyke* showing a clear vignette of a particular spot, in the medieval landscape.

Most people lived by some sort of road or path, but neither word was in use in that sense in the surname period. 'Road' is connected with the verb 'to ride' and signified the act of riding or a clearing through the woods where a horseman could go. The meaning of its northern version, *Royd*, never developed beyond this stage. In the South an intrusive 'h' has given us *Rhodes*. Here again, as with Christian names like Robert, we see how Saxons tended to aspirate an initial R. In the Dorset Subsidy Roll of 1327 one can see not only 'atte Rhod' but also at the 'Rhugge' (ridge), and the 'Rhok' (rock), and several other local features.

The commonest surname relating to roads is *Lane*. A more important line of communication was generally known as the *Way*, but this was not sufficiently explicit to serve very often as a surname without some further detail such as the *Greenway* or the *Broadway*. The *Holloway* was a part of the road sunk between deep banks; the *Ridgeway* the opposite. A group of cottages lining the road was often referred to as the *Row*, sometimes with more detail as the *Woodrow* or the *Townrow*, and the very last house in the village had a significant position at the *Townsend*, spelt in a variety of ways.

Others lived in more solitary places where a wider geographical term was sufficient to describe them. To live on a *Hill* is always distinctive, and there are a number of words with this same meaning, as for instance *Downs* in the South and *Fell* in the North. *Low* (from O.E. 'hlaw') can also mean a hill, though in its other sense it is sometimes a nickname for a short man.

A *Moore* was a sparsely inhabited wasteland anywhere from Yorkshire to Devon, and a man who lived even on the edge of it, probably a shepherd or herdsman, was apt to be identified with it in other men's minds. But in connection with this name we have only to remember the tendency to call a dark man a 'moor', or even 'as black as a moor', which produced the common word 'blackamore' and the surname *Blackmore* (which can also be local), to realize that in this case geography and personalities are hopelessly mixed together.

There is less confusion when we descend into the sheltered hollows where many homesteads were placed. We have all sizes from *Hole, Dell, Dean* (O.E. 'denn' meaning a dip or depression) to the North Country *Dale* which implied a whole valley. 'Valley' itself is much too late to have made surnames, though a very few *Vales* did become established in the South. The good old English word *Bottom*, used extensively in the North and also in the Cotswolds for the lower part of a deep valley, has an unfortunate humorous connotation, and Shakespeare's contribution only added to the fun. Consequently some families with this surname have been driven to disguise it slightly by variations of spelling, such as *Botham*, but it has just the same significance as the more romantic sounding 'valley' words. *Longbottom* means exactly the same as *Langdale*, and the original Richard who gave his name, in colloquial form, to the place called *Higginbottom*, by which his family became known, probably lived in a most beautiful hollow in the hills.

Some people, of course, lived on the coast, but their numbers were small compared with those in the thousands of inland farms and villages, and there are few surnames that can be definitely attributed to them. The sea itself has made no surname, unless it is represented by the rather rare *Say* (cf Peacock and Paycock). Probably among coast dwellers it was too large and vague an expression, and a more detailed form of address such as by the *Cliff* or *Cave* was preferable, or more exactly still, the *Redcliffe* or *Radcliffe*, or the South cliff (*Sutcliffe*). These could also be inland features, and so could *Shore*, which was used of lakes and rivers as well as the coast, but to counterbalance this we should bear in mind that a sheltered harbour on the coast was often a *Poole* (as for example Poole in Dorset) and that those who lived by the *Waters* could be by the sea. Probably the most distinctive seaside name is *Sands*, written by one well-known Cornish family in the old form of spelling, *Sandys*.

Many of these common local names are closely allied with occupations. In an earlier chapter we noted that a man described as 'of the *Mill*' was probably the Miller, and that one of the most numerous of apparently local names, *Hall*, must generally have been used for a man employed there, perhaps as bailiff or steward. Something similar might be said of *House*, which can only have been used in the sense of 'the big house' of the village. The *Houseman* was certainly an employee there rather than the owner. The name *Cottage*, which is rather rare, must have distinguished its occupant from another man of the same name who lived at the *Hall*, or the *House*, or even the *Castle*. *Booth* was originally a cow-house or herdsman's hut according to Ekwall, and the man associated with it had an obvious occupation.

In the same way the men who belonged to the *Wood* must often have been woodcutters. An enormous number of such men must have been needed for this essential work, and the small number of *Sawyers*, noted previously, are not enough. A man who lived on the edge of the wood and spent his working days in it would naturally be Jack of the Wood. In the same way one who lived by the *Marsh* was often a fowler snaring the water birds that formed so large a part of the manor house diet, while the man at the *Weir* (or *Weare*) was responsible for the fish. Likewise the man who took his name from a *Pitt* presumably dug something out of it, *Clay* perhaps or *Chalk*.

Stone is another name that could be either local or occupational. In the surname period when far more of the land was in a natural, wild state than now, great rocks and boulders as well as standing stones raised up by pre-historic people were comparatively common and often used, as trees were, for boundary marks. Many early examples of the name as 'atte Stone' show that it often referred to some such local feature. And yet it could also be used as a nickname for a stone-cutter, or for one with a stony nature, the latter sense being not necessarily derogatory. That the English had always had a veneration for the qualities of stone is shown by their frequent use of the word ('stan' in O.E.) in forming Christian names. This would make it particularly apt to be used as a personal designation in later times. In fact *Stone* belongs to all our four categories.

Sometimes the suffix 'man' was added to a local feature, making surnames like *Pitman* and *Crossman* which have a very occupational sound about them, but actually the sense is not altered in any way. There is no clear distinction between *Wood* and *Woodman*; each was in all probability busy with his axe. The *Bridgeman* may have been employed taking tolls from travellers, but so may a man called plain *Bridge*, or *Bridgen*, the latter living at the bridge end. The *Stileman* only lived by the *Stile*, the *Pulman* by the *Poole*, and the *Ashman* by the *Ash* (he certainly did not collect ashes).

Another group of surnames in an occupational guise end with '-er' or '-ier'. We have *Laker*, *Streeter*, *Fenner*, *Brooker*, *Downer*, *Hillyer* and so forth. The Swedish scholar Gustav Fransson who has made a special study of this group, says that they originate almost entirely in Sussex and mean only that the families in question lived in those places.

So far we have mentioned surnames from local words still current in the language and easy to recognize, but many come from words once common but now obsolete. Some, like *Dell* and *Dene*, are vaguely familiar; others, like *Wray* and *Sykes*, have completely gone. A list of some of these unfamiliar local terms with their meanings will be found on page 342.

Once the meaning of a word was forgotten a surname from it was easily distorted into something else that sounded more familiar, and many old dialect words have suffered this fate. As an example, there is the surname *Pickles* with its lively, spicy sound. It comes from a word often seen in old deeds of Hertfordshire and adjoining counties, 'pightle', meaning a small enclosed piece of land, sometimes the site of a cottage.

Often a local word of this kind that has become a surname can give a strong hint as to the part of the country in which it originated. *Hurst* (a wooded hill) belongs to Kent and Sussex; *Coombe* (a deep valley) to the West; *Holmes* (low water meadows, once hardly more than islands) to the northern and eastern counties; *Thorpe* (a hamlet), *Thwaite* (a clearing), and *Garth* (a yard) to the North. Most of these and many others can be placed more exactly, but the subject of the distribution of place names is far too large and complex to be dealt with here. Those interested should consult *The Oxford Dictionary of English Place-Names* or the publications of the English Place-Names Society.

Before going any further, something must be said about the strange way in which many common nouns used as surnames appear to be plural without any reason. In the case of Christian names there seemed some sense in the final '-s' that attached itself to so many, in that they could be regarded as possessive, although it was seldom there when the name was first established, but adhered at a much later date. We could only conclude that a vague idea of possession, coupled with influence of Welsh names (which always took this possessive form) were the main causes. But neither reason will make any sense in explaining how *Brooke* so often became *Brookes*, or why *Coombes* is far more common than *Coombe*. It would be unusual to live beside two brooks and impossible to live in two coombes, and in any case we know from records of the fifteenth and sixteenth centuries that at that date such names were still nearly all without this final letter.

There really is no reasonable explanation of this phenomenon, though many writers have tried to find one, and all one can do is to observe the facts. In the formative period these names always appear with a preposition (most commonly 'at') and without any sign of the plural unless such a meaning is really intended. During the fourteenth century the prepositions began to disappear leaving the names as simple *Brooke, Hill, Coombe* and so on, and it is not until two or three centuries later that some of them acquired the additional 's', without apparent reason. One can see it happening gradually in old parish registers; from time to time the parson carelessly writes a name with an 's' that never had one before. He would not be inclined to do this if he had not heard it spoken that way. Like most other surname changes, its origin is verbal.

We must accept the fact that English people are very much inclined to end words with 's' on the slightest provocation. Other letters may be dropped in the course of time, but once an 's' has adhered it tends to stick, even if it has no reason to be there. But this only happened to words that were short and familiar and in frequent use. We saw with Christian names that the 's' first adhered to short forms like Will, and never to the Old English and early Norman names that had gone out of fashion by about 1250. And with local names (where the phenomenon is much less logical, there being no idea of possession) the terms that became obsolete early, like *Holt* and *Hearn*, are much less liable to have it than words that continued in use, like *Banks* and *Meadows*.

In some individual cases a particular influence can be found to account for the phenomenon. Some people, for instance, came from the town of *Wells* which naturally had the plural form. But whereas the Hundred Rolls contains eighteen examples of 'de Welles' as against seventy-five of 'atte Welle' or 'ad Fontem', which is exactly the same, the modern directory has 550 with the '-s' as against three without. In the same way *Bridges* sometimes signified, not what it seems, but that the man had come from Bruges. But this will not account for all our *Bridges*, which

275

can often be seen as 'ad Pontem' in the rolls, nor for any of the northern *Briggs*. In fact these particular explanations make no difference to the general problem.

It should not be thought that this final '-s' is just a possessive form that might append itself to any surname. It is hardly ever to be found on nicknames, even short, common ones like Brown or Young or Bull or Lamb, and very seldom indeed on names of occupation. The only ones in this latter class that regularly have it are those like *Parsons* and *Masters* where the surname nearly always started with the servant of the man named rather than himself, in which cases it had a reason to be there. The only surnames subject to this peculiarity were those consisting of common Christian names and common local nouns. The rest were apparently immune. It remains an enigma, not a very important one, but the point should be clear that anyone whose name is *Mills* should not assume that his ancestor was a multi-mill-owner.

It is true that almost all local surnames had lost their prepositions by the early fifteenth century, but in some few cases these useful little words had fitted themselves so snugly on to the nouns that followed them that they are there still. Thus 'atte Welle' which, as we have just seen, generally became *Wells*, has also survived as *Attwell* or *Atwill*. Others in this class include *Attwood, Attwater, Attridge, Attfield, Attlee, Attenborough, Atterbury* and a good many more. We noticed earlier that the last letter of 'atten' could stick to *Ash*, making it *Nash*. Likewise the first letter only of the preposition could remain, making names like *Agate, Ahearn* and *Adeane*. Other names in this class include *Bywaters, Bygraves* (meaning 'groves', not the churchyard), *Bytheway, Underwood,* and *Overbury*. In medieval rolls we can see many phrases of this sort used as names, generally written in one word, and often appearing very strange to the unaccustomed eye. Atetunhishend, for instance, from the Suffolk Subsidy of 1273, is bewildering at the first glance, but one has only to ignore the superfluous aitches and separate the words to find a well-known surname. Bynethergate from Yorkshire at the same date is much easier. There is no Nethergate in the London Directory, but there is probably one somewhere.

The survival of prepositions, which is comparatively rare among English surnames, is the normal thing in France where Dubois and Dupont are the regular equivalents of our *Woods* and *Bridges*. Some of these common French surnames inevitably found their way across the Channel during the Middle Ages, but had their prepositions dropped as if they were English, and scant respect paid to their French pronunciation. Thus we have *Boys* (which may have another source, see page 184), *Mount* and *Pont* and a few more, but none of them is at all common. Perhaps the French local word that has given us most surnames is *Travers* or *Travis* which means a crossing place, and as it seems to have been applied chiefly to a bridge or ford where a toll had to be paid we can imagine a Norman official familiarizing the word as he collected the groats.

To find topographical names of French origin one has to search about. But the English names of this type are legion, and those mentioned in this chapter are only a few of the best known. Normans may have owned most of the land officially at the beginning of the surname period, but it was the English who lived and worked among the *Hills* and *Dales*, by *Meadow*, *Grove* and *Stream*, by *Oak* and *Ash* and *Thorne*, knowing every *Stock* and *Stone*, and they spoke of these things in their native tongue.

Chapter 26

ENGLISH VILLAGES

If local names form the largest section of surnames, the biggest group within that subject is formed of the proper names of English villages and other inhabited spots. There were over ten thousand parishes in England in 1800, most of them extremely ancient, and hardly one among them has not given its name to at least one family. Added to these are the names of tiny hamlets, farms and houses, many of which cannot now be identified. Most of the surnames with these origins are individually rare. Together they form an enormous group.

The only names in this class that are common are those with very simple meanings that occur in many different places. Ekwall, in his dictionary of English Place-Names, lists over fifty villages called *Newton,* and there are about the same number each of *Norton, Sutton* and *Weston.* Of the points of the compass *Easton* is much the least numerous, because as the Anglo-Saxons progressed westwards across England the new settlement or 'tun' which had yet to be named lay always to the West, possibly to the right or left, but seldom behind them. Most of these common village names had to have a second designation later on to distinguish them from others, just as people had to have surnames (Newton Abbott, Weston-super-Mare); but to their own inhabitants they are still simply Newton or Weston; that is enough for conversation and was quite enough long ago for family names.

In the last chapter we considered surnames formed from common nouns expressing locality, and inevitably that class overlaps with village names. For instance there are at least six villages in England called *Churchill,* but there are many more

278

places where the church stands on a hill, and someone who lived on it could be called by that name. Again there are two villages in Warwickshire called Whitacre, but there were fields in many places with white, chalky soil from which such a name as *Whittaker* could arise. Or yet again there are three villages called *Hargreaves*; Professor Ekwall cannot distinguish whether the groves or woods in question were hoary or full of hares; they could be either, and likewise there could be other hoar woods, with hares in them too, where someone lived. It would be easy to give scores of such examples, but even though names of that sort could arise in many places the fact remains that hundreds of surnames do come directly from particular villages of such names, and in very many cases there is just one village which can be identified with near certainty as the place of origin of the family in question.

As regards the meaning of a village-surname, it signifies that the forbears of the family lived there, probably for many generations round about the twelfth or thirteenth century. The meaning of the place name is another matter altogether, lying farther back in the past, and does not really concern us here. An understanding of the formation of place names is necessary for recognizing them among surnames, but is a different subject, a very large one, and one on which many books have been published; therefore the student of surnames may well feel that enough has been done in tracing a name to a village.

We must next consider in what circumstances a family could acquire a village name. It could happen in two very different ways. The first was by residence there, as the principal land-owner. This was a natural statement of fact, used from the earliest recorded times and resulting in some of our oldest and most honourable names. In Anglo-Saxon Charters, where the names of thanes are given as witnesses to legal transactions, their home address is often added as an identification. Thus a list of sureties for the estates of the Abbey of Peterborough, written between 960 and 980, includes Alfweard of Denton, Othulf of Barnwell, Ogga of Southwick, Osmund of Catworth, Clac of Warmington, Grim of Castor, Eadric of Thorpe and many more. As long as these men's descendants continued as the leading men of these villages they would be spoken of by these names. But at the general upheaval of the Norman Conquest if the estates passed to newcomers the names went with them. At this stage in our history the village name had far more staying power than the family.

But some Anglo-Saxons, indeed hundreds of them, did keep their homes and lands by submission to the new king. Their Old English Christian names are mostly so distinct from the Norman that they can be clearly recognized in Domesday Book, and there is no reason why a number of village surnames should not have stayed with the same family since before the Conquest. Detailed evidence for such old descents does not exist. Sir Anthony Wagner tells us in his *English Genealogy* that the oldest proved line of descent from an Englishman with a territorial name is that of Turchil of Arden who held land in Warwickshire (which he had inherited from his father) in the reign of William Rufus. One of his descendants was Shakespeare's mother, Mary Arden, and others exist today. This statement serves to illustrate the extremely scholarly approach of modern genealogists, who accept nothing that is not proved at every step, and also the scarcity of such proof at this early date. But lack of evidence does not make a thing untrue. Domesday Book is full of local surnames which are still in use today, and the probability is that many of them have come all the way from that time in lineal descent, branching this way and that, with many social ups and downs, and that some few may even be pre-Conquest, although in no individual case can it be proved.

A number of people whose surnames are the names of villages mentioned in Domesday Book are inclined to say that their ancestor 'came over with the Conqueror'. This may often be true, but is hardly ever known for certain. To his principal barons William gave large estates which they divided out in small units among their knights and followers to be held on feudal tenure, and undoubtedly many of these Norman adventurers who received English manors as rewards for their loyalty and warlike prowess did settle in them and become identified with them in name. But many of these young knights remained in attendance on the king or great barons. Their estates were divided and subdivided again; the small holdings were frequently occupied by Englishmen, and it was actual occupation that gave a man the village name. Thus when a village surname does signify lordship of a manor in the Norman period there is less than an equal chance that its first bearer was of Norman blood. To my mind English ancestry is the better of the two. The English had a far longer tradition of civilization behind them than the upstart Normans.

In any case, among the minor gentry the distinction between the races had almost gone in a hundred years. The great earl or baron was still a foreigner spending much of his time in attendance on the king, which meant frequent visits to Normandy, and journeys from castle to castle, speaking French. But the man who lived in 'the Hall' of a small village, ruling the local community and only occasionally called away on duty to his overlord, spent more and more of his time at home, and spoke English. In the *Dialogue of the Exchequer* written in 1172 the author tells us that among freemen it is really impossible to tell the two races apart.

As an example of how these village names adhered to their leading families, I quote the case of the small hamlet of Hailey in Hertfordshire, which, though a separate manor in Domesday Book, was never a separate parish, consisting only of the Hall and about twenty cottages. In the early Middle Ages, when it ranked only as a quarter of a knight's fee, it belonged theoretically to various Norman barons and their under-tenants, but when the truly local records begin in the thirteenth century we find that the man on the spot, who lives in the Hall, presides at the Manor Court, pays the largest tax and is to all practical purposes Lord of the Manor, is none of these grand gentlemen but someone known simply as Richard – or Robert, or John, as the generations change – of *Hailey*. We can watch him prosper. By 1300 he has leased the larger adjoining Manor of Great Amwell and is presiding at both courts. Not long after he marries the heiress of the Manor of Chelsea, which is much bigger and grander, and thereafter appears in Chelsea records, presiding at courts there and apparently in residence. He has now gone up in the world, but he is still Richard of Hailey, or just Richard Hailey, and so his descendants would also be wherever they went.

Almost every manor in England named at least one family in this way, that of its principal resident in the century or two after the Conquest. After that such names hardly ever changed. The one just quoted is typical in several ways. The detailed records do not start until after 1200; before that we have only heard of the official owners who are not the same as the actual occupant. By that date the name Richard could belong to an Englishman as well as a Norman, so we have no evidence of his nationality, but in all probability it is already mixed, and Richard certainly talks English though he may know French too. Again, his migration to another manor is a very normal development as he rose in status.

In the Subsidy Rolls of Edward I we see a great many villages where the principal resident (he who pays the chief tax) has the village name. By the Poll Tax of Richard II there is a marked difference, a large number of these having moved into some other place, generally not far distant. Even in the twentieth century a few – a very few, such as the *Berkeleys* of Berkeley or the *Kingscotes* of Kingscote (a few miles away) – may still be found in the place where they started, but the descendants of most of the families that began in this way are not only far from their point of origin but scattered round the world.

It was natural for a landowner to take his name from his land, and in this way all the gentry who had not already got surnames of another sort were provided with them by about 1200; all very gratifying for those who have such names. But there is another side to the picture. Within a village only the leading family would use its name, but for anyone who left it and found employment elsewhere it was an equally natural designation. When a poor boy from the village of Berkeley walked the sixteen miles to Gloucester and found work with an innkeeper there, it was the most natural thing in the world for his master to call him Jack of Berkeley to distinguish him from another Jack who had come from Stroud. The idea that he might in some way be confused with the son of the great lord, who lived at the castle like a prince, would be too absurd to be entertained. In any case the words would be spoken without any thought on the subject.

And when Jack had earned enough to have a house of his own and perhaps a horse or a cow, and the tax-collector came round collecting groats for the king's subsidy, his name would be put down on the parchment as Johannes de Berkeley exactly like that of the young lord, except that the latter would be followed by the word 'armiger' to show his knightly status. Many people think that the preposition 'de' is a sure mark of a French name, but in the twelfth and thirteenth centuries every place name used as a surname, French or English, was written in that way, simply because clerks, trained in the Norman tradition, were sticklers for the niceties. By the middle of the fourteenth century these prepositions had nearly all gone, except in a few aristocratic families who were conscious of their Norman origins and liked to preserve the outward signs. But in the early days of surnames there was nothing socially significant about 'de'.

We see now that village names can take us back to early aristocracy or to obscurity, and only a great deal of genealogical research can decide the point. Fortunately few people worry about such a question, and those who do are generally quite confident that they belong to the former category.

Young men who set out to seek their fortunes in the Middle Ages nearly always made for a town or at least a larger village than the one they had left, and if one studies lists of the inhabitants of towns at this period one always sees a good many whose surnames are the names of the surrounding villages. In the rolls of about 1300 the villages are mostly near at hand, or at least in the same county. A century later, after the Black Death and the enormous changes that followed it, the range is very much wider. In early parish registers (of the sixteenth century) we can still see in every town names from nearby villages, for the same process of movement was continuing all the time, but also others from remoter parts of the country, and the same widening trend has gone on ever since. And yet, in spite of all these trouble-filled centuries, it is still the case that in small country towns a number of people, particularly of the farming and shopkeeping class, have village names belonging to the neighbourhood. At Wotton-under-Edge in Gloucestershire our postman, Mr *Stinchcombe*, had the name of a village five miles away. His family may have moved several times since the thirteenth or fourteenth century but they had not got very far. Similar examples could be found in hundreds, and I recommend anyone who has some idle minutes to spare in an old market town to look at the names on the War Memorial, pick out the village surnames and see where the families have come from. Those with far distant names may have been anywhere in the world before settling in this town, but those with fairly unusual names of nearby villages have probably been hereabouts for six hundred years at least.

The bigger the town the more people were drawn to it, and in early London records this is most evident of all. Village names were particularly suitable for surnames in cities because of their great diversity and once established there had no cause to change, unlike trade-names, which were particularly unsuitable unless every member of the family continued to practise the same craft. A country boy arriving in London might tell his new master that his name was John Miller, a name that had perfectly distinguished him in Little Wilmington. But if there was another Miller round the corner he would find he was John *Wilmington* before he could turn round. Thus London, in common with other medieval cities, had a high proportion of rare names, very many of them local, giving it the great variety it needed.

A detailed study of the London Subsidy Rolls of Edward I and II and other contemporary or earlier London records was made by Ekwall with a view to seeing where the rapid increase in population was coming from. His object was to explain certain dialect elements which ultimately prevailed in London and in Standard English, and his method was simply to take all surnames derived from known places outside London and plot them on to a map of England. Altogether he dealt with the names of some seven thousand people and found, as one would suppose, that they had come from every county in England. He had expected to find the highest numbers from the East Midlands and East Anglia, but though this proved to be true (the highest scores coming from Norfolk and Suffolk) he also discovered a very large contingent from the North, and almost as many from the South. In fact they had come from all parts, and very naturally the greatest numbers were from those counties nearest to London.

The only feature he was able to observe to fit in with his linguistic theory was that the immigrants from villages in Norfolk, Suffolk, Cambridge, Lincoln, Bedford and in fact the East Midland area in general, paid the highest taxes in London and were in a more prominent position than the rest. Some from the extreme North were also important citizens. The reason for this trend appears to be related to the Scandinavian element in the population, as all these counties noted in this way were formerly part of Danelaw. These people's success in London may have been due to the inherent Danish tendency towards enterprise and commerce, or to social conditions that enabled them to leave their native villages at an early date. It is evident in Domesday Book that far more freemen held land in the Danelaw counties than in the South and West, where the native population was more strictly bound to the soil, and unable to move without their lord's permission. Therefore more people from the Eastern counties were free to go and establish themselves in towns and rise to prominence before the less fortunate inhabitants of the South and West could get there.

This study of Ekwall's is just an instance of what can be done with surnames. Obviously they can be a valuable means of studying population movements in the Middle Ages, but very little has yet been attempted in this field.

This brings us to the question of the sort of people who made this change from country to town. For peasants holding their lands by villein service such movement was theoretically impossible. Of course they sometimes ran away, and if they could reach a town and maintain themselves there for a year and a day they had won their freedom. But during that time when they were liable to be caught and taken back to bondage they would be hardly likely to advertise the name of the village they had come from. I think it may be accepted that the majority of men who took a village name with them when they went to settle elsewhere were at least freemen, sons perhaps of village craftsmen, or of franklins, or of the reeve or the clerk, or even occasionally, of the parson; young men for whom there was no provision at home, or who wanted more than the village could offer; and of course there were always the younger sons of the lord of the manor, which brings us back to the other way of acquiring the name as landed gentry. Perhaps the distinction between the two groups is not so great after all.

One point is clear. The smaller the village that made your name the more chance there is that your family once held its manor. With a large town like *Lincoln* or *Carlisle*, your forbears lived there once but only got the name by leaving it. A bishop or earl might use the name of an important town as a title of honour, but it seldom became a regular surname in such a way, though it did so frequently for very ordinary citizens who went to live somewhere else, as for example in London where the names of most of the county towns could be found by the reign of Edward I.

To try to enumerate village names in detail is out of the question. Even such dictionaries of surnames as have been published have included only a small selection of them, and people who look in vain for their surnames in such works might often find them in a gazetteer for the British Isles. However since many surnames sprang from tiny hamlets or names of manors which have now disappeared, swallowed up perhaps in the spreading growth of cities, they may be derived from places that once existed but cannot now be found on any map.

Or again, the surname whose origin is being sought may preserve an old spelling, or a distorted or contracted one, and may look different from the place name from which it is derived. *Bristowe* is an old version of Bristol; *Bastable* of Barnstable. *Gaitskill* comes from Gatesgill in Cumberland, and *Gaskell* is another version of the same name. *Honeybun* is a corruption of Honeybourne in Devon, and *Twaddle* of Tweedale. When a family settled in an area where the original source of its surname was not known, it often came to be approximated to some more familiar word.

However, even when a surname cannot be found on any map, its form may indicate decidedly that it is a place name. All the common nouns that were discussed in the previous chapter, most of which can stand alone, can also make the final part of particular place names; and surnames with these endings are nearly always village names. I am obliged to qualify the statement because there are a few pit-falls, the chief being the Anglo-Saxon Christian names ending in 'stan' or 'burgh' already mentioned on page 250, but, except in a few cases that have been specified, the place-name origin is much the more likely, and in the great majority there is no doubt at all.

The commonest of all English place-name endings are the familiar 'ton' and 'ham', which originally meant an enclosure and a dwelling place, and developed gradually into the words 'town' and 'home'. The vast number of village names ending in '-ington' or '-ingham' can never be mistaken for anything else.

Each one implies the settlement of the tribe or family belonging to the person named in the first syllable. Thus *Winnington* is the 'tun' of Wini's people, the personal name being always a brief contracted form which is often hard to recognize as a man's name.

Another frequent place-name ending is the Old English 'burg' meaning a fortified place, which survives in different parts of the country as *Burgh, Borough, Bury* and even *Berry*, all of which exist alone, but are very common as parts of longer names. The meaning has developed as variously as the form and can apply to anything that was once fortified, from an uninhabited earthwork or a manor house to a large city.

Two very frequent place-name endings that are too brief to stand alone as common nouns are '-by' and '-ey'. The former comes from an Old Norse word for a settlement, and any surname that ends with it is almost sure to come from a village in the North. The latter signified an island or a river (O.E. 'eg' an island, and 'ea' a river, are often confused, but this fine point need not concern us here). A name ending in '-ey' is very likely a place name, though other sources are possible, and one ending in '-ley' almost certainly so (see page 269). The suffixes '-all', '-ell' and '-ill' are often contractions of '-hall', '-well' or '-hill', the vowel generally becoming the indeterminate 'e'; for instance *Bicknell* may be from Bickenhill in Warwickshire or Bickenhall in Somerset. But again it must be remembered that many French diminutives, such as *Blundell*, end in this way and each separate name must be considered as an individual problem.

As most villages began their existence with a hastily erected stockade to keep off wild beasts and enemies, so the most frequent meaning for the endings of village names is 'enclosure'. 'Tun' (later 'ton' and 'town') has already been mentioned; less known elements with the same meaning include *Worth*, which always implies a settlement of some sort, even in a case like *Woolworth*, which cannot now be found on the map; and *Hope* which seems to have been a small enclosure among fens or hills – the meaning is not very clear – and accounts for the last syllable of such places as *Stanhope, Glossop* and the Northumbrian *Blenkinsop*.

No region of England has such distinctive place names as Corn-wall, which is no wonder as they belong to an entirely different language. Among their best known elements are 'Tre-', meaning a settlement or farm; 'Pen-', a hill or headland; 'Pol-', a pool or harbour, borrowed by the English; 'Ros-', a moor or heath; 'Nan-', a valley; 'Car-' or 'Carn-', a rock or rocks; 'Lan-', a church. These half dozen words alone conjure up a complete picture of the Cornish landscape. In contrast to the English custom they are generally placed at the beginning of the place name, and any surnames beginning with one of them (such as *Trevelyan, Tremaine, Pengelly* and *Nancarrow*) is likely to be Cornish. The most distinctive of these is Tre-. Pen- and Car-, though often Cornish, may also come from Celtic place names in the North. *Carmichael,* for instance, is generally a Scottish name.

Perhaps the most interesting feature of Cornish surnames is the fact that they include a far higher proportion of local names than any other region of England, the other parts that come nearest in this respect being Devonshire (where obviously the same causes were at work) and the north-western counties where again a considerable Celtic strain must have survived in the population. This is the more strange because in the other Celtic countries, Wales, Ireland, the Highlands and Brittany, the vast majority of surnames are patronymics.

This curious discrepancy cannot be easily explained, but it is not the result of chance. Only very deep-seated causes can produce such results. We know, for instance, that Gaelic surnames, consisting almost entirely of patronymics, such as MacGregor, shared by large numbers of people, are a direct reflection of the clan system by which the lives of Highlanders were regulated from earliest recorded times and on which their lives depended. In Wales it was not so much clan loyalty as devotion to ances-tors which made every man remember his family tree in detail, so that it was a long time before he learnt to confine himself to one name only as a surname.

In Cornwall other emotions took precedence. Though sur-names there are largely local, they seldom consist of the Cornish equivalents of the common nouns like hill and lane that abound in other parts of England; for the most part they are the proper names of farms, hamlets and small villages, individual settlements created by great labour in times past, and often inhabited by the same families for many generations. It seems in fact that as the Celtic peoples were driven westwards this particular branch of them, with their backs to the sea, dug in their heels and would go no further, and their homesteads, built in stone and fortified so strongly and simply against the elements that they seem dateless, meant more to them than any other considerations; so that a family was naturally spoken of and identified not by allegiance to another person but by one of those weatherbeaten old farmhouses that still stand in sheltered hollows, each with its cluster of barns and cottages and its ancient, individual name. Perhaps it was the very nature of their life on this windswept peninsula that made the Cornish put down their roots so deep into the soil.

Chapter 27

THE NORMANS AND THEIR NEIGHBOURS

From English villages and towns we turn to those of Normandy, which provide us with that well-known group of names that formed for centuries the summit of our social structure.

The Northmen or Vikings in their mobile, marauding period had been inclined to personal nicknames like Blue Tooth or Blood Axe which were unrelated to any locality, but when they settled down they soon became land conscious. This is what happened to that branch of them known as the Normans, who, when they obtained a foothold on the mainland of Europe, changed rapidly from pirates to landowners and church-builders, and expressed their change of character by calling each other by the names of the French villages dominated by their castle keeps. They had not long been doing this when one more great raid carried them across the Channel, and the whole of England was in their grip.

Whereas in the days when Rolfe the Ganger founded the Norman state his people had not been inclined to look back to their earlier possessions, in 1066 they were very conscious of the roots they had put down in Normandy, and brought with them to England, not only the personal names, about which much has been said already, but also the surnames they had lately adopted. Some of these like Bigod and Bassett were of the old-fashioned nickname type, but the majority of the invading Normans' surnames were those of their continental homes.

Most of these names, that were destined to become so distinguished in England, represented very small places. If their owners had not found them insufficient for their energies, the urge that inspired them to such an ambitious military exploit would have been less strong. As a result of its success the great majority of William's army went up in the world, not only his fighting men but cooks, seamen and supporters of every kind. A man who had ruled one small village in Normandy found himself in possession of many in England. He might leave Englishmen in occupation of some of them if they would submit to him, and put followers of his own into others, and he himself became a much more important person than he had ever been before. The lesser men who had had no territorial distinction of their own in Normandy were happy to be known by the names of their English acquisitions, but the leading men nearly all kept the names of their Norman estates even though they now had greater ones in England. In doing so they showed their racial pride that made them wish to proclaim their Norman blood, and also that family pride and sense of continuity that was one of the chief causes of surnames becoming hereditary.

Most of these family names can be identified with Norman villages or what were so once, *Mowbray* with Montbrai in La Manche, *Mortimer* with Mortemer in Seine Inférieure, and so on. But in many cases the matter is complicated by there being several places of the same name, or the same in part. *Neville* or Neuville, for instance, meaning 'new town', occurs as often in France as *Newton* in England. There are at least five Norman villages called *Beaumont*, four called *Percy*, and several sources each for *Montagu, Sackville, Grenville, Tracy* and others. L. C. Lloyd in his great work on *Anglo-Norman Families* has traced over three hundred of them to their exact place of origin, and this intricate subject is best left to such skilled genealogists. But the point should be made that several distinct families with each of these names probably came to England in the Norman period.

Noble families cherishing their Norman ancestry have in many cases preserved the French appearance of their names from the Conquest to the present day, but more often these have been anglicized to some extent. The preposition 'de', which once preceded all place names, has generally been dropped, except for those beginning with a vowel where it has often adhered as an initial D, as in *Devereux, Darcy, Doyly, Damerel* and *Disney* from Evereux, Arci, Oilli (of which there are five Norman villages),

Aumarle and Isigny. But most Norman families increased in England, and while the heads of houses were keeping up their ancient dignity (with the assistance of clerks to do the written work), younger sons of younger sons and their progeny slipped into easy obscurity and spelt their names, if at all, by ear. Thus almost all the names of the great Norman barons that have survived, have done so in several versions, some of them very homely and English looking. *Beauchamp* can also be *Beecham*, *Beachem* and *Peachum*; *Beaumont* could turn into *Bemond* or *Beaman*; D'Aubigny, name of the Norman Earls of Arundel, became anything from *Daubeney* to *Dabney* or *Dobney*; *Beaufoy* could come to *Buffey*, *D'Oyley* to *Dolley*, and *Montford* to *Mumford*; *Mowbray* ramified into *Mumbray* and the curious imitative forms *Mummery* and *Memory*; while the great Bohuns, Earls of Norfolk, have survived only in contracted forms such as *Boon* or *Bown*. This small selection of names and spellings is enough to show that Norman names are more numerous than some might suppose.

In this gradual process of anglicization the French ending '-ville', which was quite alien to England, was often turned into '-field', simply because the latter was more familiar and the sound vaguely similar. Thus Sémerville could become *Summerfield*; Blonville, *Bloomfield*; and *Grenville*, *Greenfield* or *Grenfell*. Thomas Hardy was quite right in principle about the d'Urbervilles.

Norman place names that were in sound like English ones were soon absorbed into them. Mortain, from which one of William I's half-brothers took his title, could not possibly be kept distinct from the English *Mortons* of which there are very many originating from moorland villages in several counties, and anyone from the Norman village of Charenton would soon have his name assimilated to *Carrington*, the name of three English villages, but in such cases the chances are always heavily in favour of the English origin.

In fact, although a large group of Norman names have kept their distinctive French appearance, at least as many more have mingled with the English as completely and indivisibly as Norman blood with Saxon.

Norman villages provided surnames not only for English families but also for a number of English villages which needed further designations because their own were so common, and received the family names of their owners. Thus we have Weston Turville, Norton Fitzwarren, Moreton Valence and many more; but it was seldom indeed that a Norman name created a completely new place name north of the Channel. Our village names were ancient before the Normans even settled in Normandy, and have seldom been changed except by the natural erosion of time. A rare exception is Montacute in Somerset, where a family from the Norman village of Montaigu established itself. Another is the Welsh county of *Montgomery* which takes its name from one of the baronial families related to the Conqueror, who became Earls of Shrewsbury and exercised great powers over the southern part of the Welsh Marches. This is the most prominent Norman name on our modern map and came into use early enough to make an occasional surname for a family on coming into England from that county.

Norman barons did not confine themselves to England. They were eager to extend their suzerainty into Wales, and later Ireland as occasion offered, and in a more peaceful manner many of them settled in Scotland. During the two centuries after the Conquest relations between England and Scotland were friendly, and Scottish kings, anxious to be abreast of the times, welcomed Normans at court and even endowed them with land. *Bruce* and *Balliol* are both Norman names (from Brix and Bailleul) that entered Scotland by way of England and have in due course found their way back. *Melville* and *Sinclair* also come from place names from Normandy that took root early in Scotland.

When all the relevant surnames are plotted on to a map of Normandy, it looks like part of the Milky Way, and it is clear that every village must have sent its contribution of fighting men to join the Duke's expedition. In the rest of what is now France, though a fair sprinkling can be put in with some certainty, the density is nothing like the same; and even in Normandy it may be noticed that the invaders came thickest from the parts nearest to England, now La Manche, Calvados, and Seine Inférieure.

The district that comes nearest to Normandy in providing us with names is Flanders, or what was called Flanders in the eleventh century when William's father-in-law reigned as Baldwin

293

V, and now comprises Belgium and part of Northern France. But in this area a marked difference is apparent. From Normandy the names are mostly those of small villages and hamlets which the knights of William's army actually held by feudal tenure, and the few important towns are less well represented. *Cane* is in many cases from Caen, but it was also one of those many short Anglo-Saxon Christian names, Cana, with *Canning* as a diminutive. *Ruan* is from Rouen, but is uncommon. It may often have been assimilated into *Rowan*, but there are many rowan trees in England, especially in the North, and the English origin is the likelier.

But from Flanders the names that came into England are mostly those of towns. This is because those who came in largest numbers during the whole surname period were craftsmen and artisans. A contingent of knights, led by the Queen's nephew Gilbert of Ghent, was present at Hastings and suitably rewarded, but the main flow of immigration that followed consisted of useful workers invited by Norman kings to fill up depopulated areas or introduce new crafts. Consequently they came, not from the country, but from those tight-packed, walled towns that look so charming in illuminated manuscripts and must have smelt so strong inside; from Calais (*Callis* and *Challis*), Boulogne (*Bullen*, better known in the Tudor spelling *Boleyn*), Ghent (which in England became *Gaunt*, as we know from 'time honoured Lancaster'), Bruges (which became confused with our *Bridges*), Crécy, or *Cressy*, and many more.

From Brittany, William's other principal ally, there are fewer place names, not that Bretons did not settle freely in England, but because, like most of the Celtic race except the Cornish, they were late in developing fixed surnames and when they did so were more inclined to patronymics than place names. In this way they contributed to our vast mixture a number of typical Breton Christian names such as Alan, Brian, and Hervey, but comparatively few of locality.

As we get further from England the places that have created English surnames are fewer and more widely scattered, but the famous towns of the north of France are mostly represented. *Paris* is very often found as a surname in medieval records, as in the case of Matthew Paris, chronicler of Henry III's reign, but in later times it was nearly always turned into *Parish*, making the perfect example of the grand foreigner reduced to humble native status. In Middle English 'is' and 'ish' were often interchangeable, and in this case the familiar word was too strong for the newcomer. I know of no evidence or likelihood of 'parish' becoming a surname on its own account. As every place in England was in a parish, the word was useless for distinguishing one man from another.

Bloy and *Troy* represent Blois and Troyes, the territory ruled by our King Stephen's family. They are not common, but it would be surprising if they were totally lacking. *Charters* and *Charteris* come from Chartres, *Burge* and *Burges* occasionally from Bourges, though the latter has a good English origin also as a burgess.

The principle noticed before holds true, that people who migrated from large towns were generally of the artisan or professional classes, the aristocratic land-owning families nearly always bearing the names of small villages where their castles dominated the landscape. A distinguished name that comes from a small place about a hundred miles south of Paris is that of *Courtenay*. This famous family, whose estates were confiscated by Louis VII, moved to England in the reign of our Henry II, where in due course they became Earls of Devon and married into the royal family. Meanwhile their cousins of the same name had been ruling as Emperors in Constantinople – three of them in succession from 1216 to 1273. This name has flourished in England – there are over eighty of them in the directory, generally spelt *Courtney* – and as it is not derived from a common French place name likely to give rise to many other families, it may be supposed that the majority of them are descended from cadet branches of the noble Courtenays, though only genealogy can prove it in each separate case.

Some French place names which we have already noted as belonging to villages in Normandy from which some of our leading families have come recur in large numbers all over France. Professor Weekley has counted forty-six *Beaumonts*, no less than fifty-eight Neuvilles (*Neville*), and the same number of the aristocratic *Villiers*. Ferrières (*Ferrers*), which indicates a place with iron works, is also found in all parts of France, so that there are possibilities of French families with any of these names settling in England at almost any date to augment those that appear in Domesday Book. And yet the numbers of French names from any part except the North are on the whole so slight that the Norman origins are by far the likeliest. In the cases of the surnames mentioned above there is ample evidence of flourishing families settled in England in the early Norman period, in the most prosperous circumstances that could exist, and it is more probable that modern families with the same names are descended from them than from other French immigrants whose existence is mere supposition.

Other surnames that could come from anywhere in France, but are again most probably from Normandy, are *Meynell* which comes from the Old French 'mesnil', meaning a homestead or farm, and *Mullins* which is simply 'moulins' or 'mills'. In Normandy they would generally be windmills, a common feature of many villages, which like 'mesnil' often made part of the village name.

A pleasant group of surnames from villages in Normandy, Brittany or France proper consists of saints' names including the title 'Saint', generally in contracted form. A place was known by the dedication of its church as St Denys, St Clair, St Maur, St Pierre, St Paul, St Leger or St Aubin, and a family taking its name from the locality and migrating elsewhere became *Sidney, Sinclair, Seymour, Semper, Semple, Salinger* or *Tobin*. The first of these is the least well authenticated and could have an English origin; the others have all been traced to their sources in the cases of individual families. *St Aubyn* and *St Leger* have also remained in two words; *St John* (pronounced like one word though written as two) and *St George* have a more English appearance, but they are both Norman in origin.

Although the Conqueror's great grandson, Henry II, became by the aid of marriages, diplomacy and luck, the ruler of more than half of what is now France, and travelled constantly about his huge realm with a large retinue, there are very few surnames to show for it from his more southerly possessions. Many Frenchmen must have come to England at that time, but apparently not many of them were tempted to stay. The only inducement seems to have been commercial, and the one feature of our medieval connection with the South of France that stands out clearly among our surnames is the wine trade with Gascony and Poitou. Before the Conquest the English had made their own wine as best they could with their own sour grapes, but now under the Plantagenets a tremendous business grew up between Bordeaux and the principal English ports, shipping the much prized barrels of claret. The name Bordeaux does not seem to appear in our directory, and it is clear that the merchants who handled the business were simply called Gascons; we know them now as *Gascoigne, Gaskain* and *Gaskin*. The names *Burgoyne* and *Burgin* probably belong to the wine trade too, though Burgundy was never part of the English dominions and the wine must have come by a less direct route.

That merchants also settled in England from Poitou is amply proved by the frequent appearance of 'poitevin' in medieval records, but the word seems to have been found somewhat difficult by the English. It branches into so many versions that they all end up as rarities. In Domesday Book there is Roger Petevinus established at the start; in the Hundred Rolls there are several examples, including a lady called Presciosa Potewyne; in the Subsidy Rolls the name is to be found in almost all counties with sea ports; as far north as Newcastle, for instance, there is John Peytefin, a vintner, and in Dorset Robert Pidwin. Its modern survivals include *Potwin, Petwin, Pettifin, Puddifin*, possibly some of the *Pattens* and *Peytons* (though there is a village of that name to be considered), and certainly *Portwaine* and *Portwine*. This last has managed to retain the vinous connection, although neither part of the word has any etymological link with it. *Peto* comes direct from Poitou.

One would expect to find quite a solid group of names from Anjou and Aquitaine, both so closely linked with the Plantagenets, but there is hardly anything. The directory produces one solitary example of *Angers*, the capital town of Anjou, and two more of *Angwin*, which may represent Angevin or the Cornish 'angwin' meaning 'white'. From Aquitaine I find nothing. Either few people from these warm, gay countries chose to stay in England, or those who did had different kinds of surname, or – and this accounts for a good many – the English, troubling themselves little about foreign places so far away, called them simply *French* and had done with it.

Chapter 28

COUNTIES AND COUNTRIES

We have seen that Norman landowners brought the names of their small villages to England and made them famous there; that people of rather lower degree coming from important towns might often be known by their names; and that those who came from remoter places, as for instance the South of France, were referred to by wider geographical expressions such as *Gascoigne* or *French*.

Returning to England we find the same general principle at work, that the nearer a man was to a place when its name stuck to him the smaller it could be, and conversely that the farther away he went the wider the area required to give him a name. A man called *Bush* lived right by a bush, the man with a village name might only have gone into the next parish, though village names made such good durable labels that they would take you anywhere; but the man called *Darbyshire* or *Cheshire* had gone away to a place where the name of his village was unknown, but that of the county gave a general idea of his origin.

Nearly all the English counties have made surnames. In some cases it is the plain name *Kent* or *Cornwall*, in others we have an adjective as *Kentish*, *Cornish* or *Cornwallis*. The counties whose names consist of the county town with the addition of 'shire', most of which can be seen at full length in early records, have nearly all dropped the ending, so that now they are only *Bedford*, *Lincoln* and so forth. Many preserve the old phonetic spellings that were usual before scholars got to work to make the names look more historical. *Darby*, *Warrick*, *Lester*, *Gloster* and *Wooster* are sensible spellings; *Dossett* and *Willsher* suggest old-fashioned pronunciations, and one or two pleasant old forms like *Warricker, Dosseter* and *Devenish* are preserved.

Of the forty Old English counties all but three can be found in the London Telephone Directory (if we count the simplified forms). The numerical winner is *Kent* with a score of 260, which is not surprising for it was a prosperous, well-populated county in the surname period with a distinctive character of its own. Its inhabitants, whether 'men of Kent' or 'Kentish men', are still rather fond of saying so. And then it is a conveniently short name, not easily confused with anything else. *Cornwall* is second, and here the special character amounts to a strong racial distinction, so much so that we should perhaps class it with Wales and Scotland as another country. A Cornish migrant in the Middle Ages and those who received him would be very conscious of his place of origin. In Ekwall's enumeration of place names among early London surnames (page 116) he found few from Devon or Cornwall. He was of course counting village names as well as towns and counties; but though not many from the extreme South-West had reached London by the early period he was examining, they were on the way. In fourteenth-century Devonshire records the name *Cornish* or Cornwallish can often be found; in Dorset one sees both these and *Devenish*. If the names were formed in any number some examples of each of them would arrive in London eventually.

One of the three counties unrepresented in the modern directory I have used (though no doubt it exists as a surname elsewhere) is Northumberland. The old kingdom of Northumbria, which had had such a strong character at an early period, had suffered many vicissitudes and been broken up into different divisions by the Norman period. But its character remained in men's minds and was expressed by the vague term 'the North' which for Southerners still serves for all the old Northumbrian region. It is no mere chance that *North* (which with its cognate form *Norris* amounts to over five hundred) is seven times as numerous in the directory as the opposite party *South, Southern* and *Southeran* (with a mere seventy). Likewise there is a very similar preponderance of *West* (seven hundred) to *East* (110). The general movement was always from country to town, and from small towns to larger ones, the truth of which is demonstrated by the very small numbers of *London* as a surname. Most of the principal medieval cities were on the East side of England; York, Lincoln, Norwich as well as London. Bristol is an exception, but western lands lay beyond that. Therefore the migration from country to town was far more from the North and West than the reverse, and in London especially, being in the South-East corner, a new arrival from Northumberland or Shropshire would be very likely to be spoken of in these terms.

It is said that a man could be called *West* merely by living on the west side of the village, but I think it most unlikely. In a small area where every foot of the land was known and every feature had its name, such a vague term is totally out of place. *Westbrook*, *Westwood* and *Westlake* each specify a well-defined area; *Westcott* is very exact; the Yorkshire *Westoby* signifies 'west-of-the-by' (or village); the Devonshire *Westaway*, the west way or road to the West; but a man called simply *West* had come from further away than any of these.

Having now widened our scope from a single *Bush* to great areas like the *North* and the *West*, we can still go one step further and take the whole of *England* in one stride. How does a man get the name of his own country? Obviously by going away from it. He need not go very far. Over the border into Scotland or Wales will be enough, or even into Cornwall where to this day old people still speak of visitors coming 'from England'. Many Englishmen must also have gone into France in the retinues of Norman barons, and sometimes have stayed for long periods and been called 'L'Anglois' (which is quite as common a name in France as *French* is in England). If they or their sons returned to England the name would come with them, and very likely, as their speech turned again from French to English, the name would be translated too without thought. The surname *English* is more easily accounted for than *England*. In the former case we have only to imagine one Englishman in a group of Normans anywhere, but the latter could only arise if he were right out of the country. Scotland is perhaps the place where it originated most often, for English was the language of the Lowlands and there no need for translation would arise. We have exactly the same situation with the name *Scott* which should logically be found chiefly in England, but is frequent from early times in Scotland too. The borders of these two countries were never well defined in the Norman period, and there the two races met and mingled, each man very conscious of his race.

We have reached the boundaries of England and must now turn our thoughts to the neighbours, not to consider their own names which have been sufficiently touched on, but to see how the medieval Englishman referred to them and the terms he applied to them when they persistently settled within his gates. The list on page 343 shows them in numerical order as they appear in the London Telephone Directory today. It might be said that the numbers do not signify greatly because each name is backed up to a varying extent by others from the same country; but with certain reservations they do give in a neat, compact form a general picture of immigration into England in the surname period. They belong truly to that early time, for foreigners arriving at a later date came provided with their own surnames; and they are genuinely English, for it was in the vernacular speech of this country that they were first applied to the families who still have them.

The list shows at a glance that while the Normans were the most prominent, a steady infiltration from our Celtic neighbours was increasing the population.

The *Scot(t)s* have always been with us. The name was used in England before the Conquest and is found all over the country soon afterwards. Naturally it is most plentiful in Northumberland, but also appears early in London, Devon, Dorset (where it is sometimes *Scutt*), and indeed wherever one looks. In the twelfth-century list of tenants of Battle Abbey in Sussex one of them is Wulfwin Scot. In their own country the name harks back, in its earliest occurrences, to the time when several races were mingling to make a nation. It will be remembered that the Scots had originally come from Ireland and only spread gradually from Galloway across the Lowlands, but by the eleventh century the name was already used for the whole country (in 1034 Malcolm II was styled King of Scotia), so that although north of the border the name may have implied a nice racial distinction, as far as the Englishmen were concerned during the surname period a Scot meant very much what it does now. But some of the *Scotts* who came south at that time have been English for so long that their surnames must rank as Old English.

As for the Highlanders with their Celtic language, there is no sign of them in Norman England. The word 'Gael' was not used for them in England at that time. If any of them came south they were not differentiated from Scots by the English at that time; but they made little impact on English surnames until the eighteenth century when they overflowed from their wild hills to sprinkle, not only England, but the world with a scattering of Macs.

'Welsh' is an English word (from O.E. 'wealh' meaning a foreigner), and is what the Anglo-Saxons called the Celtic peoples of the West. Its adjectival form can be seen regularly in Middle English records as Waleis or Walysh, giving us the surnames *Wallis, Wallace, Walsh* and *Welsh*; the first two being the earlier. There were always Welshmen coming into England; in fact it would be more accurate to say they had never left it, and from the earliest part of our period their names are to be seen plentifully in the western counties, often in their native forms such as Rhys ap Madoc, but often again when in a more English neighbourhood, with the English tag 'le Walysh' attached to them. As with the *Scotts*, these tags adhered very early and indicate that their bearers settled in England at a remote time.

With the Scots and the Welsh, whose numbers both run into four figures, it is interesting to compare the Irish, who score a bare seventy, consisting mostly of *Ireland*. Here we see the historic truth that while the other two Celtic races came freely into England at all times, there was little migration from Ireland in the Middle Ages. They may have come as far as Scotland and Wales, having ancient links with both of those sister countries, but there is little sign of their reaching England. Indeed in the Norman period the migration was more the other way; Norman barons set out to conquer Ireland and many of them stayed on, never to return.

Before we leave the Celtic peoples there is one more large contingent to consider, the Bretons, whose national name has survived in several forms: *Bretton, Britton, Brett* and others. Like the Scots and Welsh they were well known in England before the Conquest, particularly in the South-West. The sea was a natural highway uniting the Celtic Christian peoples of the West when the Normans were still heathen, and the word 'Briton' like 'Welsh' might be used for any of them (including the Celts in

Cumberland), though in time each word came to be located in its special area. The Bretons, as we have seen, supported William in 1066, and those who came with him were rewarded with manors, chiefly in Lincolnshire, where these national expressions as well as their own Christian names made many surnames.

No racial name for the Danes can be identified clearly enough for any calculation of numbers. The early form of the word was very similar to that of the common place name 'dene' or 'dean' meaning a hollow, while the adjective 'daneis' or 'deneis' became indistinguishable from the Christian name *Dennis*, and probably accounts for at least half of its numbers. This adjective would in the normal way have developed in Middle English into Danish and *Dench* (of which latter word there are just a few examples), but before this had happened the Conquest had put an end to Scandinavian incursions, and during the surname period there was little further need for such terms, the Danish element in the country being already well absorbed into the mixture called English.

It is very noticeable that apart from the two words Dane and Danish, both in early forms that are not easy to distinguish, we have no local names from Scandinavia. The Danes brought many personal names into England before the Conquest that continued in use and gave us surnames, but seldom indeed any indication of the place of origin. One odd personal name of theirs that may be mentioned here, as the idea behind it is racial, is that of the Viking leader Halfdane, which means just what it says, and presumably signifies the son of a mixed marriage. It exists now as *Haldane*. But I am unable to produce a single place name from any Scandinavian country, acclimatized in England as a surname, to set against the hundreds of local names from Normandy and the Low Countries. In their own countries the Danes and the Swedes were extremely late in establishing fixed surnames, using largely patronymics which tended to change with each generation right down to the nineteenth century.

It might be thought that Norman influence had been sufficiently dealt with, but the generic term deserves a final notice in this racial line-up. It reminds us of the fact that over and above the Normans who came into England complete with surnames, many of them already permanent, there were still others of no particular distinction who were simply spoken of as 'Norman'. But even this does not fully account for the surname, for strange as it may seem this same word had been used by the English before the Conquest as a Christian name. In those days it simply denoted one of northern race, not this one particular branch of it that was to make itself so uncomfortably felt by all its neighbours. Several Englishmen with this name held land in the reign of Edward the Confessor, and as so many of the recorded Anglo-Saxon names became in due course surnames some few of the four hundred *Normans* in our directory may have originated in this way. But when the turn of events gave the name such a specialized and uncongenial meaning, the English very naturally dropped it as a Christian name, and it was hardly used at all (except in Scotland where the same painful associations did not apply) until Charlotte Yonge brought it into fashion again in the nineteenth century. Consequently we may take it that the meaning of the surname is for the most part racial.

From the time of the Conquest the word *French* could be used for Normans in England. Strictly speaking the Kingdom of France was a small part of the great country for which we now use the name, owning only a vague suzerainty over the rest, but already from the eleventh century its name was used for all the French-speaking duchies, bound so loosely together. In Domesday Book the Norman followers of a baron are often referred to as French men, and royal charters of that time are addressed to all subjects whether 'Franciis' or 'Angliis'. However the numbers of the surname *Norman* show that it was much used in common speech for a time.

Later in the Plantagenet period when England had a wider contact with more French provinces, the term French must have been more often used. We have seen in the previous chapter that certain regions of France, such as Gascony, impressed their character on the English mind more than others. Picardy, being close to England, was clearly well known, and we have almost as many *Pickards* as *Gascoignes*. But remoter parts like Savoy or Aquitaine, both the homes of English queens, have given no surnames at all.

The name *Francis* has largely a racial meaning in the surname period. Just as 'Wallais' and 'Wallis' developed into 'Welsh', so

'Francais' and 'Francis' became 'French'. They are only different forms of the same word, and although the Saint of Assisi, who was christened Giovanni but later called Francisco because of family connections with France, made it ever after a popular Christian name, that came about somewhat late in our surname period.

As the French developed fixed surnames at about the same time as we did in England, most of those who came here were already provided in this respect, particularly in the latter part of our period. Therefore those who were dubbed *French* or *Francis* in England must have settled here early, probably before the French provinces were lost in John's reign. They must have arrived without any great distinction of their own to supply a surname of their own language. Young landless fighting men would fill the bill, or merchants or clerks, but not in the retinue of a Norman, whose men would all be French. We must picture one Frenchman in an English group, who differs from the rest chiefly in his nationality.

The solid block of over two hundred *Flemings* reminds us once more of our close association with the Low Countries, which is always cropping up in this book. They gave us in all probability the diminutive form '-kin', the distinctive 'Han-' forms for John and the popularity of Juliana; like the Bretons large numbers of them came into England early enough to be still in need of surnames. The Low Countries seem always to have produced a superfluous population of particularly industrious people, and when from time to time an English king wished to plant a colony on some strategic but thinly populated spot, or start a new industry, there was always a supply of Flemings available for the purpose. They were not much liked; many were murdered in the Peasants' Revolt; but they multiplied none the less.

Holland, at the first glance, appears to be strongly represented, but its numbers are deceptive. There are three villages in England of this name, derived from 'hoh-land' or high land, being all on slight eminences in flattish country in Lancashire, Lincoln and Essex. These native sources must account for a good many of our *Hollands*, though many must also come from the country.

Beyond Holland our links with Europe weaken rapidly. Very few of our *Germans* come from Germany. Two bishops of Gaul in the Dark Ages were canonized as St Germain; consequently it became a regular Christian name in France and Normandy, and it is in that light that we must regard most of our *Germans*, *Jarmans* and *Jermyns*.

One more red herring must be mentioned. Professor Weekley suggested that *Pollock* might come from Polack, a name for an inhabitant of Poland, first mentioned in Hamlet. But this cannot be taken seriously. There are over a hundred *Pollocks* and they certainly have a more homely English origin, probably as a nickname for a fishmonger, like *Herring* or *Haddock*, or perhaps from some other early colloquial nickname connected with the head which was often called the 'poll' in Middle English. The ending '-oc' was a common early diminutive. The surname *Pole* is a variant of 'pool', when not from Paul. There is no evidence of Poles ever being in medieval England, and they could hardly have produced so large a group of surnames without being noticed.

In fact, though Northern France and the Low Countries have given us plentiful local surnames, we find that beyond that area the supply soon ends. From the vast confusion of Germanic states only an isolated city here and there has produced anything, the strongest representation being *Lubbock* (from Lubeck), already established in London in 1276 and amounting now to twenty-five names. *Cullen* is sometimes from Cologne, but may also be from a Scottish name.

Ranging all over Southern Europe, we see so few names that it becomes a pleasure to collect them like rare birds; twenty-five from *Spain*, twenty from Portugal in forms like *Pettingill*. Such people must in all probability have been merchants who found a profitable business in London or other ports, as the Gascons and Burgundians did, who were mentioned in the last chapter. Of course there were many such merchants, but only those who came early, stayed permanently and had descendants who have survived in the male line to the present day are to be found in our directories. No wonder there are so few.

The *Lombards* were mostly bankers who negotiated loans on a grand scale after the Jews had been expelled. Merchants from Milan dealt chiefly in silk and have left us the common noun 'milliner', but if it was developed early enough to become a surname it is lost among our more plentiful *Milners*. Venice scores thirty-five made up of some mixed spellings including fifteen examples of *Venus*, while Genoa, clearly little known in England, turned into *Jennerway* and *Jannaway*. The largest contingent in Italy comes from *Rome*, or *Roome* as it was then often pronounced, but this includes *Romer*, a nickname given sometimes to Englishmen who had made the pilgrimage to the Eternal City.

We have now reached the farthest limit from which our racial surnames come. *Moor* and *Turk* are only nicknames and do not represent real nationalities. *Rhodes* has nothing to do with the Greek island (page 271), and though the river *Jordan* was actually reached by the crusaders who gave the name to their sons, it does not indicate an inhabitant of the Holy Land.

The small numbers of the genuine regional names from the remoter parts of Europe throw into strong relief the hundreds that come from its northern coasts, and even more so the high scores of our Celtic neighbours.

SURNAMES IN AMERICA

Although this book was originally written for the English it applies equally to people of the same stock anywhere, and according to the evidence of surnames these form the great majority of Americans. Of course some with different racial origins have anglicised their names, but even so countless thousands of American families have their deepest roots in England and their surnames, created there, are by many centuries their oldest personal possessions.

In trying to discover why some surnames are so numerous, while others of apparently the same sort are so rare, I have made much use of figures from the London Telephone Directory, and this may seem to be unrelated to surnames in the States. But the pattern of names displayed in the modern directory was evolved long before the Mayflower sailed, even before Columbus made his voyages, and the same pattern is visible in America today.

This is clearly shown in the lists of the twenty-one most numerous surnames from five American cities on pages 345–6. Non-British elements can be seen as variegated threads running through the firm fabric of English names which form the bulk of the material. It was woven in the island of Britain in the days of the last of the Saxon kings, the Normans and the early Plantagenets, and its intricate design is little changed since then.

In each of these American lists the great majority of the surnames are British – in Atlanta, for instance, all – and two-thirds or more occur also among the top twenty-one in London. Some variation over a long period of time in different places is inevitable, and it is really amazing that the degree of differ-

ence in the order of surnames in these two countries, and in
those of the British Commonwealth, is so slight. London shows
a rather stronger Welsh influence than any of the American
lists; the three Commonwealth cities have each a stronger
Scottish element; and some of the American lists, particularly
that of Atlanta, are more purely English than any of them.
However, though few surnames of non-British origin appear
among these leading names, yet they play so large a part in
American life that something brief must be said of them here.

Looking first at the list for New York we find that Jewish
names are prominent. *Cohen* and *Levy* (with its variant *Levine*)
are typical Hebrew names both connected with the priesthood,
and their numbers in any district give a clear indication of the
proportion of Jews in it. The Jews have always been inclined
to adapt their surnames to changing circumstances, and most
of them date only from the late eighteenth or early nineteenth
centuries, when a number of edicts in the Germanic states of
central Europe compelled all Jews to take permanent second
names with recognizable meanings. Naturally they chose
pleasant subjects, though they often had to make heavy pay-
ments to secure the name of their choice – names such as
Rosenbaum (rose tree), *Friedmann* (man of peace), and
Goldstein (gold stone), all familiar in America. These surnames,
deliberately chosen in comparatively recent times, are of a very
different character from those that developed spontaneously in
England, France and Italy in the Early Middle Ages.

In Germany too, permanent surnames had developed in a
natural way long before the Jews took theirs, but later than in
England. Many German names have exact English counterparts
and may easily be anglicised. That is why in the New York
list *Miller*, with the probable addition of some German *Müllers*,
is higher than in London. The meaning is the same in either
case, the only question being whether the original miller
ground his corn by an English stream in the thirteenth century,
or a German one in the fifteenth. The presence of *Schwartz*
(black) and *Klein* (little) in the New York list betrays the great
number of Germans there. I have not found them so prominent
in any of the other cities I have studied.

The next nationality to make its presence felt in this way is
Swedish. The Scandinavian countries were the last in Europe

to adopt fixed surnames, and in 1901 an act was passed in Sweden compelling all families to keep permanently the names then in use instead of changing with each generation. As nearly all used patronymics of the most straightforward kind, the result was a great lack of variety, the same name being common to large numbers of people – as also in Wales. Even so no purely Swedish name qualifies for our lists. It is only when they coalesce with well established British names that their influence is felt, as in Chicago where the *Johanssons* and *Janssons* (slightly modified) have boosted the English *Johnson* into first place, for once dislodging the ubiquitous Smith. In the same city *Peterson* and *Nelson* (the latter assisted by *Nilsson*) reach the top twenty though their English numbers are very moderate, while *Anderson*, a well established name in Scotland and the north of England, is as high in most American cities as it is in Edinburgh.

In San Francisco we see the Chinese influence in the shape of *Wong*, an exotic note among the staid British names around it. *Lee* and *Young* too are both higher than they would be without some oriental aid, though both are fairly common British names, *Young* particularly so in the North.

Surnames from Spanish-speaking countries score one place in New York and one in Denver, but in the two southern cities that I have studied (Atlanta and Houston) where I most expected them I found the old-established British stock well ahead of them. However the fact the *Martin* holds its place so strongly, especially in the South, may reflect the devotion to this special saint in Italy, Spain and France, as well as England. The Spanish *Martinez* and the Italian *Martini* would only have to drop one syllable to swell the numbers of the English name. The French version is identical. And yet no great effect has been made, for Martin is fourteenth in London, and no higher than eleventh in Atlanta, thirteenth in Houston, and fifteenth in Denver. There is not much in it.

It may be wondered why no purely Italian name appears in any of these lists, even in New York, but Italian names are immensely diversified, each one that might be common having divided itself long ago into endless familiar or diminutive forms. The most numerous surname in Rome is *Rossi*, meaning 'red', but *Rossini*, *Rosetti*, *Roselli* and other forms of the same word exist also, not one of them in high numbers. In America it has sometimes been shortened to converge with the British *Ross* of totally different origin. This is a Celtic word meaning a rocky moorland, that exists in many place names. As a surname it usually indicates that its bearers' family came from the county of Ross in Scotland, but there are possible places of origin in the west of England too.

We may notice this general truth about family names: where they developed early and spontaneously, as in Italy, France and England, they display enormous variety, any tendency to repetition within one neighbourhood being countered by the natural urge to differentiate one man from another; but where they were established late under official pressure they show far more uniformity, some few of them being obliged to serve for thousands of families.

The antiquity of surnames brings us to the Irish, who probably have the oldest in the world. The hereditary surname uniting a family through succeeding generations is a European development, not found – so far as I know – in Asiatic countries, and in this respect the Irish seem to have led the way. No other country has displayed a greater fondness for the past or a stronger tendency to cherish its ancient history and the names of its heroes. The surname *O'Connor*, for instance, springs from a continuous folk memory of the legendary King Conchubar, who is supposed to have been contemporary with Christ and to have witnessed the darkness that fell over the earth at his crucifixion. In the realm of established history, Niall (or Neil) of the Nine Hostages was ruling all Ireland as High King about the year 400, and many other royal Neils came after him. Certainly there have been *O'Connors* and *O'Neils* in Ireland as far back as its records go, but it should not be supposed that they are all descended from kings any more than that all our *Wilsons* are the progeny of William the Conqueror. Many Irish surnames were definitely hereditary by the tenth century, some probably far earlier, but many also belong to much later times. The Irish may have the oldest surnames that are still in use but it was probably in England that the system first became universally established.

All the Old Irish names are patronymic, but within this limitation they display, as we should expect, a huge variety.

As in Saxon England, new names were constantly being created and old names diversified. Some, it is true, were descriptive in origin and might be classed as nicknames, but all of those that have lasted best were used as personal names, and remembered not for their meanings (some of which are given on page 331) but for the sake of the famous men who bore them. Such a one was *Kennedy* (ugly head), prince of Munster, father of the great Brian Boru who as High King defeated the invading Danes in a decisive battle in 1014. Brian is a Celtic name that came into England from Brittany but flourished chiefly in Ireland as the many *O'Briens* and *Bryants* witness.

The prefix O' means 'descendant of', while Mac originally signified more precisely 'son of', but as generations passed the distinction vanished. At a very early date 'Mac' spread to Scotland where it became typical of Highland clans, but it continued in Ireland too. The Manhattan Telephone Directory contains over six hundred different names beginning with Mac or Mc, and the majority are Irish.

In the twelfth century the English king, Henry II, determined to conquer Ireland, and the invaders he sent, as well as others who followed later, generally settled there permanently, their English and Norman names mingling with the native Irish. *Moore*, for instance, is an English name that has multiplied in Ireland but has always remained widespread in England too.

No single Irish name qualifies for our short list for New York, but in Boston they make a serious challenge to the English; I have not found them in such force in any other city outside Ireland. The Scots are much less in evidence, though they have made some contribution to *Johnson*, *Wilson*, *Anderson*, and *Thompson* (in Scotland generally spelt without the 'p'). Lowland Scots names can hardly be distinguished from Northern English, and this type of patronymic is a regular Northern form. No purely Scottish names – that is no Gaelic name – qualifies, though *Campbell* is not far off in some cities.

As for the Welsh, they have been mixed with the English for so long that it is of little use to try to separate them. Apart from their old native names (see page 75), they are responsible for the high numbers of *Jones*, *Williams*, and *Davis* (in Wales spelt *Davies*), but in many cases these families must have settled in England for generations before they migrated to America.

In comparing all these American cities with my short list for London, I have somewhat neglected English provincial cities, which have each some local character. In a brief review I may say that northern towns have a higher proportion of the '-son' type as noted above, including *Jackson, Robinson* and *Watson*, whereas southern ones are more similar to London. In an attempt to select a city as far as possible from Welsh or Scottish influence, in fact 'mere English', I took Norwich and found fewer patronymics, more occupational names, and a high proportion of plain Old English monosyllables. The first ten were *Smith, Brown, Clark, Wright, Taylor, Cook, Cooper, King, Moore, Green*, all well represented in the States.

The names that appear in these short lists are like mountains seen at a distance with only their peaks visible. It is no bad way to view an enormous subject, and as the contours of these high points remain so much the same on both sides of the Atlantic we may assume that the great masses supporting them, made up of thousands of rarer names, are of very similar character also. Indeed anyone who has travelled in the States knows that this is so.

In order to look at American names from a different angle, to take a cross-section instead of a distant view, I have made an analysis of the names of the members of the Ninetieth Congress to match those of the House of Commons given on page 77. The method has its disadvantages. I suspect that in both countries the proportion of non-British names in politics is somewhat higher than in other walks of life, but it does serve to give an assorted sample of manageable size covering the whole range of the alphabet and coming from all parts of the country. If democracy is to be trusted it should be truly representative.

This is what I find:

English	309 ⎫		
Old Welsh	11 ⎬	333	62% British
Gaelic	13 ⎭		
Irish	43 ⎫		
Germanic	56 ⎬	163	31% Non-British
Other origins	64 ⎭		
Unknown	39	39	7% ?
	535		

In this analysis I have counted all names as English that have been in use in England since the Middle Ages, but I have noted the Gaelic and Old Welsh, such as *Macdonald* and *Griffiths*, separately because they give an indication of the amount of these elements in the mixture. A name like *Williams*, though largely used by the Welsh, is Norman in origin and is taken as English.

Among non-British names, those of Germanic language predominate but not all their owners are necessarily of German stock. The Irish are unmistakable, their names being not easily confused with any other race except Gaelic. 'Other origins' include Dutch, Scandinavian, Slavonic, Italian, Spanish, Oriental and Greek, in roughly that order, but as I make no claim to know all the languages of the world I cannot be precise about the figures. For the same reason I have left thirty-nine names unclassified, the majority of them being probably non-British.

A closer analysis of the English names gives: Locality 36.5%, Relationship 34.5%, Nicknames 17%, Occupation 12%. When these figures are compared with those of England and New Zealand, given on pages 78–9, it will be seen how constant the pattern remains throughout the English-speaking world.

This cross-section, inadequate though it is in relation to the vast numbers concerned, has the advantage of giving us a random selection of less common and rare names to counterbalance the regular appearance of the giants. For instance, the three leading craftsmen, the smith, the miller, and the tailor, together with the clerk who is never far away, are here reinforced by such useful people as the *Collier*, or charcoal-burner, the *Brewster*, who brewed ale, and the button-maker, long since abbreviated to *Button*, who may be found in the records of twelfth century London working in association with the mercers.

Among the nicknames we notice *Goodling*, a typical Anglo-Saxon endearment, formed as a diminutive of 'good', just as 'darling' is of 'dear'. Speakers of Norman French may have used *Purcell* (little pig) in much the same affectionate spirit.

As usual William is to the fore among the many patronymics. What an influence one man has had on the directories of the world! The other Christian names that have made most surnames, John and Thomas, have each several saints to account for their numbers. Martin was beloved throughout Western Europe. But there was no famous St William. The Conqueror stands alone, austere and majestic, as the fountain-head of all the innumerable *Wilsons, Wilkins, Willises* and the rest of them. In this list, too, we see variations of some of the other names from his family that swept England in the twelfth century. *Hicks* and *Diggs,* for instance, represent Richard, a royal name that split into so many popular forms that none of them quite reaches the highest numbers. (For the Norman royal family see the endpapers.)

Some of the older native English names are here too. *Irwin* is Eofor-win, companion of the wild boar; *Hosmer* is Osmaer, divine and famous, which in this case has acquired a spurious 'H'. I have noticed a high proportion of these Old English names in America, particularly in New England where many of those specially associated with the old kingdom of Wessex – such as *Aylward, Aldrich* and *Alden* – seem prominent.

But it is among the local names that the cross-section method is most helpful, because owing to their great variety these names hardly ever have sufficient numbers to appear among 'the peaks'. Members of Congress bear among them the names of over sixty towns and villages in England, some seven in Scotland and six in Normandy, nearly all very small places.

Apart from these particular place names, we see many general terms for features of the landscape; some like *Hill* and *Brook* easy to understand, others of an archaic or dialect character. The meaning of some of these are given on pages 341–2. We are back very deep in the old English countryside when we speak of the *Stubblefield* and the *Taft,* the *Smathers* and the *Spong.*

The study of surnames must go hand in hand with genealogy as far as possible. The expert can only give the usual well-attested meaning of a name, while the individual who owns it may know some item of family history that throws a different light on the matter. But with English names the origin generally lies too far in the past for family tradition to help, and in these cases the name itself can often tell what human beings have forgotten.

Epilogue

English surnames are old, but full of vitality. Having outlived seven or eight centuries there is no reason why they should not last as long again, if only our race can endure. These verbal expressions, first uttered in England and Normandy in the early Middle Ages (though augmented later from other countries) still form the great majority of surnames in any English community. But that is only the beginning of their achievement. They also form the bulk of American names, though on that side of the Atlantic they have met with stronger foreign competition; they have spread round the world and are probably to be found in their purest and most concentrated form in the Antipodes. Some have expired from natural causes; others go on and on; and many rare specimens that are extinct in their native land are flourishing on some prairie, veldt, or island on the other side of the globe. In fact this enormous subject embraces the English-speaking world.

In all this time and space some surnames have experienced strange twists and turns of fortune. Many have been turned into Christian names, particularly in the United States. In England we have a more strongly developed traditional feeling as to what is a Christian name and what a surname, but in modern times the barrier has broken in many places. Take *Stanley*, for instance; first a stony lea, then a village, from which a family eventually takes its name; then a descendant of this family becomes a famous explorer and little boys are called after him, the whole process from the stony ground to the modern boy taking well over a thousand years.

Some surnames have branched into side activities, enriching and replenishing the language with new common nouns and verbs. I will quote only two. Medieval ironworkers in the Sussex Weald hammered the metal into bars which they called 'blooms', and the craftsman who did it was called a *Bloomer*. Mrs Bloomer who tried to introduce sensible garments for lady cyclists in the late nineteenth century gave the name a new connotation and the language a new noun. *Boycott* was originally a small cottage in Berkshire where someone called 'Boia' or 'boy' lived before 1066, and when Captain Boycott was cold-shouldered in Ireland in 1880 the language acquired a new verb.

Many surnames have provided names for new inventions, or for cities or other geographical features. The highest mountain in the world is called by an English surname, or rather an Anglo-Norman one. It comes from Evreux in Normandy, and is the same in origin as *Devereux*, but was well knocked about in England to produce *Everest*. It is intriguing to watch how names can pass in this way from places to families and back again to very different places.

Surnames have also occasionally travelled from one family to another. Just as apprentices sometimes took their masters' names in thirteenth-century London, so slaves attaining their freedom in the West Indies sometimes adopted the surnames of their former owners. In such ways English names have become the heritage of people of a different race.

But these diversities are all exceptional, and the great bulk of English surnames are still used for the purpose for which they sprang into being, and by the lineal descendants of their first owners. They link us by long-stretched, tenuous threads each to one ancestor, each giving one clue to his appearance, character, race, work, social standing or place of abode. Some of these clues give good hard facts; some are very slight; some obscure. The whole vast subject is an unfinished puzzle on which work is still proceeding. It will never be completely solved, but there is so much early evidence yet to be searched through, that more of the truth will come to light in time. Meanwhile the unknown draws us on and the subject is wide open.

The names that cause the most trouble to the investigator are those with two or more possible origins. Two examples of these were given in an earlier chapter (page 71). Another is *Bell*. A family with this surname could be descended from a bell-ringer, a tavern keeper, a woman called Belle, or a handsome Frenchman. Only genealogy can give the answer, and with a fairly common name it is a hard task to trace a family far enough back to find it. This is an extreme case, but there are many names where, though the general meaning is well understood, some second possibility remains to raise a doubt.

However my hope is that readers of this book are not concerned only with individual names but have a taste for the subject in general. If they have not they will hardly have reached this point. It is a subject that can add interest to our daily life, increasing our enjoyment of our language, and our awareness of the historic past manifested so plentifully on all sides. Even a slow bus journey along a crowded London street can take on new interest: *Swan* and *Edgar*, the perfect Anglo-Saxon pair; Austin *Reed*, a red-head of course; *Robinson* and *Cleaver*, we could never get far without Robin, and his partner must have been a butcher; *Mappin* and *Webb*, little Mab and the weaver. If it were just a game it might still amuse us, but it is not imaginary. These were real people who lived in England in the early Middle Ages.

If our system of names is a true mirror of our history, as I believe it is, then all the great changes in our national life must be reflected in it, showing the long trend from simplicity to ever-increasing complication. Our earliest forefathers in this island were content, as far as we know, with a single name, and that of a single syllable, if we ignore the final, unstressed vowel which would in time drop off. But as they became more civilized they found that they needed something more, and the two-part name developed; Dod became Dodric, and names like Edmund were the proper thing to have; but yet Dod lingered on colloquially.

The great upheaval of the Conquest changed everything, including names. One was no longer enough, even a double one; everyone needed another to cope with changing conditions, and Edmund, taking his father's name, became Edmund Dodd. This arrangement of two separate and complete names lasted and proved sufficient for practical purposes until the Industrial Revolution again changed the social structure of the nation. In the intervening six or seven centuries the only real change was the shift of emphasis from the first to the second name. In the eleventh century Edmund was the real name, Dodd a very minor addition; in the nineteenth, Mr Dodd's first name was hardly ever heard.

It was late in the eighteenth century that the first signs came that more was still needed. At that time we begin to see second Christian names appearing in parish registers. During the nineteenth century with its tremendous social pressures the practice grows steadily. But still the necessary diversity of names can hardly keep pace with the rapid growth of population, and so a new phenomenon develops, the double surname. A few of these had been used before 1800, generally in aristocratic families for special purposes, but the frequent habit of double-barrelling is a modern growth, just like the doubling or even trebling of Christian names.

The fearful complexity of modern life is shown in the modern Englishman's complete set of names, to which more and more may be added in the way of titles and letters. What will come next? Numbers? The authorities are inclined to give them to us already, and we all have some for particular purposes, but we are allergic to numbers and tend to resist them. Indeed, in the face of so many complications, we go to the opposite extreme and call each other by Christian names more freely than has been done since the fifteenth century. But our surnames are part of us and we would not lose them even if we could, for they are our roots in the past. Dod has become Major-General J. H. E. Millington-Dodd, DSO, OBE, MC, but the Anglo-Saxon churl is still there at the heart of the matter.

Select Bibliography

ABBREVIATIONS

L.T.D.	London Telephone Directory	**S.R.**	Subsidy Roll
O.E.	Old English	**P.T.**	Poll Tax
M.E.	Middle English	**B.M.**	British Museum
O.F.	Old French	**P.R.O.**	Public Record Office

It has been my aim throughout this book to indicate the sources of names given as examples, because their dates and places of origin add greatly to their interest, but this has often been done briefly. Where a name has been no further specified than by the name of a county, it comes from the appropriate Subsidy Roll as listed below. It was not thought necessary to give references on each occasion for common names that occur frequently in medieval sources.

Quotations, illustrating the meanings of words, if no other origin is given for them, may be found in the New English Dictionary under the word in question.

I DICTIONARIES

C. W. Bardsley. *A Dictionary of English and Welsh Surnames.* Oxford, 1901

G. F. Black. *Surnames of Scotland.* New York, 1946

F. L. Cross. *The Oxford Dictionary of the Christian Church.* Oxford, 1957

A. Dauzat. *Les noms de famille de France.* Paris, 1945

E. Ekwall. *The Oxford Dictionary of English Place-Names.* Oxford, 1936

P. H. Reaney. *A Dictionary of British Surnames.* London, 1958

E. G. Withycombe. *The Oxford Dictionary of English Christian Names.* Oxford, 1944

II STUDIES ON OLD ENGLISH AND MIDDLE ENGLISH NAMES

E. Ekwall. *Early London Personal Names.* Kungl. Humanistika Vetenscapssamfundet. No. 43. Lund, 1947

Sir Henry Ellis. *An Introduction to Domesday Book.* 1833
(An old book that is still useful if checked from other sources)
O. von Feilitzen. *Pre-Conquest Personal Names of Domesday Book.*
Nomina Germanica No. 3. Uppsala, 1937
G. Fransson. *Middle English Surnames of Occupation.* Lund, 1935
M. Redin. *Uncompounded Personal Names in Old English.* Uppsala,
1919
W. G. Searle. *Onomasticon Anglo-Saxonicorum.* Cambridge, 1897
G. Tengvik. *Old English Bynames.* Nomina Germanica No. 4.
Uppsala, 1938

III CONTEMPORARY SOURCES OF PERSONAL NAMES, A.D.
600–1600, arranged in order of the dates of the original material

The Anglo-Saxon Chronicle
Codex Diplomaticus aevi Saxonici. J. M. Kemble. 1839
Anglo-Saxon Wills. Ed. D. Whitelock. Cambridge, 1930
Anglo-Saxon Charters. Ed. A. J. Robertson. Cambridge, 1930
English Historical Documents. Ed. D. Whitelock and D. C. Douglas.
Vols 1–3, London, 1955
English Coins. G. C. Brooke. (For lists of moneyers) London, 1932
Domesday Book. Translations in the Victoria County Histories
Liber Wintonienses. Vol 4. Victoria County Histories.
Inquisitio Comitatus Cantabrigienses. Ed. N. E. S. A. Hamilton. 1876
Feudal Documents of the Abbot of Bury. Ed. D. C. Douglas. London,
1932
An Abstract of the Cartulary of Burton. Salt Archaeological Society
(Staffs). Vol 5
The Life of Wulfric of Haselbury. Somerset Record Soc. Vol 47, 1933
Chronicon Monasterii de Bello. (Battle Abbey) Anglia Christiana
Society, 1846
The Great Roll of the Pipe. 1158–1214, 35 vols
The Hundred Rolls. 2 vols, 1812–18
Feudal Aids. 6 vols, 1899–1920
The Register of Roger Martival Bishop of Salisbury. Oxford, 1959
Assize Rolls, Crown Pleas, Eyre Rolls, etc
Bedfordshire Record Society, vols 1–3
Lancashire Record Society, vols 47, 49
Wiltshire Archaeological Society, vol 16
Yorkshire Archaeological Society Record Series, vol 44
Subsidy Rolls, whole or in part, including Poll Tax returns
Cambridgeshire: *The Subsidy Roll of Edward III.* Ed. W. M.
Palmer. Norwich, 1912
Cumberland Lay Subsidy (1332). Ed. J. P. Steele. Kendal, 1912

Dorset: S.R. of 1327. Manuscript copy in Dorset County Museum

Essex: *The Great Revolt of 1381* (incl. part of P.T.). C. W. Oman. London, 1906

Hertfordshire: S.R. for the Hundred of Hertford for 1291, 1294, 1296, 1307, 1317, 1543. Unprinted Exchequer Rolls, P.R.O.

Lancashire: S.R. of 1332. Lancashire and Cheshire Record Society, vol 31

London: *Two Early London Subsidy Rolls* (1296, 1319). E. Ekwall. Lund, 1951

    Finance and Trade under Edward III (S.R. 1332). Ed. G. Unwin. Manchester, 1918

    The London Subsidy of 1412. *Archaeological Journal,* vol 44

Northumberland: S.R. of 1296. Ed. F. Bradshaw. Published privately, 1916 P.R.O.

Staffordshire: S.R. 1332. Salt Archaeological Society, vol 10

    P.T. 1379–81. Salt Archaeological Society, vol 17

Sussex: S.R. 1296, 1327, 1332. Sussex Records Society, vol 10

Warwickshire: S.R. 1332. Ed. W. Carter. Dugdale Society 6, 1926

Yorkshire: S.R. 1297, 1301. Yorkshire Archaeological Society Record Series 16, 21

    P.T. 1397 (West Riding). Yorkshire Archaeological Journal 5, 7, 9

    P.T. 1381. East Riding Antiquarian Society, No 30.

Manorial Records

Court Rolls of the Earl of Lancaster. Temp. Edward II. Lancashire and Cheshire Record Society, vol 41

Court Rolls and Rentals of Great Amwell, Hertfordshire. (Unprinted)

    1289–1532 B.M. and Westminster Abbey Muniments

    1599–1928 Hertford Record Office and Haileybury College

Parish Registers (a selection, of which the early parts have been used, with their starting dates)

Berkshire: Denchurch 1534–

Devonshire: St Andrews, Plymouth 1558–

Dorset: Gussage All Saints 1560– ; Swanage 1563– ; Almer 1530–

Hertfordshire: Great Amwell 1558– ; Hunsdon 1546–

Shropshire: Shipton 1538–

Somerset: Swainswick 1557–

Suffolk: St Nicholas, Ipswich 1539–

Yorkshire: Huggate 1539–

London: Christchurch, Newgate St 1541– ; St Clement, Eastcheap 1539– ; St Martin-in-the-Fields 1550– ; St Mary Aldermanbury 1548– ; St Vedast, Foster Lane 1558–

Indexes of Wills, for Devonshire, Cornwall, Lincoln, Norwich, and the Prerogative Court of Canterbury. British Record Society Publications

Registers of the Universities of Oxford and Cambridge

Registrum Annalium Collegii Mertonensis. H. E. Salter. Oxford, 1923

IV GENERAL

Butler's Lives of the Saints, revised edition. Ed. H. Thurston and D. Attwater. Aberdeen, 1956

H. C. Darby Ed. *An Historical Geography of England.* Cambridge, 1936

B. Dickins and R. M. Wilson Ed. *Early Middle English Texts.* Cambridge, 1950

E. Duckett. *The Wandering Saints.* London, 1959

E. Ekwall. *Variation in Surnames in Medieval London.* Lund, 1945

E. Ekwall. *Studies on Population in Medieval London.* Stockholm, 1956

C. L. Ewen. *History of British Surnames.* London, 1951

E. A. Freeman. *The Norman Conquest of England.* Oxford, 1879

J. P. Hughes. *How you got your Name.* London, 1959

L. C. Lloyd. *The Origins of some Anglo-Norman Families.* Harleian Society, 1951

A. Longnon. *Les Noms de Lieu de la France.* Paris, 1923

C. M. Matthews. *Haileybury Since Roman Times.* London, 1959

The Paston Letters. Everyman Edition, 1924

A. W. Pollard. *English Miracle Plays.* Oxford, 1927

A. L. Poole. *Domesday Book to Magna Carta.* Oxford, 1953

Sir M. Powicke. *The Thirteenth Century.* Oxford, 1953

C. Roth. *A History of the Jews in England.* London, 1941

John Russell's Boke of Nurture. Ed. F. J. Furnivall. London, 1868

L. F. Salzman. *English Industries in the Middle Ages.* Oxford, 1923

L. F. Salzman. *English Trade in the Middle Ages.* Oxford, 1931

A. H. Smith. *English Place-name Elements.* Cambridge, 1956

D. M. Stenton. *English Society in the Early Middle Ages.* London, 1952

F. M. Stenton. *Anglo-Saxon England.* Oxford, 1943

W. E. Tate. *The Parish Chest.* Cambridge, 1951

Sir A. Wagner. *English Genealogy.* Oxford, 1960

E. Weekley. *The Romance of Names.* London, 1912

E. Weekley. *Surnames.* London, 1916

D. Whitelock. *The Beginnings of English Society.* London, 1951

H. B. Woolf. *Early Germanic Principles of Name-giving.* Baltimore, 1939

Appendices

CLASSIFIED LISTS OF
SURNAMES

NOTES ON THE APPENDICES

In nos 1, 2, 3, 7 and 8 the order of surnames (or, in some cases, groups) is determined by the numbers of examples in the London Telephone Directory of 1961–2 (L.T.D.). These are approximate only, but every care has been taken to make them as accurate as possible. Small variations of number are unimportant, but the large differences indicate at a glance which names were common in the Middle Ages.

Nos 4 and 5 are selected to show the derivations of two interesting classes of surnames of which none is individually numerous. They are given alphabetically.

No. 6 includes a list of each kind.

It has not been possible to include all variations of spelling: and where the pronunciation and derivation are identical, as in Bird, Byrd, the alternative has often been omitted from the list, though included in the count.

An asterisk * indicates that a name has another considerable origin besides the one implied by its position on the list. For further information, consult the chapters indicated, or the index.

Appendix 1

THE MOST NUMEROUS SURNAMES OF OCCUPATION AND OFFICE
(Chapters 7–12)

All with over a hundred examples in the L.T.D. are included. Varied forms of the same word with identical meanings have been added together. Where the meaning is the same but the root word different, the names are placed together but the numbers given separately.

CRAFTSMEN AND DEALERS

5750	Smith, Smythe, Smithson, Smithers
2570	Taylor, Taylorson
2490	Miller, Mellor, Mylne, Milner, Mulliner, Milliard, Mill/s
1790	Baker, Baxter, Backer, Backhouse, Bacchus
1610	Webb, Webster, Webber, Weaver
1450	Wright, Wrightson
1360	Turner
1350	Cooper, Cowper
1250	Walker; 365 Fuller; 280 Tucker
770	Chapman
730	Mason, Machin
500	Barker; 150 Tanner
500	Wheeler
390	Fletcher
350	Potter
330	Skinner

OFFICIALS AND SERVANTS

2740	Clark/e, Clarkson
1230	Cook/e, Coke, Cookson
1080	Hunt/e, Hunter
1070	Bailey, Baillie, Bayley, Bayliss
1040	Ward/e, Warden, Warder
900	Carter
860	Parker
860	Marshall, Mascall
820	Knight
800	Fisher
700	Shepherd, Sheppard
680	Reeve/s, Grieve, Greaves, Graveson
660	Gardiner, Gardner
630	Chamberlain, Chambers, Chalmers
620	Page, Paige, Paget
610	Butler
570	Day* (dairyman)
560	Kemp, Camp, Campion, Champion

CRAFTSMEN AND DEALERS, *continued*

280 Carpenter
270 Butcher
260 Hooper
260 Chaundler
240 Brewer, Brewster, Broster
240 Slater, Slatter
230 Tyler
230 Waller
230 Glover
210 Goldsmith
210 Salter, Saltman, Salt
190 Dyer; 120 Lister
190 Collier
160 Sawyer
140 Saddler
135 Marchant, Merchant
120 Mercer
120 Spicer
120 Draper
110 Cartwright; 65 Wainwright
110 Naylor
100 Spooner
90 Cutler
90 Plummer
80 Thatcher, Thacker, Thaxter

OFFICIALS AND SERVANTS, *continued*

540 Spencer
520 Forrester, Forrest, Forster, Foster;* 210 Woodward
430 Parson/s
420 Hayward, Heywood, Haywood
380 Porter
310 Fowler
300 Barber
300 Harper
280 Chaplin, Caplin, Caplan
240 Leach, Leech
230 Archer; 170 Bowman
200 Falconer, Faulkner, Falkner
190 Squire
190 Farmer
160 Sargeant, Sargent
160 Singer
135 Herd, Heard, Hurd
130 Batchelor
120 Vickers, Viccars
110 Proctor
100 Launder, Lander, Lavender
100 Piper

Appendix 2

THE MOST NUMEROUS SURNAMES FROM NICKNAMES (Chapters 12–17)

These have been grouped according to their types, but it will be seen how varied they are and how hard to classify. Some overlap with occupation and status. Many were personal names before the Conquest. All nicknames with over a hundred examples (L.T.D.) are given, with a few more in some groups.

FROM DESCRIPTIONS

2960	Brown/e	195	Short
1900	White	190	Small, Smale
1900	Green/e*	185	Crisp, Cripps (curly haired)
1180	Read/e, Reed, Reid (red)		
1110	Young	180	Whitehead
800	Gray, Grey	170	Pollard (short haired)
700	Black, Blake	160	Wild/e
640	Gold, Gould	160	Good/e
550	Sharp/e	145	Moody, Mudie (brave)
500	Long, Lang	130	Blythe, Bligh, Bly
300	Bright, Burt	130	Ballard (bald)
270	Keen, Kean/e	120	Stark/e, Starkey (inflexible)
260	Armstrong		
250	Pratt (cunning)	115	Strong, Strang
250	Dunn/e (dark)	110	Crook (crooked)
245	Fry/e (free)	110	Swift
210	Hoar/e	110	Gay
210	Smart	100	Turnbull (strong)
200	Wise	100	Blackman
200	Beard, Baird	100	Snell (bold)

FROM METAPHORS

Birds			*Animals*	
800	Cock/s, Cox		700	Hart/e
380	Bird		610	Fox
240	Peacock, Pocock		280	Bull
220	Finch		230	Lamb
200	Jay		170	Todd
195	Swan		135	Buck
170	Drake		120	Wolf/e
150	Crowe		115	Hogg
140	Hawke		110	Bullock
135	Partridge		100	Hare
130	Spink/s, Pink		100	Fitch/ett
115	Crane		90	Brock
115	Nightingale		90	Kidd
100	Rook			
95	Woodcock		*Other Comparisons*	
80	Dove		420	May*
80	Sparrow		340	Steele
75	Raven		315	Winter
65	Pye*		300	Frost
65	Wren		250	Summers, Somers
60	Coote		90	Snow
50	Heron		90	Flint

FROM STATUS

(largely ironical)			*(largely factual)*	
1500	King		750	Newman
450	Bishop		700	Palmer
260	Abbott		660	Freeman
200	Prior, Pryor		470	Goodman
175	Pope		360	Franklin
160	Angel		350	Burgess
140	Earle		340	Mann
120	Monk		260	Bond
120	Nunn		240	Child/s
100	Baron		210	Ayre, Ayer/s, Eyre (heir)
100	Lord		150	Master/s
100	Loveman, Leaman, Lemon (lover)		110	Cousin/s
			100	Friend
60	Darling		90	Guest

FROM NORMAN NICKNAMES

700 Russell (red haired)
550 Grant (tall)
500 Barratt*, Barrett* (cunning)
450 Curtis, Curtoys (courteous)
350 Hardy (brave)
270 Blunt, Blount, Blundell, Blunden (fair)
230 Bassett, Bass (short)
230 Noble

210 Lovell, Lovett (little wolf)
200 Beal/e (handsome)
140 Durrant, Durand (unyielding)
130 Pettitt, Petty (small)
130 Prince
120 Jolliffe, Jolly (gay)
100 Corbett, Corbin (little crow)

SOME SURNAMES FROM CELTIC NICKNAMES

Old Welsh

610 Lloyd, Floyd (grey)
220 Vaughan (little)

210 Gough, Gooch, Goudge (red)
50 Gwynn/e (white)

Gaelic

Bain, Bayne (fair)
Begg (small)
Cameron (crooked nose)
Campbell (crooked mouth)

Dougall, Dowell (dark stranger)
Duff, Dow (black)
More (big)
Roy, Roe (red)

Old Irish

Boyd (yellow haired)
Doyle (dark stranger)
Finn (fair)
Flynn (red)

Kennedy (ugly head)
Murdoch (seafarer)
Murphy (sea fighter)
Sullivan (black eyed)

No numbers are given for the Gaelic and Irish names because they developed in different conditions from those of the English name system. (See pp. 73–5 and 311–14)

Appendix 3

SURNAMES FROM MEN'S CHRISTIAN NAMES (Chapters 18–22)

Each name is followed by its principal derivatives, their variety and numbers showing its popularity in the Middle Ages. The numbers represent the total for each group. All that score over 500 (L.T.D.) are given, but many more would score over 100.

Predominantly Welsh names are in parentheses. The Fitz- names have not been included because so many of them are Irish, but a small number of them might be added to each of the leading men's names.

7730   JOHN   (Jones), Johns, Johns(t)on, Jacks, Jackson, Jackman, Jaggs, Janes, Jennings, Jenkins/on, Jinks, Hanson,* Hankin,* Hanks,* Hancock*

6580   WILLIAM   (Williams), Williamson, Wilson, Wills, Willis, Wilkins/on, Wilkie, Willett, Wilmot, Mott, Wilcock/s, Wilcox, Gillam, Gillett*

5400   DAVID   Dawe/s, Dawson, Dawkins, Dowson, Davy, Davis, (Davies), Davison, Davidson, Day,* Dakins

4860   ROBERT   Roberts/on, Robson, Robbie, Robey, Robbins, Robin/son, Robens, Dobb/s, Dobson, Dobbie, Dobie, Dabbs, Nobbs, Hobbs, Hobson, Hopkins/on, Hobart, (Probert, Probyn)

4250   RICHARD   Richards/on, Ricks, Ricketts, Rix/on, Rigg/s, Dicks, Dickens/on, Dixon, Dickie, Dicker/son, Diggens, Hicks/on, Hitchens, Hickie, Hitchcock, Hiscock, Higgs/on, Higgins, Hignett,(Pritchard, Pritchett, Prickett)

4030   HENRY   Harris, Harrison, Harriman, Harry, Henderson, Hawkins, (Parry, Perry)

3600   THOMAS   Thomason, T(h)om(p)son, Thoms, Tom(p)kins, Tonkins, Tonks, Tombs, Tomlin/son, Tomsett, Tamlin, Tampling

2680   SIMON   Simmon(d)s, Symonds, Simms, Symes, Simpson, Simpkins, Simcox

2570 NICHOLAS Nic(h)ols/on, Nickells, Nicks, Nickson, Nixon, Collins,* Colletts, Collis/on

2570 PETER Peters/on, Pears/e, Pierce, Pearson, Pearman, Perkin, Parkin/son, Perks, Parks, Perrin, Perrot, Parrot, Parr

2450 WALTER Walters, Waters/on, Watts, Watson, Watkins/on, Watkiss

2200 HUGH Hughes, Hewes, Hewson, Huson, Huggett, Huggins, Hutchins/on, Hutchings, Hewlet, Hewett, Hewitson, Hullett, Hullis, How/es,* Howkins, Hudson,* (Pugh)

2135 PHILIP Phillips/on, Phelps, Phipps, Philpots, Potts, Filkins

(1950 LLEWELLYN, Lewis)

1885 GILBERT Gilbertson, Gilbey, Gibbs, Gibson, Gibbons

1825 MARTIN Martins, Martinet, Martell

1820 MAURICE Morris/on, Morrice, Morse, Morson

1810 ALEXANDER Saunder/s, Sander/son

1800 ADAM Adams/on, Adkins, Atkins/on, Aitkins, Adcock, Addis/on, Addy, Adey

1800 STEPHEN Stephens/on, Stevens/on, Stenson, Stimson

(1640 EVAN Evans, Bevan, Bevin)

1630 ALAN Allan/son, Allen, Alleyn, Alcock

1610 ANDREW Andrews, Anderson

1590 ROGER Rogers/on, Hodge/s, Hodgson, Hodgett, Hodgkin/son, Hodgekiss, Hodson, Dodge, Dodgson, Dodson, Dodd/s,* (Prodger)

1480 LAURENCE Lawrence, Lawrie, Laws/on, Lowry, Lorkins, Larkins

1470 ELIAS Ellis, Elliot, Ellison, Elliman

1450 EDWARD Edwards, Edkins

1340 RALPH Rolfe, Rolphe, Randolph, Randall, Randle, Rendell, Rand/s, Ranson, Ransome, Rankin, Hands,* Hanson,* Hansome,* Hankin,* Hancock,* Ralf, Relph, Rawle, Rawlins/on, Rawlings, Hawling, Rawkins, Rawson

(1250 RHYS Rice, Reese/e, Reece, Price, Preece)

1240 BENEDICT Bennett, Bennison, Benson

1230 BARTHOLOMEW Barthelmy, Bartle, Bartley, Bartlett, Bate/s, Betts, Bateman, Batt/y, Batten, Batcock, Tolley

1200 MATTHEW Matthews, Mathieson, Matt/s, Matson, Mattin, Mayhew, May,* Makins/on, Maycock

1200 MICHAEL Mi(t)chell, Michie/son

1070 JAMES Jam(i)eson, Jemmet

(1070 MORGAN)

900 JACOB Jacobs/on

(850 HOWELL   Howells, Powell)
(830 GRIFFITH   Griffiths, Griffin)
810 PAGAN   Pain/e, Payne, Pannell
810 HOWARD   Howerd, Heward, Hewart
750 HARVEY   Hervey, Harvie
720 HAMO   Hammond, Hammett, Hamlet, Hamlyn, Hambling, Hampson
700 PATRICK   Patterson, Paterson, Pattison, Paton
620 GREGORY   Gregson, Grigg/s, Grieg, Greer, Grierson
620 GEOFFREY   Geffers, Geffin, Jeffrey, Jefferson, Jeffs, Jepp, Jepson, Jeffcock, Jeffcot
610 REYNALD   Reynolds, Rennell, Rennie
590 NEIL   Neal/e, Neel/d, Neld, Nelson, Neilson
575 GERALD/GERARD   Garrett, Garratt, Garrard, Garrod, Jarred, Jerrold, Jarrett
570 HUMPHREY   Humphreys, Humphriss (Pumphrey, Boumfrey)
540 HARDING
510 AUGUSTINE   Austin, Austen

Appendix 4

SURNAMES FROM PRE–CONQUEST PERSONAL NAMES (Chapters 1 and 23)

A A SELECTION OF PRE-CONQUEST MEN'S NAMES

These are arranged in alphabetical order, showing their structure and the modern surnames derived from them. A few are of Scandinavian or continental origin (see pp. 247–8) but all were current in Anglo-Saxon England. Those in brackets are familiar forms of any name in their group. For meanings see Glossary.

Aelf-heah	Afflick, Elfick, El-phick, Elvidge	Blaec-mann	Blackman
-raed	Alfred, Alford, Elford	-stan	Blackston
-ric	Allridge, Aldridge	Brun-stan	Brunsdon
-sige	Elsey, Elsie	-wine	Brunwin (Browning)
-weald	Allwood, Ellwood	Burg-heard	Burkard, Burkett
-wig	Alvey, Elvey, Elphee	-ric	Burridge, Burrage
-wine	Alvin, Elvin, Elfin	-weard	Burward
Aethel-beorht	Allbright, Albutt, Albert	Cen-weard	Kenward
-frith	Alfrey	-wig	Kenway (Kenning)
-gar	Algar, Elgar	Ceol-mund	Chillman
-geat	Aylet, Allett, Ellett, Aylott, Elliot	-wig	Kellaway
		Cuth-beald	Cobbold, Cutbill, Cobb*
-heard	Allard, Ellard		
-maer	Aylmer, Ailmer, Elmer	-beorht	Cuthbert, Cobbett, Cubit
-noth	Alnutt, Allnatt	-maer	Cutmore, Cudmore
-raed	Elldred, Aldred	-ric	Cutteridge
-ric	Aldrich, Aldridge, Allwright, Ethe-ridge	-wulf	Culf, Cuff, Cuttle (Cutts, Cutting)
		Cyne-beald	Kemble, Kimball
		-maer	Kenmore
-stan	Alston, Atherston	-ric	Kerrich, Kenrick, Kendrick
-weard	Allward, Aylward, Allard	-weard	Kenward
-wig	Allaway, Elwes	-wig	Kenway (Kenning)
-wine	Aylwin, Alwin, Allen (Ayling)	Deor-mann	Dearman
		-weard	Deards
Beald-ric	Baldrey, Baldrick, Baldright	-wine	Darwin (Dearing)
		Dude-mann	Dodmann
-wine	Baldwin (Balding)	Dun-stan	Dunstan (Dunning)
Beorht-mann	Brightman	Ead-gar	Edgar, Egger, Agar
-maer	Brightmore, Brimmer	-mund	Edmunds, Edmonds/on, Edmans, Edmeades
-wig	Brighty		

335

A *Continued*

Ead-raed	Erret
-ric	Edrich
-wacer	Edicker
-weard	Edwards/on
-wig	Eddy
-wine	Edwin
-wulf	Eddols
Eald-gar	Algar
-noth	Allnutt
-raed	Aldred, Allred, Allard
-ric	Oldridge
-stan	Alston
-wig	Allaway, Aldway
-wine	Alden, Aldan, Auden
Ealh-here	Alger
-wine	Alchin
Ecg-beort	Agbert
-wulf	Edgell
Eofor-wacer	Earwaker
-wine	Erwin, Irwin, Urwin
Gar-mund	Garman
-wig	Garraway
Glaed-mann	Gladman
-wine	Gladwin (Gladding)
God-here	Godder
-leof	Goodliffe
-maer	Gummer
-mann	Goodman
-ric	Goodrich, Goodridge
-weard	Godward, Goddard
-wig	Goodway
-wine	Godwin, Goodwin (Gooding)
Gold-mann	Goldman
-wine	Goldwyn (Golding)
Grim-bald	Grimble, Gribble
Heathu-wig	Hathaway
Here-beorht	Herbert
-weald	Harold, Harrell, Harrod
-weard	Harward
Hwit-heard	Whittard
-mann	Whiteman (Whitting)
Leof-gar	Loveguard
-geat	Levet
-god	Lovegood
-maer	Lemmer
-mann	Loveman, Leaman
-raed	Leverett
-ric	Leveridge, Loveridge
-sige	Livesey, Lewsey, Lovesay
-sunu	Leveson
-weard	Livard
-wig	Leavey
-wine	Lewin, Leven, Levin (Loving)

Maer-geat	Merrett
Maer-ric	Merrick
North-mann	Norman
Os-beorn	Osborn/e
-god	Osgood, Hosegood
-mund	Osmond, Osman
-wald	Oswald, Oswell, Ostwald
-wig	Osway
-wine	Oswin (Hoskins)
Raed-wig	Redway, Reddaway
-wine	Readwin
-wulf	Ralf, etc
Sae-beorn	Seaborn
-fugol	Seavel, Seffle
-mann	Seaman
-wulf	Self
Sae / Sige -beorht	Seabert, Seabright
-gar	Siggers, Sayers, Sears
-ric	Search, Surridge
-weald	Sewell
-weard	Seward
Snel-gar	Snelgar (Snelling)
Stan-heard	Stannard
-maer	Stammer/s (Stanning)
Swet-mann	Sweetman (Sweeting)
Theod-ric	Tedrick, Terry, etc
Thur-beorn	Thorburn
-god	Thurgood, Thorogood
-kettill	Thirkettle, Thirkill, Thirkell
-mund	Thurman, Thorman
-stan	Thurston
Wig-beorht	Wybird, Whybird
-beorn	Wyborn, Wyburn
-maer	Wymer
-mund	Wyman, Whyman
Wine-beald	Winbolt
-beorn	Winborne, Wenborn, Wenban (Winning)
Wulf-frith	Woolfrey
-gar	Woolgar
-geat	Woolvet, Wolfit, Woolett
-maer	Woolmer, Woolmore
-noth	Woolner, Woolnough, Woolnut
-ric	Woolridge, Wooldridge, Woolveridge
-sige	Woolsey, Wolsey
-stan	Woolstan, Wolston
-weard	Woolard, Woolford
-wig	Woolway
-wine	Wooland, Wollen, Woolland

B SOME PRE-CONQUEST WOMEN'S NAMES WITH THE SURNAMES DERIVED FROM THEM

Aelf-flaed	Allflatt	Leof-daeg	Loveday, Lowdy
Aethel-flaed	Allflatt	Mild-burg	Milborrow
-gyth	Aylett	-thryth	Mildred
-gifu	Ayliffe	Rim-hild	Rimmell
-thryth	Audrey, Awdry	Sae-faru	Seaver
Beald-gyth	Baldey	-burg	Seaber, Seabury
Beorht-gifu	Berriff	Stan-burg	Stanberry, Stanbury
Cwen-hild	Quennell	-hild	Stanhill
Ead-gyth	Eade, Eady, Edis, Eddis, Eddison	Swan-hild	Swannell
		Swet-leofu	Sweetlove
Eald-gyth	Aldis, Aldous	Thur-hild	Turrell
God-gifu	Goodeve	Tun-hild	Tunnell
-gyth	Goodey, Goody	Wig-burg	Wybrow, Whybrow, Wybrew
-leofu	Goodliffe		
Gunn-hild	Gunnell	Wulf-gifu	Wolvey
-or	Gunner		

C GLOSSARY OF PRE-CONQUEST THEMES USED IN FORMING COMPOUND PERSONAL NAMES

Many of these were also used separately as personal names, cf Appendix 2

aelf	elf	heard	brave
aethel	noble	heah	high
b(e)ald	bold	heathu	war
beorht	bright	helm	helmet
beorn	child	here	army
blaec	black	hild	war
brun	brown	hwit	white
burg	fortress	kettill	cauldron
cen	keen	leof	beloved
ceol	ship	maer	famous
cuth	famous	mund	protection
cwen	queen	noth	courage
cyne	family	os	divine
deor	dear	raed	good counsel
dun	dark	ric	rule
ead	riches	rim	hoar frost
eald	old	sae	sea
ealh	temple	sige	victory
ecg	sword	snel	bold
eofor	wild boar	stan	stone
flaed	beauty	sunu	son
frith	peace	Thur	Thor
fugol	bird	theod	tribe
gar	warrior	thryth	strength
Geat	a legendary hero	wacer	watchman
gifu	gift	weald	power
glaed	glad	weard	guard
god	good	wig	warrior
grim	fierce	wine	friend
gunn	battle	wulf	wolf
gyth	battle		

D SOME SINGLE-THEME PRE-CONQUEST PERSONAL NAMES WITH SURNAMES DERIVED FROM THEM

For many of these early names no meaning can be given with certainty. Some are complete in themselves, some seem like nicknames though used alone. Some are abbreviations of longer names, as Tubbi may be of Thurbeorn, or Bugge of Burgric. These are the 'pet-names' of the Anglo-Saxon period, as Tom and Dick are of later times. They account for many short surnames of which these are only a selection.

Old English

Beda	Beade
Bondi (a farmer)	Bond, Bondy, Bundy
Botta	Bott, Botting
Budda (a bud)	Budd, Budden
Bugge	Bugg, Buggins
Bynni	Binns, Binney
Cada	Cade
Cana	Cane*, Canning
Ceada	Chadd
Cobbe (a round object)	Cobb*
Cola (coal)	Cole, Colling
Cyppe	Kipps, Kipping
Dodda	Dodd
Huda	Hudd
Manni	Mann*

Ogga	Ogg
Pymma	Pym, Pim
Wada (a sea giant)	Wade
Wigga (a beetle)	Wiggs
Wini (a friend)	Winn, Wynne

Of Danish Origin (see p. 24)

Haki (a hook)	Hake
Knut (a knot)	Knott
Orm (a serpent)	Orme, Oram
Stori (big)	Storey
Svein (a youth)	Swain
Tofi	Tovey
Toki	Tooke
Tubbi	Tubby
Tukka	Tuck
Tunni	Tunney

Appendix 5

SURNAMES FROM WOMEN'S CHRISTIAN NAMES (Chapter 24)

See also p. 337

ALICE   Allis, Allison
AGATHA   Aggass, Agg, Tag
AGNES   Annis, Annett, Annott, Annison, Anson
AMICIA   Ames, Amies, Amison, Amey
BEATRICE   Beatty, Beeton, Beaton
CASSANDRA   Cass, Casson, Case
CECILY   Cecil, Sisley, Sisson
CHRISTINA   Christie, Kitts*
CONSTANCE   Custance, Cust, Cussans, Cuss
DENISE   Dennis,* Denny
EDITH   (see Eadgyth, page 329)
ELEANOR   Ellinor, Ellen, Elson, Nelson*
ELIZABETH   Bethell, Lilley*
EMMA   Emms, Emmett, Empson
EVE   Eves/on, Eaves, Evetts
GUINEVERE   Gaynor
ISABEL   Isbell, Ibbs, Ibson, Ibbott, Ibbotson, Nibbs, Tibbs, Niblet, Libby, Bibby
ISEULT   Isitt, Izot, Izzet, Izzard
ISMENIA   Emeny, Imeny
JOYCE   Joicey, Joy
JULIAN   Julyan, Jolyan, Jewett, Jowett, Gillett,* Gill*
JOAN   (indistinguishable from John)
KATHERINE   Catlin, Cattling, Caton, Cattell, Catt, Kitson*
LETTICE   Letts, Letson, Leeson
LUCY   Lucey, Luce
MABEL   Mabb/s, Mabbet, Mabbot, Mably, Mapp, Mappin, Mobbs
MAGDALEN   Maudling, Maddison
MARGARET   Margretts, Maggs, Magson, Margery, Margetts, Margetson, Margerison, Moggs, Poggs, Pegson, Meggeson, Moxon

MARY Maris, Marrison, Marriott, Marryat, Marion, Mallett, Malleson, Mollison

MATILDA Maude, Mault, Mold, Mould, Mawson, Tilly, Tilley, Tillett, Tillson, Tillotson

MURIEL Merrell, Merrill

OLIVIA Oliffe

PETRONEL Parnell, Purnell

ROSAMUND Rosamond, Roseman, Rosoman

ROSE (Norman French Rohese) Rose,* Royce

SIBYL Sibley, Sibbs, Sibson, Sibbett

THEOPHANIA Tiffany, Tiffin

Appendix 6

SURNAMES FROM LOCAL WORDS
(Chapters 25 and 26)

All of these may also be parts of compound place names and are helpful in recognising local names among surnames. The letters N, S, E and W indicate the region (North etc) in England to which the word chiefly belongs. Sc is for Scotland which is also generally included in North. Those that have no such letters are widespread.

A THE MOST NUMEROUS

1900	Green/e*	550	Well/s
1450	Lee, Lea, Leigh, Ley	530	Ford
1350	Wood/s	500	North, Norris*
1350	Hill/s	460	Holmes
1230	Hall	450	Field/s
1220	Moore, Muir (Sc)	435	Lane
900	Brook, Brooke/s	370	Bridges*, Briggs (Sc)
800	Mill/s	340	Marsh
710	West	330	Heath

B SOME NAMES FROM ARCHAIC AND DIALECT WORDS WITH THEIR MEANINGS

The final 's' was generally a later addition and the original meaning singular.

Beck N	a brook	Craig Sc	a rock
Bourne S	,,	Croft	an enclosed
Burns N	,,		field
Bury, Berry,		Dean/e	a hollow
Brough	a fortified place	Dell	,,
Carr N	a bog	Dingle	,,
Cleeve, Clive	a cliff	Downe/s	hills
Clough N	a ravine	Fell NW	a mountain
Coombe/s SW	a deep valley	Garth N	an enclosed yard

Gill* N	a deep valley	Spong	a projecting piece of a field
Groves, Graves	a small wood		
Hale	a corner in a valley	Stead	a farm, or homestead
Hawes	a place enclosed by a hedge	Stock	a tree stump
Hearn, Hurn	a corner or nook	Stow	a place with a church, the name of several towns
Hurst SE	a wooded hill		
Holt S	a wood		
Holmes NE	low, grassy islands	Stubbs	stumps of trees
		Syke/s	a small stream
Hope NE	a small en-closure among fens	Taft NE Toft	the site of a former dwelling
Hough N Howe/s S	a spur of high land	Thorpe NE	a farm or hamlet
Kerr (see Carr)		Thwaite NE	a meadow
Law* N		Twitchell	a narrow path
Low* S	a hill	Wick/s,	
Lynch	a stretch of sandy ground	Weeks	a dairy farm or hamlet (in Scotland 'wick' means an inlet of the sea)
Mear/s	a lake		
Peal, Peel N	a defensive tower		
Rhode/s, Royd/s NE	a clearing	Worth, Worthy	a fenced homestead
Rudge S Rigg/s N	a ridge	Wray N	a nook, or corner
Scales NE	temporary huts		
Shaw	a wood		
Slade	a steep slope		
Smeath, Smather/s	a smooth, flat place		

Appendix 7

SURNAMES FROM COUNTRIES
(Chapters 27 and 28)

1280	Scott, Scotland, Scotcher, Scutt
1180	Wallis, Wallace, Walsh, Welsh, Welch
†950	Francis,* France, French
†420	Norman, Normand
400	Holland* (Some come from English villages of this name)
390	Breton, Britten, Britton, Brittain, Brett
†280	Dane,* Dennis,* Dench
260	England, English, Inglis
240	Fleming, Flanders, Flinders
220	Cornwall, Cornwell, Cornell, Cornish, Cornwallis
†110	German,* Germaine,* Jermyn,* Jarman*
85	Rome, Romer, Room/e
70	Ireland
70	Gascoigne, Gaskain, Gaskin
65	Pickard
35	Florence
35	Veness, Venis, Venus
30	Burgoyne, Burgin
30	Lorraine, Loring
30	Spain, Spanier
20	Portugal, Pettengale, Pettingell, Puttergill

† These numbers are uncertain owing to confusion between personal and country names. In the surname period Francis and Norman were both generally racial implying a Frenchman. Dennis could be a Christian name from St Denys or an early form of Danish. German in its various forms generally came from St Germain but was occasionally racial.

Appendix 8

THE LEADING SURNAMES OF THE ENGLISH SPEAKING WORLD

These are taken from directories of 1961–6, the top twenty-one in each city, in numerical order. In this list names have been counted individually (in contrast to Appendix 3, where those with the same derivation have been added together), but slight variations of spelling, such as Clark/e, Thom(p)son and Davi(e)s, have been disregarded.

CARDIFF	DUBLIN	EDINBURGH	LONDON
Jones	Murphy	Smith	Smith
Davies	Kelly	Thomson	Jones
Williams	O'Byrne	Brown	Brown
Thomas	O'Connor	Robertson	Clark
Evans	Ryan	Wilson	Taylor
Morgan	O'Brien	Scott	Davies
Lewis	Walsh	Anderson	Williams
Jenkins	Doyle	Stewart	Johnson
Rees	Daly	Miller	Harris
Griffiths	Smith	Macdonald	Green
James	O'Reilly	Johnson	White
Phillips	O'Neill	Campbell	Wilson
Edwards	Kennedy	Young	Lewis
Roberts	Sullivan	Mitchell	Martin
Richards	Burke	Henderson	Thompson
Harris	Farrell	Mackenzie	Evans
Price	Brennan	Murray	King
Hughes	Nolan	Watson	Phillips
Morris	Carroll	Reid	Miller
Lloyd	Macarthey	Ross	Edwards
Owens	Moore	Allen	Wright

NOTE: It will be seen that the names of Wales, Scotland, and Ireland are entirely different, except for the single case of Smith which occurs in two of them, but that England shares names with both

Wales and Scotland. The Welsh names score in London out of proportion to the rest, because their lack of variety makes their numbers concentrated. Many of them are also English, but it is the Welsh numbers that make them so high on the London list. Without them it would read: Smith, Brown, Clark, Taylor, Johnson, Green, White, Wilson, Martin, Thompson, King, Miller, Wright, Lee, Baker, Turner, Cooper, Robinson, Walker, Hall, Jackson.

SYDNEY	TORONTO	WELLINGTON (N.Z.)	NEW YORK
Smith	Smith	Smith	Smith
Brown	Brown	Brown	Brown
Johnson	Johnson	Wilson	Johnson
Jones	Wilson	Thompson	Cohen
Williams	Thompson	Taylor	Williams
Wilson	Macdonald	Johnson	Miller
Thompson	Taylor	Williams	Davis
Davis	Clark	Clark	Jones
Taylor	Campbell	Jones	Green
Clark	Jones	Anderson	Lee
Stewart	Miller	Martin	Harris
White	Davis	Macdonald	Schwartz
Martin	White	Young	White
Macdonald	Stewart	Miller	Levy
Anderson	Martin	White	Levine
Walker	Scott	Campbell	Wilson
Miller	Williams	King	Lewis
Campbell	Young	Harris	Rodriguez
King	Robinson	Davis	Friedman
Scott	King	Robinson	Taylor
Harris	Walker	Scott	Clark

NOTE: In distant parts of the Commonwealth the proportions of surnames have remained remarkably constant, the only variations being caused by the size of the Welsh or Scottish element. The Irish do not appear, having a great variety of surnames which do not combine with any others. It is apparent that in each of the three Commonwealth cities shown, the Scottish element is higher and the Welsh lower than in London; and it is notable that their three lists contain only twenty-three different names as against the sixty-two for Cardiff, Dublin and Edinburgh.

In New York, though Jewish, German and Spanish names reach the top twenty, British names still predominate.

ATLANTA	CHICAGO	DENVER	SAN FRANCISCO
Smith	Johnson	Smith	Smith
Johnson	Smith	Johnson	Johnson
Jones	Williams	Miller	Lee
Williams	Brown	Anderson	Williams
Brown	Anderson	Brown	Brown
Davis	Jones	Williams	Anderson
Jackson	Miller	Jones	Wong
Wilson	Davis	Davis	Jones
Harris	Jackson	Wilson	Davis
Moore	Harris	Moore	Miller
Martin	Thomas	Clark	Wilson
Thomas	Nelson	Thompson	Thompson
White	Wilson	Peterson	Young
Thompson	Peterson	White	Taylor
Walker	White	Martin	White
Turner	Taylor	Taylor	Martin
Miller	Thompson	Thomas	Sullivan
Clark	Moore	Martinez	Murphy
Taylor	Martin	Lewis	Kelly
Anderson	Green	Allen	Moore
Green	Robinson	Green	Clark

NOTE: These four cities together with New York (p. 345) have been chosen as being widely spaced in different parts of the United States. Comment on the five lists will be found in Surnames in America.

The leading surnames of Houston and Boston were also studied. The former proved almost identical with Atlanta, only two names (Robinson and Lewis) qualifying in Houston that just failed in Atlanta. The variation of order was minimal. Boston proved a stronghold of the Irish, the first six names being Smith, Sullivan, Murphy, Johnson, Kelly, Brown, in that order. In the rest of the list only Cohen breaks the interweaving of English and Irish.

Index of Surnames

Subject Index

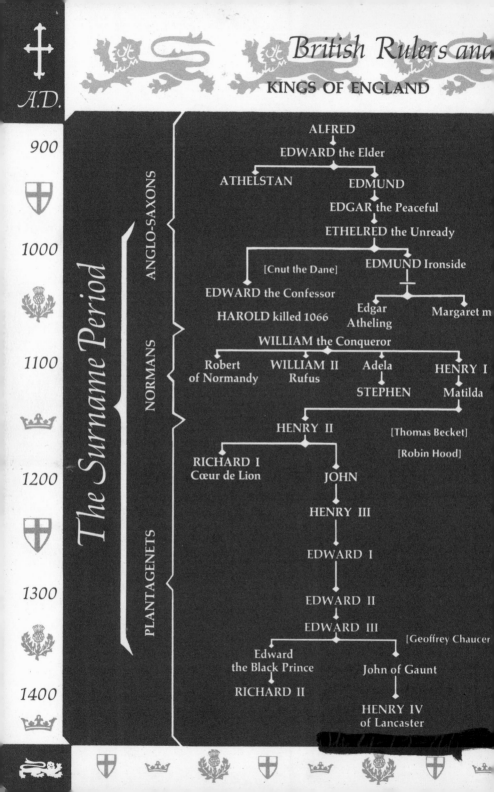

900

1000

1100

1200

1300

1400

The Surname Period

ANGLO-SAXONS

NORMANS

PLANTAGENETS

ALFRED

EDWARD the Elder

ATHELSTAN   **EDMUND**

EDGAR the Peaceful

ETHELRED the Unready

[Cnut the Dane]   **EDMUND** Ironside

EDWARD the Confessor

HAROLD killed 1066   Edgar   Margaret m
                                Atheling

WILLIAM the Conqueror

Robert   **WILLIAM II**   Adela   **HENRY I**
of Normandy   **Rufus**

STEPHEN   Matilda

HENRY II   [Thomas Becket]

                    [Robin Hood]

RICHARD I
Cœur de Lion   **JOHN**

HENRY III

EDWARD I

EDWARD II

EDWARD III   [Geoffrey Chaucer

Edward   John of Gaunt
the Black Prince

RICHARD II

HENRY IV
of Lancaster